THINK AND GROW RICH

THE 21ST-CENTURY EDITION

Annotated with Updated Examples

NAPOLEON HILL

Edited by Bill Hartley and Ann Hartley
with commentary by Bill Hartley

A PUBLICITY PHOTO OF THE AUTHOR, NAPOLEON HILL, 1955

Photograph courtesy of the Napoleon Hill Foundation

NEGLECTING TO BROADEN THEIR VIEW

HAS KEPT SOME PEOPLE

DOING ONE THING ALL THEIR LIVES.

— NAPOLEON HILL

grants, PR, FR
&
Tech writing
Sales
phys reason
outreach

ISBN 10: 1-932429-35-2
ISBN 13: 978-1-932429-35-0

10 9 8 7 6 5 4 3 2

CONTENTS

PLEASE WRITE IN THIS BOOK

This special edition of *Think and Grow Rich* is a book that is meant to be worked in. It is designed specifically so you can make notes in the margins and we have intentionally had the type set so that the lines are far enough apart to make it easy for you to underline the ideas and phrases that catch your attention.

When an idea flashes into your mind, when you suddenly "get it," the concept always seems so clear that you're sure you'll be able to remember it later. However, when something comes to you like that, it's usually because a number of bits and pieces have suddenly fallen into place in just the right way. Unfortunately, the feeling of the moment that made the idea happen is hard to hold on to . . . and even harder to recall.

Insights that flash into your consciousness can fade quickly if you don't write down something to capture that fleeting feeling of "ahah!" The editors of this edition strongly urge you to use the spaces provided to write down key words and reminders that you can use later to trigger your memory.

Our hope is that you will make this your own personalized version of *Think and Grow Rich*. When you have finished working your way through this book it should be filled with notes to yourself, it should point out the passages you find particularly relevant to your life, and it should be a record of your personal progress that you can go back and refer to at those times when you can't quite recall what it was that got you so motivated and inspired.

From the editors

THE SECRET OF SUCCESS

1

In every chapter of this book, mention is made of the money-making secret that has made fortunes for the exceedingly wealthy men whom I have carefully analyzed over a long period of years.

The secret was first brought to my attention by Andrew Carnegie. The canny, lovable old Scotsman carelessly tossed it into my mind when I was but a boy. Then he sat back in his chair, with a merry twinkle in his eyes, and watched carefully to see if I had brains enough to understand the full significance of what he had said to me.

When he saw that I had grasped the idea, he asked if I would be willing to spend twenty years or more preparing myself to take it to the world, to men and women who, without the secret, might go through life as failures. I said I would, and with Mr. Carnegie's cooperation I have kept my promise.

Luck!
right place,
right time.
Availed himself
of resources

NOTES & COMMENTS

Why reinvent the wheel?

uh oh :)

COMMENTARY

In 1908, during a particularly down time in the U.S. economy and with no money and no work, Napoleon Hill took a job as a writer for Bob Taylor's Magazine. *He had been hired to write success stories about famous men. Although it would not provide much in the way of income, it offered Hill the opportunity to meet and profile the giants of industry and business—the first of whom was the creator of America's steel industry, multimillionaire Andrew Carnegie, who was to become Hill's mentor.*

Carnegie was so impressed by Hill's perceptive mind that following their three-hour interview he invited Hill to spend the weekend at his estate so they could continue the discussion. During the course of the next two days, Carnegie told Hill that he believed any person could achieve greatness if they understood the philosophy of success and the steps required to achieve it. "It's a shame," he said, "that each new generation must find the way to success by trial and error, when the principles are really clear-cut."

Carnegie went on to explain his theory that this knowledge could be gained by interviewing those who had achieved greatness and then compiling the information and research into a comprehensive set of principles. He believed that it would take at least twenty years, and that the result would be "the world's first philosophy of individual achievement." He offered Hill the challenge—for no more compensation than that Carnegie would make the necessary introductions and cover travel expenses.

It took Hill twenty-nine seconds to accept Carnegie's proposal. Carnegie told him afterward that had it taken him more than sixty seconds to make the decision he would have withdrawn the offer, for "a man who cannot reach a decision promptly, once he has all the necessary facts, cannot be depended upon to carry through any decision he may make."

It was through Hill's unwavering dedication that this book was eventually written.

For detailed information on the life of Hill, read or listen to the audiobook of A Lifetime of Riches: The Biography of Napoleon Hill *by Michael J. Ritt Jr. and Kirk Landers. Michael Ritt worked as Hill's assistant for ten years and was the first employee of the Napoleon Hill Foundation, where he served as executive director, secretary, and treasurer. The material in his book comes from his own personal knowledge of Hill as well as from Hill's unpublished autobiography.*

This book, *Think and Grow Rich,* contains the Carnegie secret—a secret that has been tested by thousands *[now millions]* of people in almost every walk of life. It was Mr. Carnegie's idea that the magic formula, which gave him a stupendous fortune, ought to be placed within reach of people who do not have the time to investigate how others had made their money. It was his hope that I might test and demonstrate the soundness of the formula through the experience of men and women in every calling. He believed the formula should be taught in all public schools and colleges. He said that if it were properly taught, it would revolutionize the entire educational system, and the time spent in school could be reduced to less than half.

In chapter 4, on faith, you will read the astounding story of the organization of the giant United States Steel Corporation. It was conceived and carried out by one of the young men through whom Mr. Carnegie proved that his formula will work for all who are ready for it. This single application of the secret, by Charles M. Schwab, made him a huge fortune in both money and opportunity. Roughly speaking, this particular application of the formula was worth $600 million.

These facts give you a fair idea of what reading this book may bring to you, provided you know what it is that you want.

COMMENTARY

According to one method of calculation, through inflation alone it would have taken approximately twenty dollars in 2001 to buy what one dollar would have bought in 1901. However, to find the contemporary equivalent value of $600 million is not simply a matter of multiplying by the increase in the cost of living. Although there are other factors and variables in calculating buying *power, and even by conservative estimates, the $600 million would translate into at least $12 billion at the beginning of the twenty-first century.*

The secret was passed on to thousands of men and women who have used it for their personal benefit. Some have made fortunes with it. Others have used it successfully in creating harmony in their homes. A clergyman used it so effectively that it brought him an income of upwards of $75,000 a year *[approximately $1.5 million in contemporary terms].*

Arthur Nash, a Cincinnati tailor, used his near-bankrupt business as a "guinea pig" on which to test the formula. The business came to life and made a fortune for its owners. The experiment was so unique that newspapers and magazines gave it millions of dollars' worth of publicity.

The secret was passed on to Stuart Austin Wier, of Dallas, Texas. He was ready for it—so ready that he gave up his profession and studied law. Did he succeed? You will read the answer in chapter 6, Specialized Knowledge.

While I was the advertising manager for the LaSalle Extension University, I had the privilege of seeing J. G. Chapline, president of the university, use the formula so effectively that he made LaSalle one of the great extension schools of the country.

The secret is mentioned no fewer than a hundred times throughout this book. It has not been directly named, for it seems to work more successfully when it is merely left in sight, where those who are ready, and searching for it, may pick it up. That is why Andrew Carnegie passed it to me without giving me its specific name.

If you are ready to put it to use, you will recognize this secret at least once in every chapter, but you will not find an explanation of how you will know if you are ready. That would deprive you of much of the benefit you will receive when you make the discovery in your own way.

If you have ever been discouraged, if you have had difficulties that took the very soul out of you, if you have tried and failed, if you were ever handicapped by illness or physical affliction, the story of my own son's discovery and use of the Carnegie formula may prove to be the oasis in the Desert of Lost Hope for which you have been searching.

This secret was extensively used by President Woodrow Wilson during the world war *[and by President Roosevelt during the Second World War]*. It was passed on to every soldier in the training received before going to the front. President Wilson told me it was a powerful factor in raising the funds needed for the war.

A peculiar thing about this secret is that those who acquire and use it find themselves literally swept on to success. However, as is often pointed out in this book, there is no such thing as something for nothing. The secret cannot be had without paying a price, although the price is far less than its value.

Another peculiarity is that the secret cannot be given away and it cannot be purchased for money. Unless you are intentionally searching for the secret, you cannot have it at any price. That is because the secret comes in two parts, and in order for you to get it, one of those parts must already be in your possession.

The secret will work for anyone who is ready for it. Education has nothing to do with it. Long before I was born, the secret had found its way into the possession of Thomas A. Edison, and he used it so intelligently that he became the world's leading inventor, although he had only three months of schooling.

The secret was passed on to Edwin C. Barnes, a business associate of Mr. Edison's. He used it so effectively that he accumulated a great fortune and retired from active business while still a young man. You will find his story at the beginning of the next chapter. It should convince you that riches are not beyond your reach, and that no matter where you are in life, you can still be what you wish to be.

NOTES & COMMENTS

Jesus must have had it!

Start now on the road to your goal

NOTES & COMMENTS

saw the big
in something
small

Money, fame, recognition, and happiness can be had by you if you are ready and determined to have these blessings.

How do I know these things? You should have the answer before you finish this book. You may find it in the very first chapter, or on the last page.

While I was doing the research that I had undertaken at Andrew Carnegie's request, I analyzed hundreds of well-known men. Many of them attributed the accumulation of their vast fortunes to the Carnegie secret. Among these men were:

Henry Ford *[founder of the Ford automobile company, he started with no money and little education yet became one of the most successful self-made businessmen in American history]*

William Wrigley Jr. *[a traveling salesman who found that his customers liked the chewing gum he gave away as a premium better than they liked the goods he sold, so he started his own company]*

John Wanamaker *[known as The Merchant Prince, he created the world's first department store and was hailed for his innovations in marketing, customer service, and employee benefits]*

James J. Hill *[known as The Empire Builder, he built the transcontinental Great Northern Railway, encouraged homesteading in the West, then established shipping routes linking America with Asia]*

George S. Parker *[a school teacher who grew tired of fixing his students' pens, he created a new design, founded the Parker pen company, and turned a simple idea into a fortune]*

E. M. Statler *[the son of a poor pastor, he started as a bellboy and worked his way up until he was able to start his own chain of Statler Hotels, famous for their luxury and "service with a smile"]*

Henry L. Doherty *[starting at age 12 as an office boy for Columbia Gas, he went on to acquire 53 utilities companies, and patented 140 innovations for natural gas and oil production]*

Cyrus H. K. Curtis *[beginning with a small agricultural weekly, he turned it into* Ladies' Home Journal, *created* Saturday Evening Post, *then assembled one of the largest newspaper empires]*

George Eastman *[inventor and founder of the Eastman Kodak Company, he created many of the innovations that popularized photography and transformed the motion-picture industry]*

Charles M. Schwab *[the right-hand man of Andrew Carnegie, he was president of Carnegie Steel Company, brokered the deal that formed U.S. Steel, and went on to found Bethlehem Steel]*

Theodore Roosevelt *[26th president of the United States of America, 1901–09]*

John W. Davis *[a lawyer and political leader, he was Solicitor General under president Woodrow Wilson, and later appointed ambassador to Great Britain]*

Elbert Hubbard *[philosopher, publisher of* The Fra *magazine, and founder of the Roycrofters artists' colony, he was also the author of many bestsellers including* A Message to Garcia]

Wilbur Wright *[a bicycle-shop owner who, with his brother Orville, became the first American to fly motor-powered heavier-than-air aircraft; they pioneered the aviation industry]*

William Jennings Bryan *[newspaper publisher, presidential nominee, Secretary of State under President William McKinley, but perhaps best known as the lawyer who defended creationism at the Scopes Monkey Trial]*

Dr. David Starr Jordan *[educator, scientist, and author of over 50 books, he was the nation's youngest university president at Indiana University, and become the first president of Stanford University]*

J. Ogden Armour *[inherited his family's meat-packing business, turned it into a conglomerate with more than 3,000 products, was an owner of the Chicago Cubs, and a director of National City Bank]*

Arthur Brisbane *[a crusading journalist and syndicated columnist, he was sought after by every major news organization and was the most-read and highest-paid editorial writer of his day]*

Dr. Frank Gunsaulus *[a Chicago preacher who delivered such a powerful sermon that Philip D. Armour gave him a million dollars with which to start the Armour Institute of Technology, and Gunsaulus was made president]*

Daniel Willard *[president of the B&O Railroad for more than thirty years, he was honored by having the city of Willard, Ohio, named for him]*

King Gillette *[a traveling salesman and born tinkerer, he was trying to shave on a moving train when he came up with the idea of the safety razor, which became the foundation of a corporate giant]*

Ralph A. Weeks *[president of International Correspondence Schools, he helped finance Napoleon Hill's Intra-Wall Institute, established to educate and rehabilitate prison inmates]*

Judge Daniel T. Wright *[instructor at Georgetown Law School, where Napoleon Hill was studying when* Bob Taylor's Magazine *gave him the assignment to write a profile of Andrew Carnegie]*

John D. Rockefeller *[with $1,000 savings, plus another $1,000 borrowed from his father, he started a kerosene company which he grew into the giant Standard Oil and one of the world's greatest fortunes]*

Thomas A. Edison *[inventor and entrepreneur, he perfected the electric light bulb, the phonograph, the motion-picture camera, and owned the rights to more than 1,000 patented inventions]*

Frank A. Vanderlip *[a poor boy who became a journalist, social reformer, and self-made millionaire, he was president of the National City Bank, now Citibank, and was Assistant Secretary of the Treasury]*

F. W. Woolworth *[a clerk in a general store, he pioneered the idea of fixed-price selling and self-service, and forever changed retail selling with his chain of Woolworth 5 and 10 Cent Stores]*

Col. Robert A. Dollar *[starting with a small schooner bought to haul lumber down the West Coast, he built the Dollar Steamship Company, the largest fleet of luxury liners sailing under the U.S. flag]*

Edward A. Filene *[founder of the Boston-based stores, he devised revolutionary methods of distribution and merchandising, and became famous for originating the bargain-basement concept]*

Edwin C. Barnes *[the only man Thomas Edison ever had as a partner, he took Edison's failing dictating machine, the Ediphone, and sold it so successfully that it became a fixture in offices and made him a multimillionaire]*

Arthur Nash *[a Cincinnati clothing manufacturer who used his bankrupt business as a guinea pig for the Carnegie secret and was so successful that the newspapers made him famous as "Golden Rule Nash"]*

Clarence Darrow *[famed as a lawyer, public speaker, and defender of the underdog, he was perhaps best known as the lawyer at the Scopes Monkey Trial who defended teaching the theory of evolution]*

Woodrow Wilson *[28th president of the United States of America, 1913–21]*

William Howard Taft *[27th president of the United States of America, 1909–13]*

Luther Burbank *[world-renowned horticulturist who introduced over 800 varieties of new plants in his effort to improve the quality of plants and thereby increase the world's food supply]*

NOTES & COMMENTS

Edward W. Bok *[though he had only six years' schooling, by the age of 20 he was editor of* Ladies' Home Journal, *which he helped to build into the world's most widely circulated magazine]*

Frank A. Munsey *[a telegraph operator who quit to launch* Argosy *magazine, and then parlayed his fortune into a newspaper empire that included the* Washington Times *and the* New York Herald]

Elbert H. Gary *[chairman of U.S. Steel, at the time the largest corporation in the world, he spearheaded the construction of its first major project, the Gary Works steel plant, and the city of Gary, Indiana]*

Dr. Alexander Graham Bell *[best known as the inventor of the telephone, he also perfected recording devices, advances in aircraft, and was a co-founder of the National Geographic Society]*

John H. Patterson *[president of National Cash Register, he was known as an advertising visionary and a genius at motivating his sales force, which made NCR the leader in its field]*

Julius Rosenwald *[a small manufacturer who foresaw the future of mail-order, he bought 25 percent of Sears, Roebuck, & Co., and together with Richard Sears built it into an icon of American business]*

Stuart Austin Wier *[a construction engineer Hill met in the Texas oil fields who, inspired by the Carnegie secret, went to law school after age forty, and was also involved in the publishing of* Napoleon Hill's Magazine]

Dr. Frank Crane *[a noted psychologist, essayist, and author of the book* Four Minute Essays *on such subjects as The Price of Liberty, Pragmatism, The Duty of the Rich, and How to Keep Friends]*

J. G. Chapline *[president of the LaSalle Extension University at the time Napoleon Hill worked in the university's advertising and sales department, where Hill first realized his talent for motivating people]*

Jennings Randolph *[airline executive, congressman, then U.S. Senator from West Virginia, he was a lifelong admirer of Napoleon Hill, and it was he who encouraged Hill to act as adviser to President Franklin Delano Roosevelt]*

These names represent a small fraction of well-known Americans whose achievements, financial and otherwise, prove that those who understand and apply the Carnegie secret reach high positions in life.

COMMENTARY

As Napoleon Hill says, the preceding list includes only some of the more than 500 multimillionaires and extraordinarily successful individuals whom Hill interviewed prior to writing Think and Grow Rich. *It does not include the equally impressive list of people he came in contact with after the publication, nor does it include the names of those who did not have the opportunity to meet Napoleon Hill personally but who attribute their success to having read this book.*

It is said that Napoleon Hill and Think and Grow Rich *have made more millionaires than any other person in history. It might equally well be said that Napoleon Hill inspired more motivational experts than any other man in history.*

It is practically impossible to find a motivational speaker who does not draw upon Hill's work. His influence can be seen in the writings of his early peers, Dale Carnegie and Norman Vincent Peele. Later, successful authors and speakers such as W. Clement Stone, Og Mandino, and Earl Nightingale worked directly with either Napoleon Hill or with the Napoleon Hill Foundation. Echoes of Hill's principles can also be found in books by people as diverse as Wally "Famous" Amos, Mary Kay Ash, Ken Blanchard, Adelaide Bry, Chicken Soup for the Soul *authors Jack Canfield and Mark Victor Hansen, Debbie Fields, Shakti Gawain, John Gray, Susan Jeffers, Bruce Jenner, Charlie "Tremendous" Jones, Tommy Lasorda, Art Linkletter, Joan Lunden, Dr. Maxwell Maltz, James Redfield, Dr. Bernie Siegel, Jose Silva, Brian Tracey, Lillian Vernon, and Dennis Waitley. Steven Covey, author of* The Seven Habits of Highly Effective People *has often spoken of the influence of Napoleon Hill. Anthony Robbins, arguably the*

NOTES & COMMENTS

most successful motivational author and speaker at the beginning of the twenty-first century, has acknowledged Napoleon Hill as a personal hero.

I have never known anyone who was inspired to use the Carnegie secret who did not achieve noteworthy success. On the other hand, I have never known any person to distinguish themself, or to accumulate riches of any consequence, without possession of the secret. From these two facts I draw the conclusion that the secret is more important for self-determination than anything you receive through what is popularly known as "education."

Somewhere, as you read, the secret will jump from the page and stand boldly before you, if you are ready for it. When it appears, you will recognize it. Whether you receive the sign in the first chapter or the last, stop for a moment when it presents itself, and make a note of the time and place. You will want to remember, because it will mark the most important turning point of your life.

Remember, too, as you go through the book, that it deals with facts and not with fiction. Its purpose is to convey a great universal truth through which you, if you are ready, may learn what to do and how to do it. You will also receive the needed stimulus to make a start.

As a final word of preparation, may I offer one brief suggestion that could provide a clue how the Carnegie secret might be recognized? It is this: achievement, and all earned riches, have their beginning in an idea. If you are ready for the secret, you already possess one-half of it. Therefore, you will recognize the other half the moment it reaches your mind.

COMMENTARY

Unlike much of the business and motivational literature available, with Think and Grow Rich *it is not intended that readers skip around from chapter to* chapter, taking a concept here and an idea there to solve the problem of the moment. This book is written as a carefully integrated whole, to be read in its entirety from beginning to end. Concepts that are introduced in one chapter recur in other chapters where their meaning and significance rely upon the reader having already assimilated the earlier knowledge. The chapters are designed to build upon one another in such a way that every word is to be read, every idea is to be considered, and every concept is to be understood and absorbed.

Think and Grow Rich *is often called the first Philosophy of Personal Achievement, and a philosophy is more than a collection of solutions to business problems. A philosophy is a system of principles that will guide your thoughts and actions, and provide you with a code of ethics and a standard of values. This book will not just change what you think, but it will literally change the way you think.*

In preparing this new and updated edition, every aspect of Think and Grow Rich *has been analyzed to ensure its relevance to the current business climate. In those instances where material might be considered dated or out of step with contemporary practices, the original text has been updated or augmented with relevant new material.*

A hallmark of the original edition of Think and Grow Rich *is that in every chapter Napoleon Hill cites real-life examples based on his own firsthand knowledge of America's most successful self-made multimillionaires. In this edition every one of Hill's stories has been retained, and the editors have added contemporary examples and modern parallels which clearly demonstrate that Hill's principles are as up-to-date as today, and are still guiding those who succeed.*

In addition to contemporary examples, where the editors felt it would be of interest to the reader, we have included marginal notes that provide relevant information about more recent developments. Where applicable, we have also suggested books and other materials that complement various aspects of Napoleon Hill's philosophy.

NOTES & COMMENTS

On a more technical note, the editors have approached the written text as we would that of a living author. When we encountered what modern grammarians would consider run-on sentences, outdated punctuation, or other matters of form, we opted for contemporary usage.

Those readers familiar with earlier editions will notice that the chapter numbers have been changed in this edition. Originally, Think and Grow Rich *began with an unnumbered chapter,* A Word from the Author. *In this edition, that text appears as chapter 1 and is renamed* The Secret of Success. *The chapters that follow are renumbered sequentially and proceed in their original order. The chapter that was previously titled* The Mystery of Sex Transmutation *has been retitled* Sexuality: Charisma and Creativity, *and the text has been restructured and annotated to reflect the role of women in contemporary society.*

All editorial commentary is clearly set off in a font and style that is different from the original text.

BOTH POVERTY AND RICHES

ARE THE OFFSPRING

OF THOUGHT.

As you think it, so it is

Law of attraction

THOUGHTS ARE THINGS

THE MAN WHO "THOUGHT" HIS WAY INTO PARTNERSHIP WITH THOMAS A. EDISON

Truly, "thoughts are things." And powerful things, when they are mixed with definiteness of purpose, persistence, and a burning desire for their translation into riches, or other material objects.

Some years ago, Edwin C. Barnes discovered how true it is that you really can *think and grow rich.* His discovery did not come about at one sitting. It came little by little, beginning with a burning desire to become a business associate of the great Thomas Edison.

One of the chief characteristics of Barnes' desire was that it was definite. He wanted to work *with* Edison, not *for* him. Pay close attention to the story of how he turned his desire into reality, and you will have a better understanding of the principles that lead to riches.

When this desire, or this thought, first flashed into his mind he was in no position to act upon it. Two problems stood in his way. He did not know Mr. Edison, and he did not have enough money to buy a train ticket to West Orange, New Jersey, where the famed Edison laboratory was located.

These problems would have discouraged the majority of people from making any attempt to carry out the desire. But his was no ordinary desire!

THE INVENTOR AND THE TRAMP

Edwin C. Barnes presented himself at Mr. Edison's laboratory and announced that he had come to go into business with the inventor. Years later, in speaking about that first meeting, Mr. Edison said about Barnes:

> He stood there before me, looking like an ordinary tramp, but there was something in the expression of his face which conveyed the impression that he was determined to get what he had come after. I had learned, from years of experience with men, that when a man really desires a thing so deeply that he is willing to stake his entire future on a single turn of the wheel in order to get it, he is sure to win. I gave him the opportunity he asked for, because I saw he had made up his mind to stand by until he succeeded. Subsequent events proved that no mistake was made.

It could not have been the young man's appearance that got him his start in the Edison office. That was definitely against him. It was what he thought that counted.

Barnes did not get his partnership with Edison on his first interview. What he did get was a chance to work in the Edison offices, at a very nominal wage.

Months went by. Nothing happened to bring nearer the goal that Barnes had set as his definite major purpose. But something important was happening in Barnes' mind. He was constantly intensifying his desire to become the business associate of Edison.

Psychologists have correctly said, "when one is truly ready for a thing, it puts in its appearance." Barnes was ready for a business association with Edison. And he was determined to remain ready until he got what he was seeking.

He did not say to himself, "Ah well, what's the use? I guess I'll change my mind and try for a salesman's job." But he did say, "I came here to go into business with Edison, and I'll accomplish my goal if it takes the remainder of my life." He meant it. What a different story people would tell if only they would adopt a definite purpose and stand by that purpose until it had time to become an all-consuming obsession.

Maybe young Barnes did not know it at the time, but his bulldog determination, and his persistence in focusing on a single desire, was destined to mow down all opposition and bring him the opportunity he was seeking.

When the opportunity came, it appeared in a different form and from a different direction than Barnes had expected. That is one of the tricks of opportunity. It has a sly habit of slipping in by the back door. And often it comes disguised in the form of misfortune, or temporary defeat. Perhaps this is why so many people fail to recognize opportunity.

Mr. Edison had just perfected a new device, known at that time as the Edison Dictating Machine. His salesmen were not enthusiastic about the machine. They did not believe it could be sold without great effort. Barnes saw his opportunity. It had crawled in quietly, hidden in a queer-looking machine that interested no one but Barnes and the inventor.

Barnes knew he could sell the Edison Dictating Machine, and he told Edison so. Edison decided to give him his chance. And Barnes did sell the machine. In fact, he sold it so successfully that Edison gave him a contract to distribute and market it all over the nation. Out of that business association Barnes made himself rich in money, but he did something infinitely greater. He proved that you really can *think and grow rich*.

How much actual cash that original desire of Barnes' was worth to him, I have no way of knowing. Perhaps it brought him two or three million dollars *[three million dollars in the early years of the twentieth century would be comparable to more than fifty million dollars in terms of buying power at the beginning of the twenty-first century]*. But the amount becomes insignificant compared with the greater asset he acquired: the definite knowledge that an intangible impulse of thought can be transmuted into material rewards by the application of known principles.

Barnes literally *thought* himself into a partnership with the great Edison! He thought himself into a fortune. He had nothing to start with, except knowing what he wanted, and the determination to stand by that desire until he realized it.

THREE FEET FROM GOLD

One of the most common causes of failure is the habit of quitting when you are overtaken by temporary defeat. Every person is guilty of this mistake at one time or another.

During the gold-rush days, an uncle of my friend R. U. Darby was caught by "gold fever" and he went west to Colorado to dig and grow rich. He had never heard that more gold has been mined from the thoughts of men than has ever been taken from the earth. He staked a claim and went to work with pick and shovel.

After weeks of labor, he was rewarded by the discovery of the shining ore. He needed machinery to bring the ore to the surface. Quietly he covered up the mine and returned to his home in Williamsburg, Maryland. He told his relatives and a few neighbors about the strike. They got together the money for the machinery and had it shipped. R. U. Darby decided to join his uncle, and they went back to work the mine.

The first car of ore was mined and shipped to a smelter. The returns proved they had one of the richest mines in Colorado. A few more cars of that ore would clear their debts. Then would come the big killing in profits.

Down went the drills. Up went the hopes of Darby and Uncle. Then something happened. The vein of gold ore disappeared! They had come to the end of the rainbow, and the pot of gold was no longer there. They drilled on, desperately trying to pick up the vein again —all to no avail.

Finally, they decided to quit.

They sold the machinery to a junkman for a few hundred dollars, and took the train back home. The junkman called in a mining engineer to look at the mine and do a little calculating. The engineer advised that the project had failed because the owners were not familiar with "fault lines." His calculations showed that the vein would be found just three feet from where the Darbys had stopped drilling. And that is exactly where it was found!

The junkman took millions of dollars in ore from the mine because he knew enough to seek expert counsel before giving up.

Long afterward, Mr. Darby recouped his loss many times over when he made the discovery that desire can be transmuted into gold. The discovery came after he went into the business of selling life insurance.

Never forgetting that he lost a huge fortune because he stopped three feet from gold, Darby profited by the experience in his newly chosen field. He simply said to himself, "I stopped three feet from gold, but I will never stop because men say no when I ask them to buy insurance."

Darby became one of a small group of men who sell over a million dollars in life insurance annually. He owed his "stickability"

Don't give up 5 min before the miracle

NOTES & COMMENTS

to the lesson he learned from his "quitability" in the gold-mining business.

Before success comes in anyone's life, that person is sure to meet with much temporary defeat and, perhaps, some failure. When defeat overtakes a person, the easiest and most logical thing to do is to quit. That is exactly what the majority of people do.

More than five hundred of the most successful people this country has ever known told me their greatest success came just one step beyond the point at which defeat had overtaken them. Failure is a trickster with a keen sense of irony and cunning. It takes great delight in tripping you just when success is almost within reach.

COMMENTARY

Napoleon Hill's creed, "Every failure brings with it the seed of an equivalent success," was the inspiration for entrepreneur and motivational speaker Wayne Allyn Root to write his book The Joy of Failure. *Published in the late 1990s, it not only tells Wayne's personal story of using his failures as steppingstones to success, but also recounts stories from other successful people which prove that the rich and famous got to be that way only because of what they learned from their failures. People such as Jack Welch, the hugely successful CEO of General Electric, who, early in his career, failed dramatically when a plastics plant for which he was responsible blew up. Billionaire Charles Schwab was a failure at school and university, flunking Basic English twice due to a learning disability, and then failed on Wall Street more than once before he thought of the idea that grew to make him very rich indeed. Sylvester Stallone, Bruce Willis, Oprah Winfrey, Bill Clinton, Steven Jobs, Donald Trump, and a host of other equally well-known achievers all had to fail in order to learn the lessons that ultimately made them successes. Every one of them was a failure, but none of them was defeated.*

Charles F. Kettering, who patented more than two hundred inventions including the automobile ignition, the spark plug, Freon for air conditioners, and the automatic transmission, said, " From the time a person is six years old until he graduates from college he has to take three or four examinations a year. If he flunks once, he is out. But an inventor is almost always failing. He tries and fails maybe a thousand times. If he succeeds once, then he's in. These two things are diametrically opposite. We often say that the biggest job we have is to teach a newly hired employee how to fail intelligently. We have to train him to experiment over and over and to keep on trying and failing until he learns what will work. Failures are just practice shots." ✳

A FIFTY-CENT LESSON IN PERSISTENCE

Shortly after Mr. Darby received his degree from the "University of Hard Knocks," he witnessed something that proved to him that *no* ✳ does not necessarily mean NO.

One afternoon he was helping his uncle grind wheat in an old-fashioned mill. The uncle operated a large farm on which a number of sharecropper farmers lived. Quietly the door was opened, and a small child, the daughter of a tenant, walked in and took her place near the door.

The uncle looked up, saw the child, and barked at her roughly, "What do you want?"

Meekly, the child replied, "My mom says to send her fifty cents."

"I'll not do it," the uncle retorted. "Now you run on home."

But she did not move.

The uncle went ahead with his work, not noticing that she did not leave. When he looked up again and saw her still standing there, he said, "I told you to go on home! Now go, or I'll take a switch to you."

But she did not budge.

The uncle dropped a sack of grain he was about to pour into the mill hopper, and started toward the child.

Darby held his breath. He knew his uncle had a fierce temper.

Handwritten note in margin:
No is the second best answer
① yes
② NO
③ I have to think about it

NOTES & COMMENTS

When the uncle reached the spot where the child was standing, she quickly stepped forward one step, looked up into his eyes, and screamed at the top of her voice, "My mom's gotta have that fifty cents!"

The uncle stopped, looked at her for a minute, put his hand in his pocket, took out half a dollar, and gave it to her.

The child took the money and slowly backed toward the door, never taking her eyes off the man whom she had just conquered. After she had gone, the uncle sat down on a box and looked out the window into space for more than ten minutes. He was pondering, with awe, over the whipping he had just taken.

Mr. Darby, too, was doing some thinking. That was the first time in all his experience that he had seen a child deliberately master an adult. How did she do it? What happened to his uncle that caused him to lose his fierceness and become as docile as a lamb? What strange power did this child use that made her master of the situation? These questions flashed into Darby's mind, but he did not find the answer until years later, when he told me the story.

Strangely, the story of this unusual experience was told to me in the old mill, on the very spot where the uncle took his whipping.

As we stood there in that musty old mill, Mr. Darby repeated the story, and finished by asking, "What can you make of it? What strange power did that child use, that so completely whipped my uncle?"

The answer to his question will be found in the principles described in this book. The answer is full and complete. It contains enough details and instructions for you to understand and apply the same force that the little child accidentally stumbled upon.

Keep your mind alert and you will learn exactly what strange power came to the rescue of the child. You may catch a glimpse of the power in this chapter, or it may flash into your mind in some later chapter. If you stay alert to the possibility, somewhere you will find the idea that will quicken your receptive powers and place at your command this same irresistible power. It may come in the form of a single idea. Or it may come as a complete plan, or a purpose. It may even cause you to go back over your past experiences of failure or defeat. And, in doing so, it may bring to the surface some lesson by which you can regain all that you lost through defeat.

After I had explained to Mr. Darby the power unwittingly used by the little child, he mentally retraced his thirty years as a life insurance salesman. As he did so, it became clear to him that his success was due, in no small degree, to the lesson he had learned from the child.

Mr. Darby pointed out: "Every time a prospect tried to bow me out, without buying, I saw that child standing there in the old mill, her big eyes glaring in defiance, and I said to myself: 'I've got to make this sale.' The better portion of all sales I have made were made after people had said no."

He also recalled his mistake in having stopped only three feet from gold. "But," he said, "that experience was a blessing in disguise. It taught me to keep on keeping on, no matter how hard the going may be—a lesson I needed to learn before I could succeed in anything."

Mr. Darby's experiences were commonplace and simple enough, yet they held the answer to his destiny in life. In fact, to him the experiences were as important as life itself. And he was able to profit from these two important experiences, because he analyzed them and found the lesson they taught.

But what if you don't see the events of your life as being experiences of such profound significance? And what about the young person who doesn't yet have even minor failures to analyze? Where and how will they learn the art of converting defeats into the stepping-stones to opportunity?

That is exactly why this book was written—to answer those questions.

To convey my answer I have constructed thirteen principles. These principles work individually or together as catalysts. The specific answer that *you* are looking for may already be in your own mind.

Yes

No

I have to think about it

NOTES & COMMENTS

Reading these principles may be the catalyst that causes your answer to suddenly come to you as an idea, a plan, or a purpose.

One sound idea is all you need to achieve success. These thirteen principles contain the best and most practical ways and means of creating ideas.

SUCCESS CONSCIOUSNESS

Before I go any further in the description of these principles, you should know this: When riches begin to come, they come so quickly, and in such great abundance, that you will wonder where they have been hiding during all those lean years.

This is an astounding statement, especially when you take into consideration the popular belief that riches come only to those who work hard and long.

When you begin to *think and grow rich,* you will observe that riches begin with a state of mind, with definiteness of purpose, with little or no hard work. What you need to know now is how to acquire the state of mind that will attract riches. I spent twenty-five years researching the answer to that question because I, too, wanted to know "how wealthy men become that way."

What you will learn is that as soon as you master the principles of this philosophy, and begin to apply those principles, your financial status will begin to improve. Everything you touch will begin to transmute itself into an asset for your benefit. Impossible? Not at all!

One of the main weaknesses the average person suffers is too much familiarity with the word *impossible.* We know all the rules that will not work. We know all the things that cannot be done. This book was written for those who seek the rules that have made others successful, and are willing to stake everything on those rules.

Success comes to those who become success conscious.

Failure comes to those who allow themselves to become failure conscious.

The object of this book is to help you learn the art of changing your mind from failure consciousness to success consciousness.

Another weakness is the habit of measuring everything, and everyone, by your own impressions and beliefs. Some of you reading this will have trouble believing that you can *think and grow rich*, because your thought habits have been steeped in poverty, misery, failure, and defeat.

This kind of thinking reminds me of the story about the man who came from China to study at the University of Chicago. One day President Harper met this young man on campus and stopped to chat with him for a few minutes. He asked what had impressed him as being the most noticeable characteristic of the American people.

"Why," the student exclaimed, "the unusual shape of your eyes."

It's all a matter of perspective and habit.

The same is true of your belief in what a person can achieve. If you have formed the habit of seeing life only from your own perspective, you may make the mistake of believing that *your* limitations are in fact the proper measure of limitations.

THE "IMPOSSIBLE" FORD V-8 MOTOR

When Henry Ford decided to produce his famous V-8 motor, he chose to build an engine with the entire eight cylinders cast in one block. Ford instructed his engineers to produce a design for the engine. The design was drawn up on paper, but the engineers agreed, to a man, that it was simply impossible to cast an eight-cylinder engine block in one piece.

Ford said, "Produce it anyway."

"But," they replied, "it's impossible!"

Desire: Knowing clearly what you WANT

"Go ahead," Ford commanded, "and stay on the job until you succeed. No matter how much time is required."

So the engineers went ahead. Six months went by. Nothing happened. Another six months passed, and still nothing. The engineers tried every conceivable plan to carry out the orders, but the thing seemed out of the question. "Impossible!"

At the end of the year Ford again checked with his engineers And again they told him they had found no way to carry out his orders.

"Go right ahead," said Ford. "I want it, and I'll have it." They went ahead, and then, as if by a stroke of magic, the secret was discovered.

The Ford determination had won once more!

Henry Ford was a success because he understood and applied the *principles* of success. One of these principles is desire: knowing clearly what you want. Remember this Ford story as you continue reading this book. Pick out the lines in which the secrets of his stupendous achievement have been described. If you do this, if you can put your finger on those particular principles that made Henry Ford rich, you may equal his achievements in almost any calling for which you are suited.

COMMENTARY

To those readers who may interpret Ford's actions as nothing more than obstinacy, the editors would point out that he was employing a technique that has become a common part of strategic planning in many industries including aerospace, computers, medicine, and the military.

When launching large, complicated, long-term projects the planners often know that at certain points along the way they will need components that simply do not yet exist. The fact that at the beginning there is no way to get from A to B does not deter them. There are many parts of the project they can get started on now, and they just assume that by the time they get to the point where they will need a technology or a device, they will have solved the problem of making it. And they have been proven right time and again.

Stated simply, the technique is to clearly know what you want to accomplish, have faith in your ability to do it, and persist until you have accomplished your goal.

WHY YOU ARE "THE MASTER OF YOUR FATE"

When the famed English poet William Henley wrote the prophetic lines "I am the master of my fate, I am the captain of my soul," he should have informed us that the reason we are the masters of our fate, the captains of our souls, is that we have the power to control our thoughts.

He should have told us that it is because in some way our brains become "magnetized" with the dominating thoughts that we hold in our minds. And it is as though our magnetized minds attract to us the forces, the people, and the circumstances of life that are in sync with our dominating thoughts.

He should have told us that before we can accumulate riches in great abundance, we must magnetize our minds with intense desire for riches. That we must become "money conscious" until the desire for money drives us to create definite plans for acquiring it.

But, being a poet, Henley contented himself by stating a great truth in poetic form, leaving those who followed him to interpret the philosophical meaning of his lines.

Little by little the truth has unfolded itself, until I have come to know with certainty that the principles described in this book hold the secret of mastery over our economic fate.

PRINCIPLES THAT CAN CHANGE YOUR DESTINY

We are now ready to examine the first of these principles, and as we do I ask you to maintain a spirit of open-mindedness. Remember, as you read, that these principles are not my invention. Nor are they the

NOTES & COMMENTS

Particle physics
The Secret
See it, feel it

NOTES & COMMENTS

invention of any one person. These principles have worked for literally millions of people. You, too, can put them to work for you and your own enduring benefit. You will find it easy, not hard, to do.

Some years ago I delivered the commencement address at Salem College in Salem, West Virginia. I emphasized with so much intensity the need to have a burning desire, that one of the members of the graduating class became completely convinced and made it a cornerstone of his own philosophy. That young man became a congressman and an important factor in President Franklin D. Roosevelt's administration. He wrote me a letter in which he so clearly stated his opinion of the principle of desire outlined in the next chapter, that I have chosen to publish his letter as an introduction to that chapter. It gives you an idea of the rewards to come.

My dear Napoleon:

My service as a member of Congress having given me an insight into the problems of men and women, I am writing to offer a suggestion, which may become helpful to thousands of worthy people.

In 1922, you delivered the commencement address at Salem College, when I was a member of the graduating class. In that address, you planted in my mind an idea, which has been responsible for the opportunity I now have to serve the people of my state, and will be responsible, in a very large measure, for whatever success I may have in the future.

I recall, as though it were yesterday, the marvelous description you gave of the method by which Henry Ford, with but little schooling, without a dollar, with no influential friends, rose to great heights. I made up my mind then, even before you had finished your speech, that I would make a place for myself, no matter how many difficulties I had to surmount.

Thousands of young people will finish their schooling this year, and within the next few years. Every one of them will be seeking just such a message of practical encouragement as the one I received from you. They will want to know where to turn, what to do, to get started in life. You can tell them, because you have helped to solve the problems of so many, many people.

There are thousands of people in America today who would like to know how they can convert ideas into money, people who must start from scratch, without finances, and recoup their losses. If anyone can help them, you can.

If you publish the book, I would like to own the first copy that comes from the press, personally autographed by you.

With best wishes, believe me,

Cordially yours,

Jennings Randolph

Since that time in 1922, I watched Jennings Randolph rise to become one of the nation's leading airline executives, a great inspirational speaker, and a United States senator from West Virginia.

Thirty-five years after I made that speech, it was my pleasure to return to Salem College in 1957 and deliver the baccalaureate sermon. At that time, I received an honorary Doctor of Literature degree from Salem College.

COMMENTARY

As you begin the next chapter, the editors would like to reinforce the earlier statement that what you are reading is not just a collection of theories out of which you can cherry-pick what you like.

The thirteen principles of success were proven by the real-life experiences of the long list of famous successful people cited earlier by Napoleon Hill.

NOTES & COMMENTS

His techniques are also practiced and endorsed by the contemporary experts and authors whom the editors mentioned, following Hill's list. More than 60 million people have purchased copies of the book that you are now holding in your hands.

If this book has proven to be that successful, surely you owe it to yourself to give it every chance to work for you too. Read it. Don't question it. Do it. If you don't, if you think that you know better than Napoleon Hill, if you decide to pick and choose the parts that you will believe or follow, then if you don't succeed you will never know if your failure lies with this book or with you.

WHATEVER

THE MIND OF MAN

CAN CONCEIVE AND BELIEVE

IT CAN ACHIEVE.

CHAPTER

3

DESIRE

THE STARTING POINT OF ALL ACHIEVEMENT

The First Step Toward Riches

When Edwin C. Barnes climbed down from the freight train in West Orange, New Jersey, he may have resembled a tramp but his thoughts were those of a king.

As he made his way from the railroad tracks to Thomas A. Edison's office, his mind was at work. He saw himself standing in Edison's presence. He heard himself asking Mr. Edison for an opportunity to carry out the one consuming obsession of his life—a burning desire to become the business associate of the great inventor.

Barnes' desire was not a hope. It was not a wish. It was a pulsating desire, which transcended everything else. It was definite.

A few years later, Edwin C. Barnes again stood before Edison, in the same office where he first met the inventor. This time his desire had been translated into reality. He was in business with Edison. The dominating dream of his life had become a reality.

NOTES & COMMENTS

Barnes succeeded because he chose a definite goal, placed all his energy, all his willpower, all his effort—he put everything he had into achieving that goal.

Five years passed before the chance he had been seeking made its appearance. To everyone, except himself, he appeared to be just another cog in the Edison business wheel. But in Edwin Barnes' own mind, he was the partner of Edison every minute from the very day that he first went to work there.

It is a remarkable illustration of the power of a definite desire. Barnes won his goal because he wanted to be a business associate of Mr. Edison's more than he wanted anything else. He created a plan by which to attain that purpose, and he burned all bridges behind him. He stood by his desire until it became the dominating obsession of his life—and finally, a fact.

When he went to West Orange he did not say to himself, "I will try to induce Edison to give me a job of some sort." He said, "I will see Edison, and put him on notice that I have come to go into business with him."

He did not say, "I will keep my eyes open for another opportunity, in case I fail to get what I want in the Edison organization." He said, "There is one thing in this world that I am determined to have, and that is a business association with Thomas A. Edison. I will burn all bridges behind me and stake my entire future on my ability to get what I want."

He left himself no possible way of retreat. He had to win or perish!

That is all there is to the Barnes story of success.

ALLOW YOURSELF NO RETREAT

A long while ago, a great warrior faced a situation in which he had to make a decision that ensured his success on the battlefield. He was about to send his armies against a powerful foe whose men

Which battle?

outnumbered his. He loaded his soldiers into boats, sailed to the enemy's country, and unloaded the soldiers and equipment. Then he gave the order to burn the ships that had carried them. Addressing his men before the first battle, he said, "You see the boats going up in smoke. That means we cannot leave these shores alive unless we win! We now have no choice—we win or we perish!"

They won.

Every person who wins in any undertaking must be willing to burn his ships and cut all sources of retreat. That is the only way you can be sure of maintaining the state of mind known as a *burning desire* to win. It is essential to success.

how to cultivate?

The morning after the great Chicago fire a group of merchants stood on State Street, looking at the smoking remains of what had been their stores. They went into a conference to decide if they would try to rebuild or if they would leave Chicago and start over in a more promising section of the country. They decided to leave. All except one.

The merchant who decided to stay and rebuild pointed a finger at the remains of his store and said, "Gentlemen, on that very spot I will build the world's greatest store, no matter how many times it may burn down."

That was in 1871. The store was built. It still stands there today. The Marshall Field's Department Store is a towering monument to the power of that state of mind known as a burning desire. The easy thing would have been for Marshall Field to do exactly what his fellow merchants did. When the going was hard, and the future looked dismal, they pulled up and went where the going seemed easier.

Mark well this difference between Marshall Field and the other merchants. It is that difference which distinguishes those who succeed from those who fail.

Every human being old enough to understand the value of money wishes for it. But wishing will not bring riches. Desiring riches, with a state of mind that becomes an obsession, then planning definite ways and means to acquire riches, and backing those plans with persistence—a persistence which does not recognize failure—that's what will bring riches.

COMMENTARY

In other of his writings, Napoleon Hill uses the term definiteness of purpose *as being interchangeable with* desire. *The following explanation is adapted from the Napoleon Hill Foundation's book* Believe and Achieve.

Desire or Definiteness of Purpose is more than goal setting. In simplest terms, your Desire is your road map to achieving an overall career objective. Your goals represent specific steps along the way.

Having a Desire or Definiteness of Purpose for your life has a synergistic effect on your ability to achieve your goals. As you become better at what you do you devote all of your resources toward reaching your objective, you become more alert to opportunities, and you reach decisions more quickly. Every action you take ultimately boils down to the question: Will this goal help me reach my Desire, my overall objective, or won't it?

Your purpose will become your life; it will permeate your mind, both conscious and subconscious.

SIX WAYS TO TURN DESIRE INTO GOLD

The method by which your desire for riches can be transmuted into its financial equivalent consists of six definite, practical steps:

1. Fix in your mind the exact amount of money you desire. It is not sufficient merely to say "I want plenty of money." Be definite about the amount. (There is a psychological reason for such definiteness explained in subsequent chapters.)

2. Determine exactly what you intend to give in return for the money you desire. (There is no such reality as "something for nothing.")

3. Establish a definite date when you intend to possess the money you desire.

4. Create a definite plan for carrying out your desire and begin at once, whether you are ready or not, to put this plan into action.

5. Now write it out. Write a clear, concise statement of the amount of money you intend to acquire, name the time limit for its acquisition, state what you intend to give in return for the money, and describe clearly the plan through which you intend to accumulate it.

6. Read your written statement aloud, twice daily. Read it once just before retiring at night, and read it once after arising in the morning. As you read, see and feel and believe yourself already in possession of the money.

It is important that you follow the instructions in these six steps. It is especially important that you observe and follow the instructions in the sixth step. You may complain that it is impossible for you to "see yourself in possession of money" before you actually have it. Here is where a burning desire will come to your aid. If you truly desire money so keenly that your desire is an obsession, you will have no difficulty in convincing yourself that you will acquire it. The object is to want money, and to become so determined to have it that you convince yourself you will have it.

If you have not been schooled in the workings of the human mind, these instructions may appear impractical. It may help you to

NOTES & COMMENTS

know that the information they convey was given to me by Andrew Carnegie, who made himself into one of the most successful men in American history. Carnegie began as an ordinary laborer in the steel mills, but managed, despite his humble beginning, to make these principles yield him a fortune of considerably more than $100 million. *[In today's terms, the value of Carnegie's fortune would be at least $20 billion, and probably a good deal more.]*

It may be of further help to know that the six steps were carefully scrutinized by the famed inventor and successful businessman, Thomas A. Edison. He gave his stamp of approval, saying they are not only the steps essential for the accumulation of money, but also for the attainment of any goal.

COMMENTARY

In the time since Napoleon Hill wrote these words, advances in our understanding of both the physiology of the brain and the psychology of the mind have yielded a much greater understanding of human motivation. Even so, the methods used by modern motivational experts are essentially the same techniques advised by Hill. Research studies confirm that there is sound psychological basis for doing as Hill advises: be very specific when setting goals, perform the physical act of committing those goals to paper, and repeat your stated goal aloud to yourself often.

These techniques have gained wide acceptance among modern experts in the field. The psychological principle at work is similar to that which underlies autosuggestion and self-hypnosis—concepts that will be discussed in greater depth in chapter 5, Autosuggestion, and in chapter 13, The Subconscious Mind.

Hill's instruction to "see yourself as you will be when you have already achieved your objective" is also a specific technique. Today it is commonly taught by motivational experts under the term "creative visualization." In chapter 4 on faith and in chapter 5 on autosuggestion, Hill elaborates on his method.

Before moving on, the editors would like to reinforce Hill's advice to follow his instructions to the letter. The editors know there is a tendency for the reader to assume that it is enough for them just to intellectually understand a concept. As you read Hill's six points, you probably found yourself thinking, "Sure, some people might need to write things down, but I'm not a kid. I get the idea." Or, "Okay, I understand that saying it out loud might help some less sophisticated people, but I already understand the point intellectually." If you feel that way, let us remind you that many of the most successful people whom you admire did not think they were too smart or too sophisticated to follow Hill's instructions. The editors would again point out that if Napoleon Hill believed the actual acts of writing and speaking your goals is important, and if psychologists and motivational experts agree, then you would be foolish not to follow this simple advice. Just do it.

The steps call for no hard labor. They call for no sacrifice. To apply them does not call for a great amount of education. But the six steps do call for enough imagination to see, and to understand, that the accumulation of money cannot be left to chance or luck.

You may as well know, right here, that you can never have riches in great quantity unless you can work yourself into a white heat of desire for money, and actually believe you will possess it.

THE POWER OF GREAT DREAMS

If you are in this race for riches, you should be encouraged by the following truth: The world in which we live is demanding new ideas, new ways of doing things, new leaders, new inventions, and new methods, styles, versions, and variations of everything all of the time. Behind all this demand for new and better things, there is one quality that you must possess to win, and that is definiteness of purpose— the knowledge of what you want, and a burning desire to possess it.

NOTES & COMMENTS

If you truly desire riches, remember that the real leaders of the world have always been people who harnessed, and put into practical use, the intangible, unseen forces of opportunity. Leaders are the people who convert those opportunities into cities, skyscrapers, factories, transportation, entertainment, and every form of convenience that make things easier, faster, better, or just make life more pleasant.

In planning to acquire your share of the riches, don't let anyone put you down for being a dreamer. To win the big stakes in this changing world, you must catch the spirit of the great pioneers, whose dreams have given to civilization all that it has of value. It is that spirit which serves as the life-blood of our own country—your opportunity and mine, to develop and market our talents.

A burning desire to be and to do is the starting point from which the dreamer must take off. Dreams are not born of indifference, laziness, or lack of ambition.

If the thing you wish to do is right, and you believe in it, go ahead and do it. Never mind what "they" say if you meet with temporary defeat. "They" do not know that every failure brings with it the seed of an equivalent success.

Marconi dreamed of a system for sending sound from one place to another without the use of wires. It may interest you to know that Marconi's "friends" had him taken into custody, and examined in a psychiatric hospital, when he announced he had discovered a principle by which he could send messages through the air. Evidence that he did not dream in vain may be found in every radio *[and television set, cellular phone, communications satellite, and every other "wireless" device]* in the world.

Fortunately, the dreamers of today fare better. Today your world is filled with an abundance of opportunity that the dreamers of the past never knew.

If you doubt this is true, if you are feeling crushed because of a recent failure, you are about to learn how your failure can be your most valuable asset. Almost everyone who succeeds in life gets off to a bad start, and passes through many heartbreaking struggles, before they "arrive." The turning point in the lives of those who succeed usually comes at the moment of some crisis, through which they are introduced to their "other selves."

COMMENTARY

Napoleon Hill's concept of the "other self" is mentioned elsewhere in Think and Grow Rich, *but he does not comment on it extensively. The following elaboration is taken from his later writings:*

> *You've been thinking about your losses to the exclusion of everything else. The more you concentrate on them, the more you attract other losses. Stop thinking about them, and make up your mind that you are going to benefit from your experience. Whatever personal obstacles you face, you must start getting to know that side of your personality that knows no obstacles, that recognizes no defeats. Cultivate a friendship with the "other" you, so no matter what you are doing, you are allied with someone who shares your goals. All the philosophy and advice about persuading others will be much more useful to you if you practice it yourself.*

Sydney Porter discovered the genius that slept within his brain only after he had met with great misfortune. He was found guilty of embezzlement, and confined to a prison cell in Columbus, Ohio, and it was there that he became acquainted with his "other self."

He began to write short stories. Then, while locked in his cell, he began to sell those stories to magazines under the pen name O. Henry. Through the use of his imagination, he discovered himself to be a great author instead of a miserable criminal and outcast. By the time he was released from prison, O. Henry was the most popular short-story writer in the country.

NOTES & COMMENTS

More recently, in another prison, another kind of writer met his other self, and country music gained one of its most talented songwriters and biggest stars. As a kid, Merle Haggard's family home was a converted boxcar in Bakersfield, California. After his father died when Merle was nine, more often than not, home for young Merle was a series of juvenile detention centers. At sixteen he quit school, and for the next four years the only mark Merle Haggard made in the world was a rap sheet for stolen cars, burglaries, and bogus checks. By the age of twenty, he was serving time in San Quentin and gaining a reputation as a hard-case con.

Then he met his other self. Inspired by a concert Johnny Cash played for the inmates, plus conversations with men on death row and the time he spent in solitary confinement, Haggard learned that he had another self—and that self had something to say through his music.

When he got out of solitary Haggard asked for the hardest job the prison had to offer, he enrolled in night-school courses at the prison, straightened himself out, and won his parole after two and a half years. He went back to Bakersfield, and dug ditches during the day so he could polish his songwriting and performing at night. Within three years he had a recording contract, within five years he had his first top-ten hit, and has since gone on to become one of the most influential voices in modern country music.

Thomas Edison dreamed of a lamp that could be operated by electricity, and he began where he stood to put his dream into action. He failed more than ten thousand times. Despite his failures, he stood by that dream until finally he was driven to the discovery of the genius that slept within his brain.

COMMENTARY

Dean Kamen got to know his other self very early in life. While he was a teenager Kamen started his own company, building and selling control systems for automated sound and light shows. He was still in high school when he got the contract to automate the Times Square New Year's Eve ball. Though he went on to attend university, he never bothered to graduate because he was too busy working on something he called Auto-Syringe, the first wearable infusion pump for administering drug therapies. His invention was hailed as a medical landmark, as were many of his other breakthroughs which include a revolutionary kidney dialysis machine, an insulin pump for diabetics, an improved stent used for heart patients, and more than one hundred and fifty other devices he has patented.

One day, seeing the difficulty a man in a wheelchair was having getting up a curb, Kamen set his mind to creating a device that would liberate people confined to wheelchairs. The result is the iBot, a revolutionary wheeled device that uses computers and a system of stabilizing gyroscopes that imitate the working of the human body. It not only goes over curbs but it will even go up and down stairs, travel over almost any kind of rough ground, and will allow the user to raise themself eye-to-eye with a standing person. And it does it all without the user having to get out of the device or needing anyone's assistance.

In 2001 Kamen hit the front pages when he introduced the Segway, a one-person people-mover, based on his iBot technology. It's a two-wheel scooter-like device that zips and zooms forward, backward, left, right, and comes to a stop without the rider doing anything more than barely shifting his or her body. It is so sensitive that it is almost as though it obeys the user's thoughts. The Segway may be a world-changing invention, with possible applications for work and travel that stagger the imagination. As this is being written, the Segway is already being used to navigate large warehouses and is being tested by police departments and postal employees.

While traffic cops and city hall wrangle over whether the Segway belongs on the sidewalk or the road, Dean Kamen is dreaming a new dream. This time the dream is an invention that may literally bring light to some of the darkest corners of the earth. Kamen has developed a nonpolluting electric generator that can use almost anything as fuel. But here's the extraordinary part—he has created a revolutionary closed system so that the engine's heat is used to purify ten gallons of drinkable water every hour. This amazing invention could bring

NOTES & COMMENTS

safe drinking water to parts of the world where contaminated water kills millions, and at the same time it will provide a source of cheap, reliable, electric power.

Dean Kamen is not some academic hidden in a lab somewhere. Kamen is an inventor, but like Thomas Edison, he is also an entrepreneur and businessman creating and marketing devices that are changing the public perception of what an inventor is.

Henry Ford, poor and uneducated, dreamed of a horseless carriage. He went to work with what tools he possessed, without waiting for opportunity to favor him, and now evidence of his dream belts the entire earth. He put more wheels into operation than any man who ever lived, because he was not afraid to back his dreams.

COMMENTARY

Steven Jobs and Steve Wozniak, two university dropouts, dreamed of making and selling computers that the average person could use. Like Ford, working with the tools they possessed, they built the first Apple computer in the Jobs' family garage, and, like Ford, they weren't afraid to back their dreams. After showing their prototype to a local retailer they got an order for twenty-five machines, Jobs sold his Volkswagen and Woz sold his expensive Hewlett-Packard scientific calculator to raise $1,300 to start their new company. They took the money, convinced the local electronics suppliers to grant them a line of credit, and started production of the Apple I.

They revolutionized the computer hardware and software industries. Released in 1976, and priced at $666, the Apple I earned them $774,000. Two years later they introduced the Apple II which, in the next three years, earned $140,000,000. In 1980 Apple went public, and after the first day of trading the company had a market value of $1.2 billion. Wozniak left the company in 1981, but Jobs pushed through the development of the Macintosh in 1984. In 1985 Jobs left too, but in 1998 he came back to Apple to revitalize the floundering company with the creation of the iMac computers, the animation company Pixar, the iPod, and iTunes.

In presenting stories of contemporary successes, the editors have followed Hill's style of using real people to illustrate the principles of success. But Napoleon Hill was granted a rare privilege. Unlike anyone before or after, he had the opportunity to personally meet the most powerful and successful people and learn firsthand the dreams that inspired them, the obstacles that confronted them, and how they found the courage within themselves to overcome their failures. Hill met many of the inventors and the empire builders who laid the foundations of twentieth-century American industry while they were still news, not history. Then, for more than twenty-five years, he studied the habits and learned the secrets of the next generations who built on the foundations, forged new industries, devised new systems, and dreamed new dreams. It was only because Hill was given such unprecedented access over such a long period that he was able to compare, contrast, analyze, and then formulate a philosophy of achievement based on the real stories of real people who had used these techniques to create their success.

Think and Grow Rich *revolutionized self-help writing, and to this day is the standard against which all motivational literature is measured. Its success also helped create the market for the thousands of business biographies that tell in detail how the dreams were born, plans were made, frustrations were faced, and triumphs achieved in every sector of modern business. And because this wealth of information is now available, with little more than the click of a mouse, you can read, hear, or watch today's greatest entrepreneurs and most successful CEOs confirming, in their own words, the basic truth behind every one of the principles Napoleon Hill explains in this book.*

The products or services they sell may be different but the story of their success is the same: dreams, followed by failures, followed by lessons learned, then success. For every Henry Ford, Thomas Edison, or O. Henry that Napoleon Hill cites to make a point, today there is a Steve Jobs, Dean Kamen, or Merle Haggard proving that Hill's points are still valid.

There is a difference between wishing for a thing and being ready to receive it. No one is ready for a thing until they *believe* they can acquire it. The state of mind must be belief, not mere hope or wish. Open-mindedness is essential for belief. Closed minds do not inspire faith, courage, and belief.

Remember, no more effort is required to aim high in life, to demand abundance and prosperity, than is required to accept misery and poverty. A great poet has correctly stated this universal truth through these lines:

> I bargained with Life for a penny,
> And Life would pay no more,
> However I begged at evening
> When I counted my scanty store.
>
> For Life is a just employer,
> He gives you what you ask,
> But once you have set the wages,
> Why, you must bear the task.
>
> I worked for a menial's hire,
> Only to learn, dismayed,
> That any wage I had asked of Life,
> Life would have willingly paid.

DESIRE OUTWITS MOTHER NATURE

As a fitting climax to this chapter, I wish to introduce one of the most unusual persons I have ever known. I first saw him a few minutes after he was born. He came into the world without any physical sign of ears. When pressed for an opinion, the doctor concluded that the child might be deaf and mute for life.

I challenged that doctor's opinion. I had the right to do so. I was the child's father. I, too, reached a decision, but I expressed my opinion silently, in the secrecy of my own heart.

In my own mind I knew that my son would hear and speak. How? I was sure there must be a way, and I knew I would find it. I thought of the words of the immortal Emerson: "The whole course of things goes to teach us faith. We need only obey. There is guidance for each of us, and by lowly listening, we shall hear the right word."

The right word? Desire! More than anything else, I desired that my son should not be deaf and unable to speak. From that desire I never receded. Not for a second.

What could I do about it? Somehow I would find a way to transplant into that child's mind my own burning desire for ways and means of conveying sound to his brain without the aid of ears.

As soon as the child was old enough to cooperate, I would fill his mind so completely with a burning desire to hear, that Nature would, by methods of her own, translate it into physical reality.

All this thinking took place in my own mind, but I spoke of it to no one. Every day I renewed the pledge I had made to myself, that my son should not be deaf.

As he grew older, and began to take notice of things around him, we observed that he had a slight degree of hearing. When he reached the age when children usually begin talking he made no attempt to speak, but we could tell by his actions that he could hear certain sounds slightly.

That was all I needed to know! I was convinced that if he could hear, even slightly, he might develop still greater hearing capacity. Then something happened that gave me hope. It came from an entirely unexpected source.

We bought a phonograph. When the child heard the music for the first time, he went into ecstasies. He promptly appropriated the machine. On one occasion he played a record over and over, for almost two hours, standing in front of the phonograph, with his teeth clamped on the edge of the case. The significance of this did not become clear to us until years afterward. At the time, we had never heard of the principle of "bone conduction" of sound.

Shortly after he appropriated the phonograph I discovered that he could hear me quite clearly when I spoke with my lips touching his mastoid bone, at the base of the skull.

Having determined that he could hear the sound of my voice plainly, I began immediately to transfer to his mind the desire to hear and speak. When I discovered that my son enjoyed bedtime stories, I went to work creating stories designed to develop in him self-reliance, imagination, and a strong desire to hear.

There was one story line in particular that I emphasized over and over. Each time I told it, I gave it some new and dramatic coloring. These stories were designed to plant in his mind the thought that his affliction was not a liability but an asset of great value. As a result of my studies and personal experience, I firmly believed that every adversity brings with it the seed of an equivalent advantage. However, despite my beliefs, I must confess that I did not have the slightest idea how this disability could ever become an asset.

He Won a New World with Six Cents!

As I analyze the experience in retrospect, I can see now that my son's faith in me had much to do with the astounding results. He did not question anything I told him. I sold him on the idea that he had a distinct advantage over his older brother, and that this advantage would reflect itself in many ways. For example, the teachers in school would observe that he had no ears, and because of this they would show him special attention and treat him with extraordinary kindness. And they always did. I also sold him on the idea that when he became old enough to sell newspapers (his older brother had already become a newspaper merchant) he would have a big advantage over his brother. My reasoning was that people would pay him extra money for his wares, because they could see that he was a bright, industrious boy, despite the fact he had no ears.

When he was about seven he showed the first evidence that my method of stimulating his mind was bearing fruit. For several months he begged for the privilege of selling newspapers, but his mother would not give the project her consent.

Finally he took matters in his own hands. One afternoon, when he was left at home with the staff, he climbed through the kitchen window, shinnied to the ground, and set out on his own. He borrowed six cents in capital from the neighborhood shoemaker and invested it in papers, which he sold out. He took his earnings, reinvested in more newspapers, and kept repeating until late in the evening. After balancing his accounts, and paying back the six cents he had borrowed from his banker, he had a net profit of forty-two cents. When we got home that night, we found him in bed asleep, with the money tightly clenched in his hand.

His mother opened his hand, removed the coins, and cried. Of all things! To me, it seemed she was crying over her son's first victory. My reaction was the reverse. I laughed, for I knew that my endeavor to plant in my son's mind an attitude of faith in himself had been successful.

His mother saw, in his first business venture, a little deaf boy who had gone out in the streets and risked his life to earn money. I saw a brave, ambitious, self-reliant little businessman whose stock in himself had been increased a hundred percent. He had gone into business on his own initiative, and had won. I was not only pleased, I was impressed. He had clearly demonstrated the first signs of a resourcefulness that would go with him all through life.

The little deaf boy went through grade school, high school, and college without being able to hear his teachers, except when they

NOTES & COMMENTS

shouted loudly at close range. He did not go to a school for the deaf and we did not use sign language. We were determined that he should live like any other boy who could hear and speak. We stood by that decision, although it cost us many heated debates with school officials.

While he was in high school he tried an electronic hearing aid, but it was of no value to him.

During his last week in college, something happened that marked the most important turning point of his life. Through what seemed to be mere chance, he came into possession of another electronic hearing device, which was sent to him on trial. He was slow about testing it, due to his disappointment with a similar device. Finally he picked it up, carelessly, placed it on his head, and hooked up the battery. Suddenly, as if by magic, his lifelong desire for normal hearing became a reality! For the first time in his life he heard practically as well as any person with normal hearing.

Overjoyed because of the changed world that had been brought to him, he rushed to the telephone, called his mother, and heard her voice perfectly. The next day, for the first time in his life, he plainly heard the voices of his professors in class! For the first time in his life, he could converse freely with other people, without them having to speak loudly. Truly, he had come into possession of a changed world.

His desire was finally paying dividends. But the victory was not yet complete. He still had to find a definite and practical way to convert his disability into an equivalent asset.

Thought That Works Miracles

Intoxicated with the joy of his newly discovered world of sound, he wrote a letter to the manufacturer of the hearing aid, enthusiastically describing his experience. Something in his letter prompted the company to invite him to New York. He was escorted through the factory, and while talking with the chief engineer, telling him about his changed world, a hunch, an idea, or an inspiration—call it what you wish—flashed into his mind. It was this impulse of thought that converted his disability into an asset. An asset destined to pay dividends in both money and happiness to thousands for all time to come.

The sum and substance of that impulse was this: It occurred to him that he might be of help to the millions of people who go through life without the benefit of hearing devices, if he could find a way to tell them the story of his changed world.

For one month he carried out intensive research, during which he analyzed the entire marketing system of the manufacturer of the hearing device. Then he created a plan for reaching out to other hearing impaired people all over the world, to share with them his newly discovered changed world. When this was done, he put in writing a two-year plan, based on his findings. When he presented the plan to the company he was instantly given a position, for the purpose of carrying out his ambition.

Little did he dream, when he went to work, that he was destined to bring hope and practical relief to thousands of people who, without his help, would have been limited forever by deafness.

There is no doubt in my mind that Blair would have been deaf and unable to speak all his life if his mother and I had not managed to shape his mind as we did.

When I planted in his mind the desire to hear and talk and live as other people, there went with that impulse some strange influence that caused Nature to become bridge-builder, and span the gulf of silence between his brain and the outer world.

Truly, a burning desire has devious ways of transmuting itself into its physical equivalent. Blair desired normal hearing; now he has it! He was born with a condition that, in those days, might easily have sent a person with a less-defined desire to the street with a bundle of pencils and a tin cup.

NOTES & COMMENTS

The little "white lie" I planted in his mind when he was a child, by leading him to believe his impaired hearing would become a great asset, has justified itself. I am convinced it is a fact that there is nothing, right or wrong, that belief—plus burning desire—cannot make real. These qualities are free to everyone.

COMMENTARY

As Napoleon Hill was finishing this chapter on Desire, it was reported that the famed opera singer Madame Schumann-Heink had died. A passage in her obituary struck Hill as being so appropriate to the subject of this chapter that he was moved to comment as follows.

One short paragraph in the newspaper story about the famed opera singer Madame Schumann-Heink gives the clue to this unusual woman's stupendous success. I quote the paragraph, because the clue it contains is none other than desire.

Early in her career, Mme. Schumann-Heink visited the director of the Vienna Court Opera, to have him test her voice. But he did not test it. After taking one look at the awkward and poorly dressed girl, he exclaimed, none too gently, 'With such a face, and with no personality at all, how can you ever expect to succeed in opera? My good child, give up the idea. Buy a sewing machine, and go to work. You can never be a singer.'

Never is a long time! The director of the Vienna Court Opera may have known much about the technique of singing, but he knew little about the power of desire when it assumes the proportion of an obsession. If he had known more of that power, he would not have made the mistake of condemning genius without giving it an opportunity.

COMMENTARY

Although few readers of this edition will be familiar with Madame Schumann-Heink, every reader knows a half-dozen similar stories. It is true for every generation and every kind of music. At some time, even the biggest stars were failures. At some time, someone told them they weren't good enough. But every one of those times that they failed, their desire was bigger than their failure.

That is why you know their stories. And it's also why you've never heard about the thousands of other performers who were also told they weren't good enough. The ones you've never heard of are the ones whose desire wasn't big enough. They're the ones who believed that failure was defeat.

Several years ago one of my business associates became ill. He became worse as time went on, and finally was taken to the hospital for an operation. The doctor warned me that there was little if any chance of my ever seeing him alive again. But that was the doctor's opinion. It was not the opinion of the patient. Just before he was wheeled away, he whispered to me, "Do not be disturbed, Chief, I will be out of here in a few days."

The attending nurse looked at me with pity. But the patient did come through safely. After it was all over, his physician said, "Nothing but his own desire to live saved him. He never would have pulled through if he had not refused to accept the possibility of death."

COMMENTARY

By the 1980s the phenomenon that Napoleon Hill wrote about in the preceding paragraph was embraced by a growing segment of the population. Among the adherents were numerous medical professionals who incorporated the concept under the term "the body-mind connection," and by the turn of the twenty-first century the belief that the mind can manifest physical changes in the body had become a part of mainstream medical practice. In chapter 5, Autosuggestion, you will find further comment on the medical aspects of having a burning desire.

- Nurse
- EMT
- PPL
- GYM

NOTES & COMMENTS

⚘ I believe in the power of desire backed by faith in yourself, because I have seen this power lift people from lowly beginnings to places of power and wealth. I have seen it rob the grave of its victims; I have seen it serve as the medium by which people staged a comeback after having been defeated in a hundred different ways. And I have seen it provide my own son with a normal, happy, successful life, despite Nature's having sent him into the world without ears.

How can you harness and use the power of desire? The first part of the answer is in the technique at the beginning of this chapter. You will learn more in the next and subsequent chapters of this book.

Through some strange and powerful principle, Nature wraps up in the impulse of strong desire "that something" which recognizes no such word as impossible, and accepts no such reality as failure.

THERE ARE NO LIMITATIONS

TO THE MIND EXCEPT

THOSE WE ACKNOWLEDGE.

SUCCES

4

FAITH IN YOUR ABILITY

VISUALIZATION OF, AND BELIEF IN, ATTAINMENT OF DESIRE

The Second Step Toward Riches

Faith is the head chemist of the mind. When faith is blended with thought, the subconscious mind instantly picks up the vibration. The subconscious then translates it and transmits it to Infinite Intelligence.

The emotions of faith, love, and sex are the most powerful of all the major positive emotions. When the three are blended, they have the effect of "coloring" thought in such a way that it instantly reaches the subconscious mind. There, it is changed into a form that induces a response from Infinite Intelligence.

LAW of ATTRACTION

COMMENTARY

In the preceding paragraph Napoleon Hill uses two terms, "faith" and "Infinite Intelligence," both of which may convey to the reader a religious connotation that Hill did not intend. The following will define the meaning of the words as Hill uses them in the following chapter.

In modern usage, the word faith *has become almost interchangeable with "religious belief," which is not the way Hill uses the word. Faith, as it is used*

NOTES & COMMENTS

BLINK!

✳ here, means having confidence, trust, and an absolute, unwavering belief that you can do something. And in order for you to have faith in yourself as Hill means it, it has to be true on a subconscious level. If you have a nagging doubt in the back of your mind, or if you are just going through the motions of pretending you believe, it won't work because your subconscious will know your doubts. Unless you have absolute total confidence, unless you are convinced without question, then you don't have faith.

Hill uses the term Infinite Intelligence to identify that part of the human mind and thinking process that produces hunches, flashes of insight, and leaps of logic. Hill's concept has similarities to what psychologist Carl Jung called the "collective unconscious," and, on another level, it is very close to what contemporary psychologists refer to as "working in the flow state" or "being in the zone." Infinite intelligence is discussed in greater depth in later chapters.

Hill also uses another term, the subconscious mind, that should be commented on before the reader proceeds with this chapter. Although there are differing schools of thought, in general, modern psychology developed from the pioneering work of Sigmund Freud and Carl Jung. Each believed that the human mind operates on both a conscious and an unconscious level, but they differed on the role the subconscious plays and the way it influences attitude and action.

Through his own research and studies, Napoleon Hill developed a theory of the conscious and subconscious that is closest to the Jungian view. The following briefly describes the basis of Hill's view.

The Conscious Mind: Your conscious mind receives information through the five senses of sight, smell, taste, hearing, and touch. Your conscious mind keeps track of what you need for thinking and operating, and it filters out what you don't need. Your conscious mind (and what your memory retains) is the intelligence with which you normally think, reason, and plan.

The Subconscious Mind: Your subconscious has access to all the same information your conscious mind receives, but it doesn't reason the way your conscious mind does. It takes everything literally. It doesn't make value judgments. It does not filter, and it does not forget.

You cannot command your conscious mind to reach out and dip into your subconscious mind. However, under certain circumstances, all those forgotten facts and ideas that are always there in your subconscious can, if they are firmly rooted, influence your conscious attitudes and actions.

HOW TO DEVELOP FAITH

The following statement is very important in understanding the importance of autosuggestion in the transmutation of desire into its physical or monetary equivalent, namely: Faith is a state of mind that may be induced, or created, by affirmation or repeated instructions to the subconscious mind, through the principle of autosuggestion.

The repetition of affirmations is like giving orders to your subconscious mind, and it is the only known method of voluntary development of the emotion of faith (absolute belief that you can do something).

As an illustration, consider why you are reading this book. You want to acquire the ability to transmute the intangible thought impulse of desire into its physical counterpart, money. By following the instructions laid down in the later chapters on autosuggestion and the subconscious mind, you will learn techniques to convince your subconscious mind that you believe you will receive that for which you ask. Your subconscious will act upon that belief, and pass it back to you in the form of "faith," followed by definite plans for procuring that which you desire.

Faith in yourself and your abilities is a state of mind that you will be able to develop at will, after you have mastered the thirteen principles in this book. This is true because faith is a state of mind that will develop naturally within you when you use and apply these principles.

The emotions, or the "feeling" portion of thoughts, are what give your thoughts vitality, life, and action. The emotions of faith, love, and sex, when mixed with any thought impulse, give it even greater action. All thoughts that have been emotionalized (given feeling) and mixed with faith (absolute belief in your ability) begin immediately to translate themselves into their physical equivalent or counterpart.

However, this is not only true of thought impulses that have been mixed with faith, but it is true with any emotion. Including negative emotions.

What this means is that the subconscious mind will translate into its physical equivalent a thought impulse of a negative or destructive nature just as readily as it will act upon thought impulses of a positive or constructive nature. The following statement made by a noted criminologist illustrates the point: "When men first come into contact with crime, they abhor it. If they remain in contact with crime for a time, they become accustomed to it, and endure it. If they remain in contact with it long enough, they finally embrace it, and become influenced by it."

This is the equivalent of saying that a negative impulse of thought that is repeatedly passed on to the subconscious mind often enough is, finally, accepted and acted upon by the subconscious mind. The subconscious then proceeds to translate that impulse into its physical equivalent, by the most practical procedure available.

This also accounts for the strange phenomenon that so many millions of people experience, referred to as bad luck.

There are millions of people who believe themselves doomed to poverty and failure because of some strange force they call bad luck, over which they believe they have no control. But the truth is that they are the creators of their own misfortunes, because this negative belief in bad luck is picked up by the subconscious mind and translated into its physical equivalent.

Your belief, or faith, is the element that will determine the action of your subconscious mind. Once again let me stress that you will benefit by passing on to your subconscious mind any desire that you wish translated into its physical or monetary equivalent, in a state of expectancy or belief that the transmutation will actually take place. The subconscious mind will transmute into its physical equivalent, by the most direct and practical way available, any order that is given to it in a state of belief or faith that the order will be carried out.

At this point it should also be noted that because of the way that the subconscious operates, there is nothing to stop you from "deceiving" your subconscious mind when giving it instructions through autosuggestion. That is what I did when I "deceived" my son's subconscious mind.

To make this deception more realistic, when you call upon your subconscious mind you must conduct yourself just as you would if you were already in possession of the material thing that you are demanding.

COMMENTARY

It is an axiom of contemporary motivation theory that the subconscious mind cannot distinguish between what is real and what is vividly imagined. One of the most frequently cited studies supporting this concept was done with a group of basketball players. The players were divided into three teams, and the players on each team were tested on their ability to make free throws. The teams were then separated for a period of time and each team was given instructions which they were told would improve their abilities. One team was instructed to practice making baskets on a daily basis. The second team was instructed not to practice during the period and not to even think about basketball. The third team was also instructed not to practice during the period, but instead the members were told to spend their daily practice time visualizing in detail the process of making baskets. At the end of the experiment the teams were again tested. The team that rested showed a decrease in ability. The team that practiced showed a marked increase in ability. And the team that didn't practice but visualized making baskets showed an increase in ability almost equal to those who had practiced daily.

[Handwritten notes: I work w/ laser like focus on achieving success in all areas of my life.]

[Handwritten notes: I am clearly focused on my personal + money making goals.]

NOTES & COMMENTS

As Hill says, you can "deceive" your subconscious through autosuggestion. If you convincingly plant an idea in your subconscious, your subconscious will accept and work with the idea as though it were a fact.

But the key word is "convincingly." If you try to send a message to your subconscious but in the back of your mind you have a nagging doubt whether it will work, your subconscious will pick that up also. You will have sent mixed messages that cancel each other out. That is why Hill stresses the importance of doing it with faith. Your subconscious will not judge if it is true or false, positive or negative, but it does respond to the power of the input (how emotionalized the thought is).

It is essential for you to encourage the positive emotions as the dominating forces of your mind. But faith in yourself doesn't come from merely reading instructions. Now that you understand the theory, you must begin to apply it. By experimenting and practicing, you will develop your ability to mix faith with any order you give to your subconscious.

When you have faith in your ability, then you can give your subconscious mind instructions, which it will accept and act upon immediately. When your mind is dominated by positive emotions it will encourage the state of mind known as faith.

Faith in Yourself Is a State of Mind That You Can Create by Autosuggestion

All through the ages, religious leaders have admonished people to "have faith." They say to have faith in this, that, and the other dogma or creed, but they have failed to tell people *how* to have faith. They have not stated that "faith is a state of mind that may be induced by self-suggestion."

In language that anyone can understand, this book explains the principle through which faith in your ability to accomplish a goal may be developed where it does not already exist.

Before we begin, you should be reminded again that:

Faith is the "eternal elixir" that gives life, power, and action to the impulse of thought. The foregoing sentence is worth reading a second time, and a third, and a fourth. It is worth reading aloud!

Faith is the starting point of all accumulation of riches. Faith is the basis of all "miracles" and of all mysteries that cannot be analyzed by the rules of science.

Faith is the only known antidote for failure.

Faith is the element that, when mixed with desire, gives you direct communication with Infinite Intelligence.

Faith is the element that transforms the ordinary vibration of thought, created by the human mind, into the spiritual equivalent.

Faith is the only way the force of Infinite Intelligence can be harnessed and used.

The Magic of Self-Suggestion

It is a fact that you will come to believe whatever you repeat to yourself, whether the statement is true or false. If you repeat a lie over and over, you will eventually accept that lie as truth. Moreover, you will *believe* it to be the truth. You are what you are because of the dominating thoughts that you permit to occupy your mind. Thoughts that you deliberately place in your own mind, and encourage with sympathy, and with which you mix any one or more of the emotions, constitute the motivating forces that direct and control your every movement, act, and deed.

The following sentence is a very significant statement of truth: Thoughts that are mixed with any of the feelings of emotion become like a magnetic force, which attracts other similar or related thoughts.

A thought that is "magnetized" with one of the emotions may be compared to a seed. When it is planted in fertile soil, it germinates, grows, and multiplies itself over and over again. What was

NOTES & COMMENTS

Desire
+   => Infinite Intelligence
FAITH

originally one small seed becomes countless millions of seeds of the same kind.

The human mind is constantly attracting vibrations that are in sync with whatever dominates the mind. Any thought, idea, plan, or purpose that you hold in your mind attracts a host of its relatives. Add these "relatives" to its own force, and it grows until it becomes the prime motivator of the person in whose mind it has been housed.

Now, let us go back to the starting point. How can the original seed of an idea, plan, or purpose be planted in the mind? The answer: any idea, plan, or purpose may be placed in the mind through repetition of thought. This is why you are asked to write out a statement of your major purpose, or definite chief aim, commit it to memory, and repeat it out loud, day after day, until these vibrations of sound have reached your subconscious mind.

You are what you are because of the dominating thoughts that you permit to occupy your mind. If you choose to, you can throw off any bad influences from your past, and build your own life the way you want it to be. For instance, by taking inventory of your mental assets and liabilities, you might discover that your greatest weakness is lack of self-confidence. This can be overcome, and translated into courage, through the principle of autosuggestion. You can do this by writing out a set of simply stated, positive thought impulses, memorizing them, and repeating them until they become a part of the working equipment of your subconscious mind.

The following is an example for someone whose definite purpose is to overcome a lack of self-confidence.

Self-Confidence Formula

1. I know that I have the ability to achieve the object of my definite purpose in life. Therefore, I demand of myself persistent,

continuous action toward its attainment, and I here and now promise to render such action.

2. I realize the dominating thoughts of my mind will eventually reproduce themselves in outward, physical action, and gradually transform themselves into physical reality. Therefore, I will concentrate my thoughts for thirty minutes each day, visualizing the person I intend to become. In this way I will create in my mind a clear mental picture.

3. I know, through the principle of autosuggestion, that any desire I persistently hold in my mind will eventually find some practical means of attaining my objective. Therefore, I will devote ten minutes daily to demanding of myself the development of self-confidence.

4. I have clearly written down a description of my definite chief aim in life, and I will never stop trying until I have developed sufficient self-confidence for its attainment.

5. I fully realize that no wealth or position can last unless it is built upon truth and justice. Therefore, I will engage in no transaction that does not benefit all whom it affects. I will succeed by attracting to myself the forces I wish to use, and the cooperation of other people. I will persuade others to help me, because of my willingness to help others. I will eliminate hatred, envy, jealousy, selfishness, and cynicism, by developing love for all humanity, because I know that a negative attitude toward others can never bring me success. I will cause others to believe in me, because I will believe in them and in myself.

    I will sign my name to this formula, commit it to memory, and repeat it aloud once a day, with full faith that it will gradually influence my thoughts and actions so that I will become a self-reliant, and successful, person.

NOTES & COMMENTS

Behind this formula is a law of nature that psychologists call autosuggestion or self-suggestion. It is a proven technique that will work for your success, if it is used constructively. On the other hand, if used destructively, it will destroy just as readily. In this statement may be found a very significant truth, namely, that those who go down in defeat, and end their lives in poverty, misery, and distress, do so because of negative application of the principle of autosuggestion. All impulses of thought have a tendency to clothe themselves in their physical equivalent.

The Disaster of Negative Thinking

The subconscious mind makes no distinction between constructive and destructive thought impulses. It works with the material we feed it, through our thought impulses. The subconscious mind will translate into reality a thought driven by fear just as readily as it will translate into reality a thought driven by courage, or faith.

Just as electricity will turn the wheels of industry, and render useful service if used constructively, it will snuff out life if wrongly used. So too will the law of autosuggestion lead you to peace and prosperity, or down into the valley of misery, failure, and death. It depends on your degree of understanding and application of it.

If you fill your mind with fear or doubt, and if you do not believe in your ability to connect with and use the forces of Infinite Intelligence, then you will not be able to use those forces. The law of autosuggestion will take your lack of belief and use that doubt as a pattern by which your subconscious mind will translate it into its physical equivalent.

COMMENTARY

When you have faith in your ability to accomplish what you want, it not only firmly plants ideas in your subconscious, but it then works to reinforce itself.

When you have faith in your abilities, part of what you must have faith in is that it is possible to tap into Infinite Intelligence. And because you have faith that it will work, your conscious mind won't be resistant. When your conscious doesn't resist, your subconscious mind can send creative ideas to your conscious mind more easily. Then the more you see the power working in your life, the easier it is for you to act on faith the next time.

Will it work for you? You will never know unless you relax your resistance and just have faith that it will.

Like the wind that carries one ship east and another west, the law of autosuggestion will lift you up or pull you down, according to the way you set your sails of thought.

The law of autosuggestion, through which any person may rise to altitudes of achievement that stagger the imagination, is well described in the following verse. Observe the words that have been emphasized, and you will catch the deep meaning that the poet had in mind.

If you *think* you are beaten, you are,
If you *think* you dare not, you don't;
If you like to win, but you *think* you can't,
It is almost certain you won't.

If you *think* you'll lose, you're lost,
For out in the world we find,
Success begins with a fellow's will—
It's all in *the state of mind.*

If you *think* you are outclassed, you are,
You've got to *think* high to rise,
You've got to be *sure of yourself* before
You can ever win a prize.

Life's battles don't always go
To the stronger or faster man,
But soon or late the man who wins
Is the man who thinks he can!

COMMENTARY

As noted at the beginning of this chapter, the way in which Napoleon Hill uses the word faith *is meant to have no religious connotation. However, it would be impossible for Hill to write this chapter without acknowledging the power of religious faith. Therefore, in the following two paragraphs when Hill discusses Jesus Christ and Mahatma Gandhi as exemplifying the power of faith, he is referring to their personal faith: the absolute trust in his beliefs that Jesus exhibited, and Gandhi's total conviction and confidence in his cause. In this way, they perfectly exemplify thought impulse mixed with faith.*

If you wish evidence of the power of faith, study the achievements of men and women who have employed it. At the head of the list comes the Nazarene. The basis of Christianity is faith, no matter how many people may have perverted, or misinterpreted, the meaning of this great force.

The sum and substance of the teachings and the achievements of Christ, which may have been interpreted as "miracles," were nothing more nor less than faith. If there are any such phenomena as "miracles" they are produced only through the state of mind known as faith.

Consider Mahatma Gandhi of India, one of the most astounding examples of the possibilities of faith. Gandhi wielded more potential power than any man living in his time. And he had this power despite the fact that he had none of the orthodox tools of power, such as money, battleships, soldiers, and materials of warfare. Gandhi had no money, no home, he did not own a suit of clothes, but he did have power. How did he come by that power?

He created it out of his understanding of the principle of faith and through his ability to transplant that faith into the minds of two hundred million people.

Gandhi accomplished the astounding feat of influencing two hundred million minds to coalesce and move in unison, as a single mind.

What other force on earth, except faith, could do as much?

HOW AN IDEA BUILT A FORTUNE

COMMENTARY

Although the following story is not exclusively about faith, and it makes no mention of autosuggestion or the subconscious mind, Napoleon Hill included it at this point in every edition of Think and Grow Rich. *In fact, as Hill says, this story illustrates at least six of the thirteen principles of success. But faith is at the center of it. If the central figure, Charles M. Schwab, had not mixed his "big idea" with absolute, unwavering faith that he could pull it off, the whole history of American business would have been different.*

The event chosen for this illustration dates back to 1900, when the United States Steel Corporation was being formed. As you read the story, keep in mind the following fundamental facts and you will understand how ideas have been converted into huge fortunes.

First, the United States Steel Corporation was born in the mind of Charles M. Schwab, in the form of an *idea* he created through his *imagination*. Second, he mixed *faith* with his idea. Third, he formulated a *plan* for the transformation of his idea into physical and financial reality. Fourth, he put his plan into action with his famous speech at the University Club. Fifth, he applied and followed through on his plan with *persistence*, and backed it with firm *decision* until it had been fully carried out. Sixth, he prepared the way for success by a *burning desire* for success.

NOTES & COMMENTS

NOTES & COMMENTS

If you are one of those who have often wondered how great fortunes are accumulated, this story of the creation of the United States Steel Corporation will be enlightening. If you have any doubt that a person can *think and grow rich,* this story should dispel that doubt. You can plainly see in the story of United States Steel the application of a major portion of the principles described in this book.

This astounding description of the power of an idea was dramatically told by John Lowell, in the *New York World-Telegram,* with whose courtesy it is here reprinted.

COMMENTARY

In order for the modern reader to fully appreciate the following newspaper story, it is appropriate at this point to provide some background information about the main players.

Charles M. Schwab was Andrew Carnegie's right-hand man, and president of the Carnegie Steel Corporation.

Andrew Carnegie was a wealthy and powerful steel baron whose company controlled 25 percent of the iron and steel production in America.

J. P. Morgan was a wealthy and powerful Wall Street banker whose company had arranged the financing for many of the major industrial companies in America at the beginning of the twentieth century.

All the reader needs to know about the other men mentioned in the story is that at the beginning of the twentieth century, finance, business, and industry were dominated by a few hundred men, most of whom had amassed great fortunes through some connection with the railroads that had opened the country. These people were well known to readers of the New York World-Telegram *because of their financial influence.*

And that sets the stage for the following newspaper article which is not only a fascinating story about the power of faith in an idea, but also a wonderful example of the irreverent writing style that was used by many newspaper journalists of the day.

A PRETTY AFTER-DINNER SPEECH
FOR A BILLION DOLLARS

When, on the evening of December 12, 1900, some eighty of the nation's financial nobility gathered in the banquet hall of the University Club on Fifth Avenue to do honor to a young man from out of the West, not half a dozen of the guests realized they were to witness the most significant episode in American industrial history.

J. Edward Simmons and Charles Stewart Smith, their hearts full of gratitude for the lavish hospitality bestowed on them by Charles M. Schwab during a recent visit to Pittsburgh, had arranged the dinner to introduce the thirty-eight-year-old steel man to eastern banking society. But they didn't expect him to stampede the convention. They warned him, in fact, that the bosoms within New York's stuffed shirts would not be responsive to oratory, and that, if he didn't want to bore the Stillmans and Harrimans and Vanderbilts, he had better limit himself to fifteen or twenty minutes of polite vaporings and let it go at that.

Even John Pierpont Morgan, sitting on the right hand of Schwab as became his imperial dignity, intended to grace the banquet table with his presence only briefly. And so far as the press and public were concerned, the whole affair was of so little moment that no mention of it found its way into print the next day.

So the two hosts and their distinguished guests ate their way through the usual seven or eight courses. There was little conversation and what there was of it was restrained. Few of the bankers and brokers had met Schwab, whose career had flowered along the banks of the Monongahela, and none knew him well. But before the evening was over, they—and

NOTES & COMMENTS

NOTES & COMMENTS

with them Money Master Morgan—were to be swept off their feet, and a billion-dollar baby, the United States Steel Corporation, was to be conceived.

It is perhaps unfortunate, for the sake of history, that no record of Charlie Schwab's speech at the dinner ever was made.

It is probable, however, that it was a "homely" speech, somewhat ungrammatical (for the niceties of language never bothered Schwab), full of epigram and threaded with wit. But aside from that it had a galvanic force and effect upon the five billions of estimated capital that was represented by the diners. After it was over and the gathering was still under its spell, although Schwab had talked for ninety minutes, Morgan led the orator to a recessed window where, dangling their legs from the high, uncomfortable seat, they talked for an hour more.

The magic of the Schwab personality had been turned on, full force, but what was more important and lasting was the full-fledged, clear-cut program he laid down for the aggrandizement of steel. Many other men had tried to interest Morgan in slapping together a steel trust after the pattern of the biscuit, wire and hoop, sugar, rubber, whisky, oil, or chewing gum combinations.

COMMENTARY

The Random House College Dictionary *defines a trust as "an illegal combination of industrial or commercial companies in which the stock is controlled by a central board of trustees thus making it possible to control prices and destroy competition."*

Many of America's new industrial companies had grown so quickly that they were not yet profitable. They were saddled with huge debt incurred in raising the capital to finance their rapid expansion, and at the same time they were faced with having to cut costs and slash prices, or go out of business. The answer for many was to join up with others in related industries to form what were called trusts or combinations.

Although trusts were illegal since the passage of the Sherman Antitrust Act in 1890, companies still tried to find ways to monopolize their industries, and if their efforts weren't technically trusts they were something very close.

The one thing the large company owners who assembled these trusts needed was cash to buy up the many smaller companies they would have to own in order to effectively dominate an industry. J. P. Morgan was the banker who financed many such takeovers.

John W. Gates, the gambler, had urged it, but Morgan distrusted him. The Moore boys, Bill and Jim, Chicago stock jobbers who had glued together a match trust and a cracker corporation, had urged it and failed. Elbert H. Gary, the sanctimonious country lawyer, wanted to foster it, but he wasn't big enough to be impressive. Until Schwab's eloquence took J. P. Morgan to the heights from which he could visualize the solid results of the most daring financial undertaking ever conceived, the project was regarded as a delirious dream of easy-money crackpots.

The financial magnetism that began, a generation ago, to attract thousands of small and sometimes inefficiently managed companies into large and competition-crushing combinations had become operative in the steel world through the devices of that jovial business pirate, John W. Gates. Gates already had formed the American Steel and Wire Company out of a chain of small concerns, and together with Morgan had created the Federal Steel Company.

But by the side of Andrew Carnegie's gigantic vertical trust, a trust owned and operated by fifty-three partners, those other combinations were picayune. They might combine to their heart's content but the whole lot of them couldn't make a dent in the Carnegie organization, and Morgan knew it. The eccentric old Scot knew it, too.

COMMENTARY

Andrew Carnegie was born in Scotland and came to America when he just a boy. He made his first move to join the elite group of American tycoons when he quit his job as a bobbin boy in a cotton mill, earning $1.20 a week, and got a job as a telegraph messenger boy. He soon taught himself to operate a telegraph key, which got him hired as personal telegrapher and secretary to the head of the Pennsylvania Railroad. It wasn't long before he'd worked his way up the ranks to superintendent of the Pittsburgh division, which in turn put him in a position to become an early investor in the Pullman company which became the leading manufacturer of railway cars. Carnegie's investment in Pullman, and some successful real estate ventures, gave him the capital to go into business for himself.

At the end of the civil war Carnegie left railroading and started a company that built iron bridges for railroad companies. From building iron bridges it was a short step to starting his own steel mill, which led him to acquire control of other steel mills, then his own coal fields to supply his smelters, then his own ore boats and rail lines to haul the ore and coal. Because of Carnegie's vertical integration and his use of the most up-to-date manufacturing methods, he was able to sell top-grade steel at the lowest price. He managed to drop the price of steel from $140 a ton to $20 a ton. By 1899 the Carnegie Steel Company controlled about 25 percent of the iron and steel production in America.

The smaller steel manufacturers couldn't compete with Carnegie, so they went to J. P. Morgan for help. He arranged for the financing, and a wide-ranging alliance was put together of companies that were in the business of manufacturing products made from steel. Part of the deal was that they would not buy steel from Carnegie.

Andrew Carnegie was not about to be put out of business by a collection of small companies. He announced that he would buy or build his own manufacturing companies to produce finished goods made of steel.

From the magnificent heights of Skibo Castle he had viewed, first with amusement and then with resentment, the attempts of Morgan's smaller companies to cut into his business. When the attempts became too bold, Carnegie's temper was translated into anger and retaliation. He decided to duplicate every mill owned by his rivals. Hitherto, he hadn't been interested in wire, pipe, hoops, or sheet. Instead, he was content to sell such companies the raw steel and let them work it into whatever shape they wanted. Now, with Schwab as his chief and able lieutenant, he planned to drive his enemies to the wall.

So it was that in the speech of Charles M. Schwab, Morgan saw the answer to his problem of combination. A trust without Carnegie—giant of them all—would be no trust at all, a plum pudding, as one writer said, without the plums.

Schwab's speech on the night of December 12, 1900, undoubtedly carried the inference, though not the pledge, that the vast Carnegie enterprise could be brought under the Morgan tent. He talked of the world future for steel, of reorganization for efficiency, of specialization, of the scrapping of unsuccessful mills and concentration of effort on the flourishing properties, of economies in the ore traffic, of economies in overhead and administrative departments, of capturing foreign markets.

More than that, he told the buccaneers among them wherein lay the errors of their customary piracy. Their purposes, he inferred, had been to create monopolies, raise prices, and pay themselves fat dividends out of privilege. Schwab condemned the system in his heartiest manner. The short-sightedness of such a policy, he told his hearers, lay in the fact that it restricted the market in an era when everything cried for expansion. By cheapening the cost of steel, he argued, an ever-expanding market would be created; more uses for steel would be devised, and a goodly portion of the world trade could be captured. Actually, though he did not know it, Schwab was an apostle of modern mass production.

COMMENTARY

For J. P. Morgan, all of Schwab's talk about economies of scale and expanding markets meant only one thing. Until that night it was assumed that Andrew Carnegie would continue building his own manufacturing companies to compete with the steel trusts that Morgan had helped put together. Morgan knew that for Carnegie to do so would require an enormous amount of capital, and Morgan also knew that Carnegie had always been strongly against raising money by selling stock in his company.

What Schwab seemed to be implying was that rather than going to Wall Street for the money needed to fight the trusts, Carnegie might be interested in selling his business.

So the dinner at the University Club came to an end. Morgan went home, to think about Schwab's rosy predictions. Schwab went back to Pittsburgh to run the steel business for "Wee Andra Carnegie," while Gary and the rest went back to their stock tickers, to fiddle around in anticipation of the next move.

It was not long coming. It took Morgan about one week to digest the feast of reason Schwab had placed before him. When he had assured himself that no financial indigestion was to result, he sent for Schwab—and found that young man rather coy. Mr. Carnegie, Schwab indicated, might not like it if he found his trusted company president had been flirting with the Emperor of Wall Street, the street upon which Carnegie was resolved never to tread. Then it was suggested by John W. Gates, the go-between, that if Schwab "happened" to be in the Bellevue Hotel in Philadelphia, J. P. Morgan might also "happen" to be there. When Schwab arrived, however, Morgan was inconveniently ill at his New York home, and so, on the elder man's pressing invitation, Schwab went to New York and presented himself at the door of the financier's library.

Now certain economic historians have professed the belief that from the beginning to the end of the drama, the stage was set by Andrew Carnegie—that the dinner to Schwab, the famous speech, the Sunday night conference between Schwab and the Money King, were events arranged by the canny Scot. The truth is exactly the opposite. When Schwab was called in to consummate the deal, he didn't even know whether "the little boss," as Andrew was called, would so much as listen to an offer to sell, particularly to a group of men whom Andrew regarded as being endowed with something less than holiness. But Schwab did take into the conference with him, in his own handwriting, six sheets of copper-plate figures, representing to his mind the physical worth and the potential earning capacity of every steel company he regarded as an essential star in the new metal firmament.

Four men pondered over these figures all night. The chief, of course, was Morgan, steadfast in his belief in the divine right of money. With him was his aristocratic partner, Robert Bacon, a scholar and a gentleman. The third was John W. Gates, whom Morgan scorned as a gambler and used as a tool.

The fourth was Schwab, who knew more about the processes of making and selling steel than any whole group of men then living. Throughout that conference, the Pittsburgher's figures were never questioned. If he said a company was worth so much, then it was worth that much and no more. He was insistent, too, upon including in the combination only those concerns he nominated. He had conceived a corporation in which there would be no duplication, not even to satisfy the greed of friends who wanted to unload their companies upon the broad Morgan shoulders.

When dawn came, Morgan rose and straightened his back. Only one question remained.

"Do you think you can persuade Andrew Carnegie to sell?" he asked.

"I can try," said Schwab.

"If you can get him to sell, I will undertake the matter," said Morgan.

So far so good. But would Carnegie sell? How much would he demand? (Schwab thought about $320 million.) What would he take payment in? Common or preferred stocks? Bonds? Cash? Nobody could raise a third of a billion dollars in cash.

There was a golf game in January on the frost-cracking heath of the St. Andrews links in Westchester, with Andrew bundled up in sweaters against the cold, and Charlie talking volubly, as usual, to keep his spirits up. But no word of business was mentioned until the pair sat down in the cozy warmth of the Carnegie cottage nearby. Then, with the same persuasiveness that had hypnotized eighty millionaires at the University Club, Schwab poured out the glittering promises

NOTES & COMMENTS

of retirement in comfort, of untold millions to satisfy the old man's social caprices. Carnegie capitulated, wrote a figure on a slip of paper, handed it to Schwab and said, "All right, that's what we'll sell for."

The figure was approximately $400 million and was reached by taking the $320 million mentioned by Schwab as a basic figure, and adding to it $80 million to represent the increased capital value over the previous two years.

Later, on the deck of a trans-Atlantic liner, the Scotsman said ruefully to Morgan, "I wish I had asked you for $100,000,000 more."

"If you had asked for it, you'd have gotten it," Morgan told him cheerfully.

There was an uproar, of course. A British correspondent cabled that the foreign steel world was "appalled" by the gigantic combination. President Hadley, of Yale, declared that unless trusts were regulated the country might expect "an emperor in Washington within the next twenty-five years." But that able stock manipulator, Keene, went at his work of shoving the new stock at the public so vigorously that all the excess water—estimated by some at nearly $600 million—was absorbed in a twinkling. So Carnegie had his millions, and the Morgan syndicate had $62 million for all its "trouble," and all the "boys," from Gates to Gary, had their millions.

COMMENTARY

The thirty-eight-year-old Charles M. Schwab had his reward too. He was made president of the new corporation, United States Steel, and remained in control until 1930. When Schwab left U.S. Steel, he went on to found the mammoth Bethlehem Steel Corporation, of which he also became president.

NOTES & COMMENTS

RICHES BEGIN WITH THOUGHT

The dramatic story of big business that you have just finished is a perfect illustration of the method by which desire can be transmuted into its physical equivalent!

That giant organization was created in the mind of one man. The plan by which the organization was provided with the steel mills that gave it financial stability was created in the mind of the same man. His faith, his desire, his imagination, his persistence were the real ingredients that went into United States Steel. The steel mills and equipment acquired by the corporation, after it had been brought into legal existence, were incidental. However, careful analysis reveals that the appraised value of the properties acquired by the corporation increased in value by an estimated $600 million *[approximately $12 billion today]*. The increase in value of the assets is attributable to the mere transaction that consolidated them under one management.

In other words, Charles M. Schwab's idea, plus the faith with which he conveyed it to the minds of J. P. Morgan and the others, was marketed for a profit of approximately $600 million. Not an insignificant sum for a single idea!

The United States Steel Corporation prospered and became one of the richest and most powerful corporations in America, employing thousands of people, developing new uses for steel, and opening new markets, thus proving that the $600 million in profit that the Schwab idea produced was earned.

Riches begin in the form of thought.

The amount is limited only by the person in whose mind the thought is put into motion. Faith removes limitations! Remember this when you are ready to bargain with life for whatever it is that you ask as your price for having passed this way.

COMMENTARY

In the years since that article appeared in the New York World-Telegram, *the well-told business story has become its own genre within the publishing industry. There are bestselling books and biographies by and about the insiders who run every industry. The editors of this edition of* Think and Grow Rich *strongly encourage you to sample some of these books. They can be entertaining and inspirational, and in them you will be able to see examples of Hill's principles of success at work in the real world. And the best of them are not only entertaining and inspirational, but they are also filled with ideas and techniques you can adapt and use.*

There are literally too many bestsellers from which to select a "best-of" listing for inclusion here. Any such choice the editors might make would not necessarily be the best but merely reflective of the interests of the person doing the choosing. However, there are two books the editors recommend that are not by or about a single individual or industry. These books are In Search of Excellence *by Tom Peters and* Breakthroughs! *by P. R. Nayak and John M. Ketteringham. Each of these books deals with a broad spectrum of industries, and within each industry they single out certain companies and individuals for analysis.*

Both were published at the beginning of the business-book trend in the 1980s, but there are few books since then that better convey the importance of faith in a good idea. In Search of Excellence, *chosen by a panel of experts as the most influential book of the past twenty years, was a runaway bestseller and will likely be in print for years to come.* Breakthroughs! *may be harder to find but it will be well worth the effort.*

A QUITTER NEVER WINS,

AND A WINNER NEVER QUITS.

AUTOSUGGESTION

THE MEDIUM FOR INFLUENCING
THE SUBCONSCIOUS MIND

The Third Step Toward Riches

Autosuggestion is a term that applies to all suggestions and all self-administered stimuli that reach your mind through the five senses. Stated in another way, autosuggestion is self-suggestion. It is the way of communicating between that part of the mind where conscious thought takes place, and that which serves as the seat of action for the subconscious mind.

Through the dominating thoughts that you permit to remain in your conscious mind (it doesn't matter whether these thoughts are negative or positive), the principle of autosuggestion reaches the subconscious mind and influences it with these thoughts.

Nature has built human beings so that, through our five senses, we can have control over the material that reaches our subconscious mind. However, this does not mean that we always exercise this control. In the great majority of instances we do not exercise it, which explains why so many people go through life in poverty.

NOTES & COMMENTS

Recall what I said about the subconscious mind resembling a fertile garden, in which weeds will grow if the seeds of more desirable crops are not sown. Autosuggestion is the way you may feed your subconscious on creative thoughts, or you can, by neglecting it, permit thoughts of a destructive nature to find their way into this rich garden of the mind.

COMMENTARY

Numerous psychological studies and experiments with hypnotherapy have validated Napoleon Hill's concept that a person's subconscious mind retains everything that person ever experienced. Studies also support the theory that the subconscious is nonjudgmental, it does not filter or interpret, it simply processes information literally and stores it. For those readers who may be dubious about the subconscious, or that thoughts stored below the level of consciousness can exert enough influence to affect attitude and behavior, the following explanation should alleviate any such doubts.

There is no doubt about the existence of the conditions known by the psychological terms fixations, phobias, *and* compulsive behaviors. *These conditions occur when a child has learned something in such a powerful or dramatic way that the knowledge becomes firmly planted in the child's subconscious mind. Then, even as the child grows to adulthood and the conscious mind learns to understand that information from a mature point of view, because the childhood learning experience was so powerful, the subconscious still retains the childhood understanding of the information. The result is a fixation, phobia, or compulsive behavior that causes a response rooted in childhood, which does not make logical sense to the adult's conscious mind. That is because it does not come from the conscious. It comes from the subconscious belief that was so emotionalized it overrides the adult's logical, conscious mind.*

Hill's theory is based on exactly the same psychological principles. Thoughts do remain stored in the subconscious, they remain just as they were when they were input, and the more highly emotionalized the thoughts are when they are input, the more influence they exert on attitude and behavior. It is this aspect of the subconscious that will allow you to use autosuggestion as a tool with which to input the positive thoughts that will help you achieve the success you desire.

SEE AND FEEL MONEY IN YOUR HANDS

You were instructed, in the last of the six steps described in chapter 3 on desire, to read aloud twice daily the written statement of your desire for money. You were also directed to see and feel yourself already in possession of the money. By following these instructions, you communicate the object of your desire directly to your subconscious mind in a spirit of absolute faith. Through repetition of this procedure, you will create thought habits that reinforce your efforts to transmute desire into its monetary equivalent.

Read these steps again, very carefully, before you proceed further.

1. Fix in your mind the exact amount of money you desire. It is not sufficient merely to say "I want plenty of money." Be definite about the amount. $500,000

2. Determine exactly what you intend to give in return for the money you desire. (There is no such reality as "something for nothing.")

   6/30/2015

3. Establish a definite date when you intend to possess the money you desire.

4. Create a definite plan for carrying out your desire and begin at once, whether you are ready or not, to put this plan into action.

5. Now write it out. Write a clear, concise statement of the amount of money you intend to acquire, name the time limit for its

acquisition, state what you intend to give in return for the money, and describe clearly the plan through which you intend to accumulate it.

6. Read your written statement aloud, twice daily. Read it once just before retiring at night, and read it once after arising in the morning. As you read, see and feel and believe yourself already in possession of the money.

Remember, when reading aloud the statement of your desire (through which you will develop a "money consciousness"), that the mere reading of the words is of no consequence—unless you mix emotion, or feeling, with your words. Your subconscious mind recognizes and acts only upon thoughts that have been well mixed with emotion or feeling.

This is a fact of such importance as to warrant repetition in practically every chapter. The lack of understanding of this is the main reason the majority of people who try to apply the principle of autosuggestion get no desirable results.

Plain, unemotional words do not influence the subconscious mind. You will get no appreciable results until you learn to reach your subconscious mind with thoughts or spoken words that have been well emotionalized with belief.

Do not become discouraged if you cannot control and direct your emotions the first time you try. Remember, there is no such possibility as something for nothing. You cannot cheat, even if you desire to do so. The price of ability to influence your subconscious mind is persistence in applying the principles described here. You cannot develop the desired ability for a lower price. You, and you alone, must decide whether or not the reward (the money consciousness) is worth the price you must pay for it in effort.

Your ability to use the principle of autosuggestion will depend, very largely, upon your capacity to concentrate on a given desire until that desire becomes a burning obsession.

HOW TO STRENGTHEN YOUR POWERS OF CONCENTRATION

When you begin to carry out the instructions in the six steps, it will be necessary for you to make use of the principle of concentration. Following are suggestions for the effective use of concentration.

When you begin the first of the six steps, which instructs you to "fix in your own mind the exact amount of money you desire," close your eyes and hold your thoughts on that amount of money until you can actually see the physical appearance of the money. Do this at least once each day. As you go through these exercises, follow the instructions given in chapter 4 on faith, and see yourself actually in possession of the money.

Here is a most significant fact: the subconscious mind takes any orders given to it in a spirit of absolute faith, and acts upon those orders. But the orders often have to be presented over and over again (repeated positive affirmation) before they are interpreted by the subconscious mind. Because of this, you might consider the possibility of playing a perfectly legitimate "trick" on your subconscious mind. Make it believe (because you believe it) that you must have the amount of money you are visualizing. Make it believe that this money is already awaiting your claim, so the subconscious mind must hand over to you practical plans for acquiring the money that is yours.

Give this thought to your imagination and see what your imagination can, or will, do to create practical plans for the accumulation of money through transmutation of your desire.

NOTES & COMMENTS

Do not wait for a definite plan through which you will exchange services or merchandise in return for the money you are visualizing. Just start right now to see yourself in possession of the money, demanding and expecting that your subconscious mind will hand over the plans you need. Be on the alert for these plans, and when they appear, put them into action immediately. When the plans appear, they will probably "flash" into your mind in the form of an inspiration or intuition (from Infinite Intelligence). Treat it with respect, and act upon it as soon as you receive it.

In the fourth of the six steps, you were instructed to "create a definite plan for carrying out your desire, and begin at once to put this plan into action." Do the same thing here. Close your eyes and create in your mind a vivid image of you carrying out the instructions. Do not trust to your "reason" when creating your plan for accumulating money through the transmutation of desire. Your reasoning faculty may be lazy, and if you depend entirely upon it to serve you, it may disappoint you.

When visualizing the money you intend to accumulate, see yourself rendering the service or delivering the merchandise you intend to give in return for this money. This is important!

COMMENTARY

The basic principle underlying autosuggestion is closely related to self-hypnosis, and both techniques played an important role in the development of modern psychotherapy. Although all three concepts—autosuggestion, hypnosis, and psychotherapy—had to overcome initial public skepticism, unfortunately autosuggestion and hypnotism were hampered by events that further delayed their acceptance.

Hypnosis was an integral part of the therapies used by the major figures in the development of psychiatry including Sigmund Freud, Carl Jung, and William James. It fell out of favor as a therapeutic method when stage magicians began to use the technique in their acts. People found it difficult to give serious consideration to a method that was being used in theatres and nightclubs to make members of the audience do ridiculous things for comic effect.

Autosuggestion encountered a similar problem. French psychiatrist Emile Coué was the best known early advocate of autosuggestion. A contemporary of Sigmund Freud, Coué operated a clinic that treated patients diagnosed with psychosomatic ailments (individuals who have convinced themselves they are ill, and even show symptoms, but do not actually have a disease). Coué treated his patients with an autosuggestion technique that involved the repetition of statements he termed positive affirmations.

Coué devised a general, nonspecific phrase that would give the subconscious a positive instruction, but was open enough that it did not tell the subconscious how to do it. The positive affirmation was "Every day in every way I am getting better and better" and he instructed his patients to repeat the phrase several times a day. Improvements among his patients happened so quickly and dramatically that his method became the talk of medical and scientific circles, and the use of the phrase practically became a movement in Europe.

Word of the success Coué was having with his method spread to America and he was soon booked to do a lecture tour. At one of his early speaking engagements a cynical newspaper reporter made a joke of the technique, calling it "Hells bells, I'm well." The joke followed Coué wherever he spoke, and the press coverage was so negative he cancelled his tour and returned to practice in Europe.

Serious scientists and therapists continued to work with autosuggestion, but just as had happened when stage magicians cast doubt upon the efficacy of hypnosis, Coué's method of positive affirmation fell out of favor with the general public. It took the openness of the latter part of the twentieth century before the techniques of hypnosis and autosuggestion gained general acceptance once again.

Today, if you go on the Internet there are over 40,000 Web links featuring positive affirmations, and numerous bestsellers have been written on the

NOTES & COMMENTS

subject. Virtually every newspaper, magazine, and television news program regularly features stories on the crucial role the mind plays in personal growth and achievement. Techniques based on autosuggestion have fostered countless bestselling books, audiobooks, and video programs, and every week thousands of people attend seminars, lectures, and retreats to be inspired by motivational speakers or spiritual leaders, and to learn techniques that will help them achieve success—almost all of which are based on the basic principles Napoleon Hill advocates in this book.

When Hill instructs the reader to "close your eyes and hold your thoughts on that amount of money until you can actually see the physical appearance of the money," he is in fact describing the autosuggestion technique most widely taught by contemporary motivational experts. Today it is called Creative Visualization and it is regularly used by some of the most successful trainers of Olympic athletes and professional sports teams, it is used by NASA in training astronauts, and medical professionals use it in a variety of ways including teaching it to patients who need to elevate their autoimmune system.

Using visualization effectively is much more than simply daydreaming about something you would like to have, or a goal you would like to achieve. Visualization is a specific technique that involves the use of imagination, creativity, vivid imagery, and affirmations, all focused on creating something you wish to manifest in reality. Napoleon Hill identified the practice of visualization and wrote about it as early as 1928, in his first bestseller, Law of Success. *Since then, many other psychologists, medical professionals, motivational speakers, and authors have developed systems based on the same principles.*

Dr. Maxwell Maltz, a noted plastic surgeon, found that often it was as important for his patients to change their inner perception of themselves as it was to change their outer appearance. Dr. Maltz's landmark bestseller, Psycho-Cybernetics *draws heavily on visualization as a way to increase self-esteem and improve a wide range of abilities. The Silva Method, another variation on visualization, has been taught to millions of people by certified Silva*

Trainers who hold seminars throughout the country. Jose Silva's bestselling book, The Silva Mind Control Method, *has also sold many millions of copies.*

In 1978, fifty years after Napoleon Hill wrote about visualization in Law of Success, *Shakti Gawain published the phenomenal bestseller,* Creative Visualization, *and Adelaide Bry published* Visualization: Directing the Movies of Your Mind. *At about the same time, Dr. O. Carl Simonton, an oncologist, concluded that cancer patients who used visualizations in conjunction with chemotherapy treatments had a marked improvement over those who didn't. His bestseller,* Getting Well Again *had a profound impact, and it was followed by books from other respected medical professionals such as* Love, Medicine, and Miracles *by Dr. Bernie Segal, and* Superimmunity *by Dr. Paul Pearsal. Other bestsellers by Dr. John Sarno, Dr. Deepak Chopra, and Dr. Andrew Weil have made what once was referred to as alternative medicine, now part of mainstream medical practice.*

STIMULATE YOUR SUBCONSCIOUS MIND

The instructions given previously for the steps necessary in your desire for money will now be summarized and blended with the principles covered by this chapter, as follows:

1. Go to some quiet spot where you will not be disturbed or inter-rupted. Close your eyes and repeat aloud (so that you may hear your own words) the written statement of the amount of money you intend to accumulate. Be specific about the time limit for its accumulation, and a description of the service or merchandise you intend to give in return for the money. As you carry out these instructions, see yourself already in possession of the money.

For example, suppose that you intend to accumulate $50,000 by the first of January, five years from now, and that you intend to give your personal services as a salesperson in return for the

NOTES & COMMENTS

money. Your written statement of your purpose should be similar to the following:

By the first day of January, _____, I will have in my possession $50,000, which will come to me in various amounts from time to time during the interim.

In return for this money I will give the most efficient service of which I am capable. I will give the fullest possible quantity, and the best possible quality, of service as a salesperson of _____ (describe the service or merchandise you intend to sell).

I believe that I will have this money in my possession. My faith is so strong that I can now see this money before my eyes. I can touch it with my hands. It is now awaiting transfer to me at the time and in the proportion that I deliver the service in return for it. I am awaiting a plan for getting this money, and I will follow that plan when it is received.

2. Repeat this program night and morning until you can see (in your imagination) the money you intend to accumulate.

3. Place a written copy of your statement where you can see it night and morning, and read it just before retiring and upon arising, until it has been memorized.

COMMENTARY

The following is another suggestion, adapted from Hill's writings in Law of Success *and also in* Napoleon Hill's Keys to Success:

Surround yourself with books, pictures, mottoes, and other suggestive devices. Pick things that symbolize and reinforce achievement and self-reliance. Constantly add to your collection, and move things to new places where you can see them in a different light and in association with different things.

I had a friend who was a realtor who kept her Million Dollar Club certificate over her desk to remind herself of what she was capable. One day she took it down to dust and set it on top of a newspaper. When she picked it up again, she saw beneath it an article about the new football coach who had been hired at the university. Guess who bought a house she had been struggling to sell?

Remember, as you carry out these instructions, that you are applying the principle of autosuggestion—for the purpose of giving orders to your subconscious mind. Remember, also, that your subconscious mind will act only upon instructions that are emotionalized and handed over to it with "feeling." Faith is the strongest, and most productive, of the emotions.

These instructions may, at first, seem abstract. Do not let this disturb you. Follow the instructions no matter how abstract or impractical they may appear to be. If you do as you have been instructed, in spirit as well as in act, the time will soon come when a whole new universe of power will unfold to you.

Skepticism, in connection with all new ideas, is characteristic of all human beings. If you follow the instructions, your skepticism will soon be replaced by belief. And belief will become crystallized into absolute faith.

Many philosophers have made the statement that man is the master of his own earthly destiny, but most of them have failed to say why he is the master. The reason that man may become the master of himself, and of his environment, is because he has the power to influence his own subconscious mind.

The actual performance of transmuting desire into money is through autosuggestion. That is the principle by which you can reach, and influence, the subconscious mind. The other principles are simply tools with which to apply autosuggestion. Keep this thought in mind and you will, at all times, be conscious of the important part the principle of autosuggestion is to play in your efforts to accumulate money through the methods described in this book.

After you have read the entire book, come back to this chapter and follow, in spirit and in action, this instruction: Read the entire chapter aloud once every night, until you become thoroughly convinced that the principle of autosuggestion is sound, and that it will accomplish for you all that has been claimed for it. As you read, underscore with a pencil every sentence that impresses you.

Follow the foregoing instruction to the letter, and it will open the way for a complete understanding and mastery of the principles of success.

EVERY ADVERSITY,

EVERY FAILURE,

AND EVERY HEARTACHE

CARRIES WITH IT

THE SEED OF

AN EQUIVALENT OR

A GREATER BENEFIT.

SPECIALIZED KNOWLEDGE

PERSONAL EXPERIENCES OR OBSERVATIONS

The Fourth Step Toward Riches

There are two kinds of knowledge. One is general, the other is specialized. General knowledge, no matter how great in quantity or variety it may be, is of little use in the accumulation of money. The faculties of the great universities possess practically every form of general knowledge known to civilization. Most of the professors have little money. They specialize in teaching knowledge, but they do not specialize in the organization or the use of knowledge.

Knowledge will not attract money, unless it is organized and directed through practical plans for the specific purpose of accumulating money. Lack of understanding of this fact has been the source of confusion to millions of people who falsely believe that "knowledge is power." It is nothing of the sort! Knowledge is only *potential* power. It becomes power only when, and if, it is organized into definite plans of action and directed to a definite end.

NOTES & COMMENTS

The missing link in all systems of education is that educational institutions fail to teach their students how to organize and use the knowledge after they have acquired it.

Many people made the mistake of assuming that because Henry Ford had little schooling he was not a man of education. Those who made this mistake did not understand the real meaning of the word *educate.* That word is derived from the Latin word *educo,* meaning to educe, to draw out, or to develop from within.

An educated person is not, necessarily, one who has an abundance of general or specialized knowledge. An educated person is one who has so developed the faculties of their mind that he or she may acquire anything they want, or its equivalent, without violating the rights of others.

During the world war, a Chicago newspaper published editorials in which, among other statements, Henry Ford was called "an ignorant pacifist." Mr. Ford objected to the statements, and sued the paper for libeling him. When the suit was tried in the courts, the attorneys for the paper called Mr. Ford to the witness stand, for the purpose of proving to the jury that he was ignorant. They asked Mr. Ford a great variety of questions, all of them intended to prove that while he might possess considerable specialized knowledge about manufacturing automobiles, he was, in the main, ignorant.

Mr. Ford was asked such questions as "Who was Benedict Arnold?" and "How many soldiers did the British send over to America to put down the Rebellion of 1776?" In answer to the last question, Mr. Ford replied, "I do not know the exact number of soldiers the British sent over, but I have heard that it was a considerably larger number than ever went back."

Finally, Mr. Ford became tired of this line of questioning. In reply to a particularly offensive question, he leaned over, pointed his finger at the lawyer who had asked the question, and said: "If I should really want to answer the foolish question you have just asked, or any of the other questions you have been asking me, let me remind you that I have a row of electric push-buttons on my desk, and by pushing the right button I can summon to my aid men who can answer any question I desire to ask concerning the business to which I am devoting most of my efforts. Now, will you kindly tell me why I should clutter up my mind with general knowledge, for the purpose of being able to answer questions, when I have men around me who can supply any knowledge I require?"

That answer floored the lawyer. Every person in the courtroom realized it was the answer not of an ignorant man but of a man of education. Any person is educated who knows where to get knowledge when they need it, and how to organize that knowledge into definite plans of action. Through the assistance of his "Master Mind" group, Henry Ford had at his command all the specialized knowledge he needed to become one of the wealthiest men in America. It was not essential that he have this knowledge in his own mind.

YOU CAN GET ALL THE KNOWLEDGE YOU NEED

Before you can transmute your desire into money, you will require specialized knowledge of the service, merchandise, or profession that you intend to offer in return for fortune. Perhaps you may need much more specialized knowledge than you have the ability or the inclination to acquire. If this is true, you may bridge your weakness through the aid of your Master Mind group.

The Master Mind is defined as: "Coordination of knowledge and effort, in a spirit of harmony, between two or more people for the attainment of a definite purpose." The larger meaning of the Master Mind group is explained in greater detail in later chapters.

NOTES & COMMENTS

After reading Hill's definition of the Master Mind, many people may assume that he is describing teamwork. That would not be correct. The following explanation is adapted from the Napoleon Hill Foundation's book Believe and Achieve:

Teamwork can be achieved by any group—even one whose members have disparate interests—because all it requires is cooperation. In teamwork, people might simply be cooperating because they like the leader, or out of a sense of duty. Some team members will give 100 percent to any team that pays them enough, but they have little concern about the objective. And sometimes there is good teamwork because different members have different agendas. A board of directors may disagree, even be unfriendly, and still run a business successfully. Musical groups are made up of notoriously self-centered people who work as a team if it will help them get ahead.

Master Minds, on the other hand, are formed of individuals who have the same agenda, a deep sense of mission, and commitment to the same goal. Master Minds represent the highest order of thinking by a group of knowledgeable people, each contributing their absolute best according to their own abilities, expertise, and background. If you have ever been a part of a meeting when everything just clicked, and ideas built upon other ideas, with each member contributing until out of the group activity came the best possible idea or solution, that was a Master Mind at work.

Napoleon Hill believed that you must make the Master Mind experience a regular part of your life if you really want to succeed. How to select the right people for your Master Mind will be discussed further in chapter 11, The Power of the Master Mind.

The accumulation of great fortunes calls for power, and power is acquired through highly organized and intelligently directed specialized knowledge. That knowledge does not, necessarily, have to be in the possession of the person who accumulates the fortune.

This should give hope and encouragement to those who want to accumulate a fortune but don't have the necessary "education" to supply such specialized knowledge. People sometimes go through life suffering from inferiority complexes because they are not people of "education." The person who can organize and direct a "Master Mind" group of people who possess the knowledge needed is just as much a person of education as any other individual in the group.

Thomas A. Edison had only three months of schooling during his entire life. But he did not lack education, neither did he die poor.

Henry Ford had less than a sixth grade schooling but he managed to do pretty well by himself, financially.

Albert Einstein was working as a clerk in a patent office when he began to develop his world-altering scientific theories.

COMMENTARY

Had Einstein been born today, he might have been diagnosed in his early years as having attention deficit disorder. As a child he was slow to learn to talk. As a student he showed little promise and was expelled from at least one school. But what Einstein could do was to focus his concentration on a goal of his choice. His famous theories were the result of "thought experiments"—experiments that took place inside his mind! It is said that the breakthrough which led him to the theory of relativity came not from specialized knowledge of physics or mathematics, but from his ability to imagine what would happen if he were riding on a beam of starlight through space.

Specialized knowledge is among the most plentiful, and the cheapest, forms of service that may be had. If you doubt this, consult the payroll of any university.

IT PAYS TO KNOW HOW TO PURCHASE KNOWLEDGE
—AND IT PAYS TO KNOW WHERE TO LOOK

First of all, decide the sort of specialized knowledge you require, and the purpose for which it is needed. To a large extent your major purpose in life, the goal toward which you are working, will help determine what knowledge you need. Your next move requires that you have accurate information concerning dependable sources of knowledge. The more important of these are:

- Your own experience and education

- Experience and education available through cooperation of others (a Master Mind alliance)

- Colleges and universities

- Public libraries *[and even easier, the Internet]*

- Special training courses (through night schools and home-study courses in particular)

As knowledge is acquired it must be organized and put into use, for a definite purpose, through practical plans. Knowledge has no value except for what can be gained from its application toward some worthy end.

Successful people never stop acquiring specialized knowledge related to their major purpose, business, or profession. Those who are not successful usually make the mistake of believing that the knowledge-acquiring period ends when you finish school. The truth is that schools do little more than teach you *how* to acquire practical knowledge.

COMMENTARY

> *At this point in the original edition of* Think and Grow Rich, *Napoleon Hill included a newspaper story about education and job opportunities. Although the contemporary job market has changed considerably, the author of the article, Robert Moore, director of placements at Columbia University, made some*

comments that are perfectly aligned with the philosophy of Think and Grow Rich and still hold true today. One such comment was: "The man who has been active on the campus, whose personality is such that he gets along with all kinds of people and who has done an adequate job with his studies has a most decided edge over the strictly academic student."

One of the largest industrial companies, the leader in its field, in writing to Mr. Moore concerning prospective seniors at the college, said: "We emphasize qualities of character, intelligence and personality far more than specific educational background."

Although few would argue that education is valuable, as Moore implies above and as Hill noted earlier about Edison, Ford, and Einstein, academic accomplishment has never been a sure indicator of success. The October 27, 2003, issue of Time magazine made a similar point in their cover story about the changes being made in the SAT exam. Although the article's primary focus is on the efforts to make the SAT less biased, it also notes that recent research indicates that neither the SAT nor IQ tests have proven to be very reliable predictors of future real-world achievement.

In his bestselling book Emotional Intelligence, author Daniel Goleman has created a persuasive argument that the way in which a person handles themselves and their relationships, which he calls emotional intelligence or EI, is a much better indicator than IQ in predicting whether a person will be successful in life. In his later books, Working with Emotional Intelligence and Primal Leadership, Goleman applies his theory to the workplace, focusing on EI leadership techniques and comparing corporate managers' EI with their IQ to analyze which has the greatest positive effect on the financial bottom line.

Daniel Goleman's theories have caused some significant changes within educational circles and among management theorists, but their greatest impact has been on individuals who have gone through life intimidated because they believe they "aren't smart enough." For them, Goleman's books offer convincing evidence that although they may not have conventional education, their natural abilities and interpersonal skills can be far more important in achieving success.

NOTES & COMMENTS

_____

_____

_____

_____

_____

_____

_____

_____

_____

_____

_____

_____

_____

_____

_____

_____

_____

_____

_____

One of the most reliable and practical sources of knowledge available to those who need specialized schooling are night schools, extension courses, and seminars. The correspondence schools give specialized training anywhere the U.S. mails go *[or via the Internet]*. One advantage of home-study training is the flexibility of the study program, which permits you to study during spare time. Another advantage of home-study training (if the school is carefully chosen) is that most courses offer some method of personal consultation, which can be of priceless value to those needing specialized knowledge. No matter where you live, you can share the benefits.

A Lesson from a Collection Agency

Anything acquired without effort, and without cost, is generally unappreciated and often discredited. Perhaps this is why we get so little from our marvelous opportunity in public schools. The self-discipline you will learn from a program of specialized study can make up for the wasted opportunity when knowledge was available without cost. Being asked to pay, whether you make good grades or poor, has the effect of causing you to follow through with the course when you would otherwise drop it.

I learned this from experience when I enrolled for a home-study course in advertising. After completing eight or ten lessons I stopped studying. But the school did not stop sending me bills. In fact, they insisted on payment, whether I kept up my studies or not. I decided that if I had to pay for the course (which I had legally obligated myself to do), I should complete the lessons and get my money's worth.

Correspondence schools are well-organized businesses. At the time I felt that their collection system was somewhat too well organized, but I learned later in life that it was a valuable part of my education. The truth is that their collection department constituted the very finest sort of training on decision-making, promptness, and the habit of finishing what you begin. The collection system that forced me to finish the course turned out to be worth much in the form of money earned.

The Road to Specialized Knowledge

We have in this country what is said to be the greatest public school system in the world. One of the strange things about human beings is that they value only that which has a price. The free schools of America and the free public libraries do not impress people *because* they are free. This is the major reason why so many people find it necessary to acquire additional training after they finish school and go to work. It is also one of the major reasons why employers give greater consideration to employees who take specialized training courses. They have learned that those who have the ambition to give up a part of their spare time to studying at home have in them those qualities that make for leadership.

There is one weakness in people for which there is no remedy. It is the universal weakness of lack of ambition. People who give up some of their spare time to take courses seldom remain at the bottom very long. By taking such courses they open the way for the upward climb, remove many obstacles from their path, and attract the interest of those who have the power to help them.

The home-study method of training is especially suited to people who have already started working. They often find that after having left school they still need additional specialized knowledge but cannot spare the time to go back to school.

Stuart Austin Wier was a construction engineer. He followed this line of work until the Depression hit and severely limited the construction business. He took inventory of himself and decided to change his profession to law. He went back to school and took special courses to prepare himself as a corporation lawyer. He completed his training, passed the bar examination, and quickly built a lucrative law practice as a patent attorney.

NOTES & COMMENTS

NOTES & COMMENTS

Just to keep the record straight, and to anticipate the excuses of those who will say, "I couldn't go to school because I have a family to support," or "I'm too old," I will add that Mr. Wier was past forty and married when he went back to school. Moreover, by carefully selecting highly specialized courses, Mr. Wier completed in two years the work that it takes the majority of law students four years to do. It pays to know how to purchase knowledge!

A Simple Idea That Paid Off

Here is another specific example, about a salesman in a grocery store who found himself suddenly unemployed. Having had some book-keeping experience, he took a special course in accounting, familiarized himself with all the latest bookkeeping and office equipment, and went into business for himself. Starting with the grocer for whom he had formerly worked, he made contracts with more than one hundred small merchants to keep their books, at a very nominal monthly fee. His idea was so practical that he soon found it necessary to set up a portable accounting office in a light delivery truck. He now has a fleet of these bookkeeping offices "on wheels." He employs a large staff of assistants who provide small merchants with accounting services equal to the best that money can buy, at very nominal cost.

Specialized knowledge, plus imagination, were the ingredients that went into this unique and successful business. Last year the owner of that business paid income taxes of almost ten times as much as was paid by the grocery store that fired him.

COMMENTARY

It would be impossible to write a contemporary book about success without including the story of Bill Gates. And although the connection between the world's wealthiest man and Hill's story about a man who started a mobile accounting business may not be immediately obvious, the fact is that this is a very apt place to include the story of Microsoft. Just as with the mobile accountant, the two defining characteristics of Bill Gates' success are specialized knowledge and imagination.

Everyone had recognized that at an early age Bill Gates was a very bright student, but he had little interest in anything other than science and math. And when the mothers' group at his school arranged for the students to learn about computing, that became his passion. By the time he was thirteen he'd taught himself computer programming, and throughout high school and his years at university his life revolved around computer clubs and odd jobs working for companies that had something to do with computers.

Although at various times he toyed with the idea of a career in science or law, it is probably fair to say that while he was still in school Bill Gates knew, in general terms, what his "burning desire" in life would be. He paid little attention to general knowledge, but devoted himself to assembling the specialized knowledge he would need to achieve his definite major purpose.

Gates' burning desire heated up the day his friend and fellow computer-club member Paul Allen bought a copy of the January 1975 issue of Popular Electronics. On the cover was a picture of an inexpensive desktop computer, the Altair 8800, which could be built from a kit. Gates and Allen knew in their gut that there were other students just like them who would love to get their hands on one of these things. At the time, it took a lot of imagination to foresee the impact computers might have on the average person. And even though they didn't own an Altair, they decided they could write a computer program for it. That took even more imagination!

They contacted Ed Roberts, the founder of the company that made the Altair, and pitched their idea. Roberts told them he was getting offers from all over, and his policy was that whoever wrote it first would get the job. For the next two months they tore apart the manual, gleaning the specialized knowledge they would need to write the program. They were the first to deliver a workable operating system, and Roberts bought it from them for $3,000 plus a royalty on sales.

NOTES & COMMENTS

With their vision of the future burning in their imaginations, Gates and Allen used the advance and their royalties to launch a company that would be in the business of writing computer programs. They named their new company Microsoft, and called old friends from their high school computer club to staff it. Bill Gates was nineteen and Paul Allen was only a few years older. They and and their computer club friends started writing programs for Apple Computer, Commodore, and anyone else who would contract with the company for their services.

For the next five years Bill Gates and Paul Allen had their share of imaginative ideas, but mostly they concentrated on learning the specialized knowledge needed to run and grow a successful business. Then in 1980 IBM, which had finally decided to get into the small computer business, needed help getting up to speed. They approached Microsoft to write an operating system for their new computer venture. Once again, specialized knowledge and imagination were the qualities that guided Bill Gates.

In their imaginations, Gates and Allen could see an even bigger future than before, and through specialized knowledge of what computers were capable of, they knew the role they could play in that future. They then made two business moves that are the foundation of the Microsoft success. First, because IBM had such a tight schedule, Gates went to a computer programmer, Tim Patterson, and bought from him a rudimentary but already developed operating system. Gates then set to work modifying the system, and he renamed it MS-DOS—for Microsoft Disc Operating System.

The other move that was crucial to their success was the negotiation with IBM. They started from the position that they would not sell an operating system to IBM; what they would do was license the system to IBM in exchange for a royalty on every copy sold with an IBM computer. And it would not be an exclusive license, which meant that Microsoft could also license the system to other computer companies.

If you were to continue to track the history of Microsoft you would find those same qualities—a burning desire, an idea, specialized knowledge, and imagination—behind each move Bill Gates made and continues to make, just as they were behind the success of the man who started the mobile accounting business.

The beginning of the successful mobile computing business was an idea. I know this is true because I was the one who gave him that idea.

Now I'd like to pass on the story of another idea. And it was my accountant friend who, indirectly, suggested this one to me.

When I first proposed the accounting idea to him, he said, "I like the idea, but I would not know how to turn it into cash." In other words, he did not know how to market his bookkeeping knowledge after he had acquired it.

So, with the aid of a young woman copywriter, a very attractive presentation was prepared describing the advantages of the new system of bookkeeping. The brochure told the story of this new business so effectively that its owner soon had more accounts than he could handle.

There are thousands of people all over the country who need the services of a merchandising specialist capable of preparing an attractive way to market personal services.

This idea was born of the necessity to solve a specific problem, but it did not stop by serving merely one person. The woman who created the presentation has a keen imagination. She saw in her newly born brainchild the making of a new profession to serve thousands of people who need practical guidance in marketing personal services.

Spurred to action by the success of her first "prepared plan to market personal services," this woman turned to solving a similar problem for her son. He had just finished college but had been totally unable to find a market for his services. The plan she created for him was the best example of merchandising personal services I have ever seen.

When the presentation had been completed, it contained nearly fifty pages of beautifully typed, properly organized information. It told the story of her son's natural abilities, schooling, personal experiences, and a great variety of other information. The book also contained a complete description of the position her son desired, together with a marvelous word picture of the exact plan he would use in filling the position.

The preparation of the presentation required several weeks of her time, during which she sent her son to the public library almost daily to get specific data needed to sell his services to best advantage. She also sent him to all the competitors of his prospective employer, where he gathered information concerning their business methods. This was of great value in the formation of the plan he intended to use in filling the position he sought. When the plan was finished, it contained more than half a dozen very fine suggestions that would benefit the prospective employer.

You Don't Have to Start at the Bottom

You may be inclined to ask, "Why go to all this trouble to secure a job?" The answer is, "Doing a thing well is never trouble. The plan prepared by this woman for her son helped him get the job at the first interview, and at a salary fixed by himself."

Moreover—and this, too, is important—the position did not require the young man to start at the bottom. He began as a junior executive, at an executive's salary.

"Why go to all this trouble?"

Well, for one thing, this young man's planned presentation saved him no less than ten years of "working his way up."

This idea of starting at the bottom and working your way up may appear to be sound, but the major objection to it is this: too many of those who begin at the bottom never manage to lift their heads high enough to be seen by those who count. And the outlook from the bottom is not very bright or encouraging. It has a tendency to kill off ambition. You get into a rut, and you accept your fate because you form the habit of daily routine. Often this habit finally becomes so strong you don't even try to throw it off. And that is another reason why it pays to start one or two steps above the bottom. By so doing you will form the habit of looking around, of observing how others get ahead, of seeing opportunity, and of embracing it without hesitation.

A splendid example of what I mean is Dan Halpin. During his college days he was manager of the famous 1930 championship Notre Dame football team, when it was under the direction of the late Knute Rockne.

Halpin finished college at a very unfavorable time. The Depression had made jobs scarce. So, after a fling at investment banking and motion pictures, he took the first job with a potential future he could find. It was selling electrical hearing aids on a commission basis. Anyone could start in that sort of job, and Halpin knew it, but it was enough to open the door of opportunity to him.

For almost two years he worked at the job but it didn't satisfy him. He would never have risen above that job if he had not done something about his dissatisfaction. He aimed first at the job of assistant sales manager of the company, and he got the job. That single step upward placed him high enough above the crowd for him to see still greater opportunity. Also, it placed him where opportunity could see him.

In his new position he did so well selling hearing aids that A. M. Andrews, chairman of the board of the Dictograph Products Company, a competitor of the company for which Halpin worked, asked to meet with him. Mr. Andrews wanted to know something about that man Dan Halpin who was taking big sales away from the long-established Dictograph Company. When the interview was over, Halpin was the new sales manager, in charge of the Acousticon

NOTES & COMMENTS

Division of Dictograph. Then, to test young Halpin's mettle, Mr. Andrews went away to Florida for three months, leaving him to sink or swim in his new job.

He did not sink! Knute Rockne's spirit of "All the world loves a winner, and has no time for a loser," inspired him to put so much into his job that he was elected vice president of the company. Vice president was a job that most would be proud to earn through ten years of loyal effort, but Halpin turned the trick in little more than six months.

One of the major points I am trying to emphasize through this entire philosophy is that we rise to high positions or remain at the bottom because of conditions we can control. But only if we desire to control them.

I am also trying to emphasize another point—that both success and failure are largely the results of habit. I have not the slightest doubt that Dan Halpin's close association with the greatest football coach America ever knew, planted in his mind the same kind of desire to excel that made the Notre Dame football team world famous. Truly, there is something to the idea that hero-worship is helpful, provided you worship a winner.

My belief in the theory that business associations are vital factors, both in failure and in success, was clearly demonstrated when my son Blair was negotiating with Dan Halpin for a position. Mr. Halpin offered him a beginning salary of about one-half what he could have gotten from a rival company. I brought parental pressure to bear, and encouraged Blair to accept the job with Mr. Halpin. I believe that close association with people who refuse to compromise with circumstances is an asset that can never be measured in terms of money.

The bottom is a monotonous, dreary, unprofitable place for any person. That is why I have taken the time to describe how lowly beginnings can be overcome by proper planning.

MAKE YOUR IDEAS PAY OFF THROUGH SPECIALIZED KNOWLEDGE

The woman who prepared the personal-service sales plan for her son now receives requests from all parts of the country from others who want to market their personal services for more money.

But don't think that all her plan consists of is clever salesmanship to help her clients get more money for the same services they formerly sold for less. She looks after the interests of the purchaser as well as the seller of personal services. She prepares her plans so that the employers receive full value for the additional money they pay.

If you have the imagination, and seek a more profitable outlet for your personal services, this suggestion may be the stimulus for which you have been searching. The idea could earn you an income far greater than that of the "average" doctor, lawyer, or engineer whose education required several years in college.

COMMENTARY

Mary Kay Ash was literally researching and writing down specialized knowledge when the idea for a new business was born in her imagination. Mary Kay had quit her job as a very successful sales manager in the gift business because she had became discouraged by seeing the men she had trained earning more and being promoted ahead of her. She decided to write an advice book for career women, but as she assembled the knowledge women would need to get ahead, she realized she was writing a business plan for the kind of business she would like to run.

She took her life savings of $5,000, went out and found a skincare cream she liked, acquired the rights to it, and began to contact her friends and friends of friends to see if they would like to be beauty consultants for her new company. But what she was offering wasn't just a chance to sell skincare products. It was a very imaginative combination of philosophy and opportunity that gave women the chance to achieve both personal satisfaction and financial success.

NOTES & COMMENTS

The company showed a modest profit in its first year and continued to grow each year until, by the beginning of the twenty-first century, there were over one million independent beauty consultants in thirty countries, with wholesale sales of more than $1.5 billion. Three times Mary Kay Cosmetics was named as one of The 100 Best Companies to Work for in America, and Lifetime Television Network named Mary Kay the Businesswoman of the Century. She became one of the most in-demand motivational speakers, and the bestselling author of three books.

Neil Balter also started his company based on specialized knowledge and imagination. He got his specialized knowledge from his job as a carpenter's apprentice. His imagination came into play the day he was hired by a customer who wanted to clear up a messy closet by having shelves installed. Now, that kind of job must have been offered to thousands of carpenters, but not one of them had the imagination to see in it what Neil Balter saw. When he was finished the work Balter didn't just see nicely fitted shelves, he saw that he had created a solution for a problem that was common to every household in America.

He took the money he earned from the job and started his own business, California Closet Company, which specialized in shelves and fittings designed to attractively organize closet space for maximum efficiency. But Balter's imagination didn't stop once he had his own business up and running. Now he could imagine an even bigger operation, so he went out to find new specialized knowledge about operating and franchising a business. Neil Balter had licensed more than one hundred California Closet franchises when Williams-Sonoma offered to buy the company for $12 million.

Lillian Vernon's specialized knowledge was in an area that many women had, but they didn't have the imagination she had. To quote from her autobiography, An Eye For Winners: "Handbags. I knew about those, why not sell them, and belts to match. Didn't every teenage girl, strolling along the street, anywhere in the United States, sport a handbag and belt? And my handbags would offer something special: each one would be personalized with initials. I knew with absolute certainty that teenagers would go for items that made them feel unique." She believed enough in her idea that she spent $495 to take a small ad in Seventeen magazine. The ad brought in $32,000 in orders!

That was when Lillian Vernon started to gather other specialized knowledge—about renting space, manufacturing products, warehousing, and shipping—all of which she'd need to grow her idea of bags and belts into a direct-response business featuring a whole array of distinctively monogrammed items. Within a few years she needed more specialized knowledge—about product photography, layout, printing, and direct mail—as she imagined having her own catalog.

She started by mailing a 16-page, black-and-white catalog to 125,000 customers who had bought products from her in the past. At the beginning of the twenty-first century Lillian Vernon was still picking the merchandise and overseeing the design of her catalogs, many of which now run well over one hundred full-color pages, are mailed to millions of people many times each year, and generate approximately $250 million in annual sales.

There is another story about gathering specialized knowledge that is so good we will use it to conclude this editorial comment. It actually comes from the Napoleon Hill archives, and although he did not include it in Think and Grow Rich, he often used it as an example in his lectures and seminars.

There was a young man who started out working for the railroad in 1893 as a machinist at five cents an hour. He was always taking courses and learning what he could about steam engines, and by 1905 he had worked his way up through the ranks until he was superintendent of motive power for Chicago Great Western in Oelwein, Iowa. Then he did something that must have made his friends think he had taken leave of his senses. He was attending the Chicago Automobile Show when a red-and-white Locomobile caught his attention. He put up his life savings of $700 and convinced a friend to co-sign a loan for $4,300 so he could buy the car. He promptly took it home, put it into a shed, jacked it up, and proceeded to take it apart, piece by piece. Then he put it back together again. Then he took it apart and put it back together again. After doing that a few more times, he had learned what he wanted to know.

NOTES & COMMENTS

And that was how Walter P. Chrysler gathered the specialized knowledge he needed to get himself out of railroading and into the automobile business.

There is no fixed price for sound ideas!

Behind all ideas is specialized knowledge. But remember, specialized knowledge is more abundant and more easily acquired than ideas. Because of this truth, there are ever-increasing opportunities for the person capable of helping men and women sell their personal services. Capability means imagination—the one quality needed to combine specialized knowledge with ideas to create organized plans that will yield riches.

If you have imagination, this chapter may present you with an idea that is the beginning of the riches you desire. Remember, the idea is the main thing. Specialized knowledge may be found just around the corner—any corner.

HAPPINESS IS FOUND IN DOING,

NOT MERELY IN POSSESSING.

IMAGINATION

THE WORKSHOP OF THE MIND

The Fifth Step Toward Riches

The imagination is literally the workshop where all plans are created. It is where the impulse, the desire, is given shape, form, and action through the aid of the imaginative faculty of the mind.

It has been said that we can create anything that we can imagine.

Through the aid of imagination we have discovered and harnessed more of Nature's forces during the past fifty years than during the entire history of the human race previous to that time. And even with all we have accomplished, we have come nowhere near the limit of what we are capable. Our only limitation, within reason, lies in the development and use of our imagination. The human imagination offers so much possibility, it is as though we have merely discovered that we have an imagination, and have just started to use it in a very elementary way.

NOTES & COMMENTS

TWO FORMS OF IMAGINATION

The imaginative faculty functions in two forms. One is known as "synthetic imagination" and the other as "creative imagination."

COMMENTARY

In modern usage, the word synthetic *has taken on a negative connotation, implying that something is artificial, not the real thing. Today the word* synthesized, *which is defined as "something made up from component parts," would better describe what Hill had in mind and has been substituted here accordingly.*

Synthesized imagination. Through this faculty you arrange old concepts, ideas, or plans into new combinations. Synthesized imagination does not *create* anything. It merely works with the material of experience, education, and observation with which it is fed. It is the faculty used by most inventors, with the exception of those geniuses who draw upon the creative imagination when they cannot solve problems through synthesized imagination.

Creative imagination. Through the faculty of creative imagination, the finite human mind has direct communication with Infinite Intelligence, the faculty through which "hunches" and "inspirations" are received. It is by this faculty that all basic, or new, ideas are handed over to mankind. It is through this faculty that we pick up "vibes" from other people, and in that way, one individual may tune in or communicate with the subconscious minds of others. *[This concept is explained in greater detail later.]*

The creative imagination works automatically, but only when your conscious mind is motivated, energized, and working at such a high rate that it becomes very perceptive and receptive, such as when the conscious mind is stimulated through the emotion of a strong desire.

The great leaders of business, industry, and finance, and the great
artists, musicians, poets, and writers became great because they developed the faculty of creative imagination.

COMMENTARY

*At this point it should be noted that both kinds of imagination are equally
valuable to you, and they work together so seamlessly it is often hard to tell
where one ends and the other begins. For instance, when Jeff Bezos created
the idea of Amazon.com was it synthesized imagination or creative imagination? At the time, many people were getting onto the idea of the Internet as a
sales medium. From this, it could be concluded that he was drawing upon
experience, education, and observation, which would mean he was using
synthesized imagination. But why did he decide to sell books? Was that synthesized or creative? Did that idea come out of something in his subconscious
that just felt like books were the right thing? And what about that name?
Calling a bookstore Amazon didn't make sense to anyone but Bezos, but it
certainly caught the public's attention. How important was the name in the
store's success? Was that choice creative or synthesized?*

*Now, take it a step further. What about eBay? Amazon had already shown
that you could sell a lot of goods on the Internet. When Pierre Omidyar hit
on the idea of selling things on the Internet by turning it into an auction
house, what part was synthesized and what part was creative?*

*The answer is, it doesn't matter. Whether you are consciously assembling
the parts of a plan, or if subconsciously the pieces fall into place and suddenly
hit you in a flash of inspiration, all that matters is that you are putting your
imagination to work. And the more you use it the better both the synthesized and
the creative will work for you.*

Desire is a thought, an impulse. It is nebulous and ephemeral. It is
abstract, and of no value, until it has been transformed into its physical counterpart. While the synthesized imagination is the one that will

NOTES & COMMENTS

be used most frequently in the process of transforming desire into money, there will be circumstances and situations that demand the use of the creative imagination as well.

Both the synthesized and the creative imagination become more alert and receptive with use. And though your imaginative faculty may have become weak through lack of use, you can revive it. Just as any muscle or organ of the body develops the more it is used, your imagination also becomes more receptive in direct response to the amount that you use it.

Use Your Synthesized Imagination

First let us focus attention on the development of the synthesized imagination. This is the faculty that you will use more often in converting desire into money.

Transformation of the intangible impulse of desire into the tangible reality of money calls for the use of a plan, or plans. To make plans you must use your imagination. Mainly, this will require you to use your synthesized imagination as you draw upon your experience, your education, and your observations.

COMMENTARY

The following is adapted from Hill's later writing and appears in Napoleon Hill's Keys to Success:

> *An excellent example of synthesized imagination is Edison's invention of the light bulb. He began with one recognized fact that other people had discovered: a wire could be heated by electricity until it produced light. The problem was that the intense heat quickly burned the wire out and the light never lasted more than a few minutes.*
>
> *Edison failed more than ten thousand times in his attempt to control this heat. When he found the method, it was by applying*

another common fact that had simply eluded everyone else. He realized that charcoal is produced by setting wood on fire, covering it with soil, and allowing the fires to smolder. The soil permits only enough air to reach the fire to keep it burning without blazing, and that way the wood isn't burned up.

When Edison recognized this fact, his imagination immediately associated it with the idea of heating the wire. He placed the wire inside a bottle, pumped out most of the air, and produced the first incandescent light. It burned for eight-and-a-half hours.

Everything that Edison used to make the electric light was widely known, but the way he synthesized the knowledge changed the world. And made him a very wealthy man.

W. Clement Stone called the process the R2A2 formula— Recognize and Relate, Assimilate and Apply. If you do that with everything you see, hear, think, and experience it will give you a new way of looking at familiar things. If you do that, you can achieve what others believe is impossible.

Later in this chapter you will read of other fortunes that grew from even simpler synthesized ideas, and these stories should lead you to conclude that the combination of ideas is nothing that you couldn't have thought of yourself. That alone should start your own imagination synthesizing ideas. However, even though these stories will inspire you, and you will be anxious to get started, this is not yet the point for you to start making plans. Here, and throughout Think and Grow Rich, *Napoleon Hill reminds the reader that this book is meant to be read all the way through before beginning to put the philosophy into practice. There are other ideas to be assimilated from later chapters that will influence your imagination and therefore affect the plans you may develop.*

Read the entire book through, then come back to this chapter and begin to put your imagination to work on the building of a plan for transforming your desire into money. Examples and instructions for

NOTES & COMMENTS

creating plans are given in almost every chapter. Carry out the instructions that are best suited to your needs, and put your plan in writing. The moment you complete this, you will have definitely given concrete form to your intangible desire.

Now read that sentence once more in a slightly different way: "The moment I put my plan in writing, I will have definitely given concrete form to *my* desire."

Now read it aloud, and realize what you are telling yourself.

Desire is only a thought. Through synthesized imagination your experience, education, and observations will give it shape, form, and action. From the moment you follow those instructions and write out your desire and your plan, you will have actually taken the first of a series of steps that will enable you to convert the thought into its physical counterpart.

COMMENTARY

Synthesized imagination plays a role in every phase of a business plan. In fact some of the most successful companies actually get started from synthesized imagination, when an entrepreneur, drawing upon his or her education, experience, and observations, takes an idea from one source and gives it a new application.

That is exactly what happened with Ruth Handler. She and her husband, along with another partner, had started a small manufacturing company which had evolved into toy manufacturing. The success of their business depended on coming up with new toy ideas. Watching her young daughter at play, Ruth Handler noticed that she was fascinated with cutout books that featured teenage-girl or career-women paper dolls that she could cut out clothes for. She also knew that little girls loved to play dress-up in grown-up clothes. These ideas (drawn from Ruth Handler's education, experience, and observations) synthesized themselves in her imagination and came together as a new idea: Ruth Handler announced that they should make a lifelike teenage-girl doll. Not a paper doll but a real, three-dimensional, grown-up doll with a woman's figure, and they could also make grown-up clothes to fit so that girls could play dress-up with the doll.

In honor of the source of inspiration, Ruth Handler named the new doll after her daughter, Barbie.

As obvious as it seems now, until Ruth Handler, no one had the imagination to make and market a doll the way she did. And certainly no one had ever made endless collections of tiny women's fashions for a doll to wear.

Previously we mentioned Jeff Bezos creating Amazon by combining the idea of a bookstore with the Internet, and Pierre Omidyar doing the same thing with auctions when he launched eBay. Mary Kay Ash took the idea of women running their own businesses and added the idea of door-to-door sales. Anita Roddick took the trend of all-natural ingredients, combined it with cosmetics, and created The Body Shop empire. Bernard Marcus and Arthur Blank took the concept of the supermarket, combined it with hardware, and created Home Depot. Thomas Stemberg and Leo Kahn did the same thing with office supplies and launched Staples. Once the connections are made, it may seem obvious, but making these supposedly obvious connections has brought success to many people.

Napoleon Hill says imagination is like a muscle that can be strengthened through use. Just as there are specific exercises that will build and improve physical muscles, specific exercises have been developed to improve and build imagination, and it is commonly accepted that creativity developed in one area will affect your creativity in others. Dr. Edward De Bono, one of the most highly regarded experts in the field, has written more than twenty five books including the bestsellers Lateral Thinking, *and* Six Thinking Hats *that are literally designed to make you think. Dr. Betty Edwards' bestseller,* Drawing on the Right Side of the Brain, *uses drawing techniques to awaken creativity. Dr. Gabriel Rico's bestseller* Writing the Natural Way *uses a technique called Clustering as a way to break writer's block, and Tony Buzan uses a similar method for opening your mind that he terms Mind Mapping. In their bestseller,* Superlearning, *Sheilah Ostrander*

NOTES & COMMENTS

and Lynn Schroeder show ways to use classical music, and Roger von Oech suggests puzzles and riddles as stimuli in A Whack on the Side of the Head.

TAPPING INTO CREATIVE IMAGINATION

The earth on which you live, you yourself, and every other material thing are the result of evolutionary change, through which bits of matter have been organized and arranged in an orderly fashion.

As far as science has been able to determine, the entire universe consists of but four things: time, space, matter and energy. Moreover—and this statement is of stupendous importance—this earth, every one of the billions of individual cells of your body, and every sub-atomic particle of matter, began as an intangible form of energy. Through the combination of energy and matter has been created everything perceptible, from the largest star in the heavens down to and including man himself.

Desire is a thought impulse. Thought impulses are forms of energy. When you begin the process of acquiring money by using the thought impulse of desire, you are drafting into your service the same "stuff" that Nature used in creating this earth, as well as every material form in the universe including your body and your brain in which the thought impulses function.

COMMENTARY

Although recent developments in physics (gauge theory, string theory, membrane theory, and others) have advanced our understanding of matter and energy, Hill's preceding description remains in accord with modern science. The newer theories are variations on, and refinements of, the basic concept that everything in the universe is either time, space, matter, or energy, and as Einstein stated, energy and matter are in fact different forms of the same thing.

As Hill says, everything from the stars to the solar system to the earth to you, your brain, and that little spark called a thought are all the same "stuff."

As when a tablecloth is spread out, there are folds and bumps in the fabric that are all different from each other, but they are all still tablecloth. Like the folds and bumps in the tablecloth, energy and matter are the same thing in different forms. Therefore you (matter), your thoughts (energy), and everybody else (matter) and their thoughts (energy), and all other things (matter) are not just interconnected but are in essence all the same thing. Hill calls this interrelation of everything to everything else Infinite Intelligence.

In the chapter on faith he made his first mention of Infinite Intelligence being the source of hunches, intuition, and flashes of inspiration. In the chapter on autosuggestion he proposed that the subconscious mind is the connection with Infinite Intelligence. In this chapter Hill elaborates that creative imagination is the receiver through which these flashes of insight come to us from Infinite Intelligence.

Under some circumstances, when your mind is operating at a high rate, your creative intelligence receives not just an idea but also a flash of intuition. You get a hunch or a premonition about something or somebody. That flash could not come from your conscious or your subconscious because neither ever had the information. Because everything is a part of everything else, your creative imagination (energy) pulled the thought (energy) directly from the common pool of Infinite Intelligence (energy) that contains not just your sub-conscious (energy) but all other subconscious minds (energy) as well.

Infinite intelligence is a complex concept, and for those readers who find themselves questioning the process, be assured that Hill expands on the theory in later chapters. The editors advise the reader to set aside any questions for the moment, and focus on the logical and practical application Hill had in mind.

You are engaged in trying to turn your desire into its physical or monetary counterpart, and there are laws of physics and principles of psychology that can help you. But first you must give yourself time to become familiar with these laws, and learn to use them. Through repetition, and by describing these principles from every conceivable angle, I hope to reveal to you the secret through which every great fortune has been accumulated. Strange and paradoxical as it may seem, the "secret" is not a secret. It is made obvious in the earth, the stars, the planets, in the elements above and around us, in every blade of grass, and every form of life within our vision.

Do not be discouraged if you do not fully understand or accept this theory. I do not expect that you will accept all that is in this chapter on your first reading. Assimilate as much as you can now while you read this for the first time. Later, when you reread and study it, you will discover that something has happened to clarify it and give you a broader understanding of the whole. Above all, do not stop nor hesitate in your study of these principles until you have read the book at least three times. Then, you will not want to stop.

HOW TO MAKE PRACTICAL USE OF IMAGINATION

Ideas are the beginning points of all fortunes. Ideas are products of the imagination. Following are two true stories about ideas that have yielded huge fortunes. I hope that these stories will convey how important a role imagination can play in turning an idea into success, and that they will illustrate the method by which imagination may be used in accumulating riches.

The Enchanted Kettle

In the late 1880s an old country doctor drove to town, hitched his horse, quietly slipped into a drug store by the back door, and began "dickering" with the young drug clerk.

For more than an hour, behind the prescription counter, the old doctor and the clerk talked in low tones. Then the doctor left. He went out to the buggy and brought back a large, old-fashioned kettle, a big wooden paddle (used for stirring the contents of the kettle), and deposited them at the back of the store.

The clerk inspected the kettle, reached into his inside pocket, took out a roll of bills, and handed it over to the doctor. The roll contained exactly five hundred dollars—the clerk's entire savings!

The doctor handed over a small slip of paper on which was written a secret formula. The words on that small slip of paper were worth a king's ransom. But not to the doctor. Those magic words were needed to start the kettle to boiling, but neither the doctor nor the young clerk knew what fabulous fortunes were destined to flow from that kettle.

The old doctor was glad to sell the outfit for five hundred dollars. The clerk was taking a big chance by staking his entire life's savings on a mere scrap of paper and an old kettle. He never dreamed his investment would start a kettle to overflowing with gold that would one day surpass the miraculous performance of Aladdin's lamp.

What the clerk really purchased was an idea!

The old kettle and the wooden paddle, and the secret message on a slip of paper, were incidental. The miracle of that kettle only began to take place after the new owner mixed with the secret instructions an ingredient of which the doctor knew nothing.

See if you can discover what it was that the young man added to the secret message, which caused the kettle to overflow with gold. Here you have a story of facts stranger than fiction—facts that began in the form of an idea.

Just look at the vast fortunes of gold this idea has produced. It has paid, and still pays, huge fortunes to men and women all over the world who distribute the contents of the kettle to millions of people.

The old kettle is now one of the world's largest consumers of sugar, thus providing jobs to thousands of men and women engaged in growing sugar cane, and in refining and marketing sugar.

The old kettle consumes, annually, millions of glass bottles *[and plastic bottles, and cans]*, providing jobs to huge numbers of workers.

NOTES & COMMENTS

The old kettle gives employment to an army of clerks, stenographers, copywriters, and advertising experts throughout the nation. It has brought fame and fortune to scores of artists who have created magnificent pictures describing the product.

The old kettle has converted Atlanta, which was a small southern city, into the business capital of the South, where it now benefits, directly or indirectly, every business and practically every resident of the city.

The influence of this idea now benefits every civilized country in the world, pouring out a continuous stream of gold to all who touch it. Gold from the kettle built and maintains one of the most prominent colleges of the South, where thousands of young people receive the training essential for success.

If the product of that old brass kettle could talk, it would tell thrilling tales in every language. Tales of love, of business, of professional men and women who are daily being stimulated by it.

I am sure of at least one such tale of romance, for I was a part of it, and it all began not far from the very spot on which the drug clerk purchased the old kettle. It was there that I met my wife, and it was she who first told me of the enchanted kettle. It was the product of that kettle we were drinking when I asked her to accept me "for better or worse."

Whoever you are, wherever you may live, whatever your occupation, just remember every time you see the words *Coca-Cola*, that its vast empire of wealth and influence grew out of a single idea. And that idea, the mysterious ingredient the drug clerk—Asa Candler—mixed with the secret formula was . . . imagination!

Stop and think of that for a moment.

Keep in mind that the steps to riches described in this book are the very same principles through which the influence of Coca-Cola has been extended to every city, town, village, and crossroads of the world.

Now here's the most important thing to remember: the ideas you create may have the possibility of duplicating the enormous success of this worldwide thirst-killer.

COMMENTARY

Harlan Sanders, too, had a recipe and a magic kettle. Actually, his kettle was a pressure cooker, but neither his cooker nor his recipe of eleven herbs and spices would be mentioned here if he hadn't also had imagination.

Harlan Sanders owned and operated a successful motel and café in Corbin, Kentucky. But when the new interstate highway came through, it bypassed Sanders' location. In a short time his business went broke, leaving him with little more than his recipe for fried chicken and a way to make it quickly in a pressure cooker.

At sixty-two years of age, the Colonel, as people called him, had to find a new way to make a living. That's when the magic ingredient, imagination, came in. He decided he wasn't going to sell fried chicken anymore; instead, he would sell his method for making it. He packed his recipe and cooker into the back of his car and hit the road to demonstrate his fried chicken to other restaurant owners. In the first two years he managed to sell five franchises. Two years later he'd sold two hundred. Four years later he was up to six hundred locations when he was approached by an investment group to sell his company.

Recognizing that the magic wasn't just in the kettle or the recipe, the new owners asked Colonel Sanders to stay on as spokesman for the company, which he did until his death in 1980. Today there are almost twelve thousand KFC locations in more than eighty countries, with sales of nearly $10 billion a year.

Debbie Fields was a twenty-year-old housewife who loved to bake cookies. She had no formal education and no business experience, but she had a recipe and an imaginative idea that people would like to buy fresh, hot, soft cookies from a walk-up store. The businesspeople and bankers she approached told her she was crazy, but she and her husband continued to pitch her idea to banker after banker until they finally wore one down enough to give Debbie

NOTES & COMMENTS

Fields a loan to open a store in Palo Alto, California. By noon on her first day she still hadn't sold a cookie, so she went out into the street and gave away samples. That did it. Her walk-in-try-a-sample cookie store took off. Today Mrs. Fields stores are all across America, Harvard Business School uses her methods as a case study in efficiency, and Debbie Fields has become a bestselling author, an in-demand motivational speaker, and a television personality.

Wally "Famous" Amos was a Los Angeles talent agent who copied a cookie recipe off the back of a bag of Nestle's chocolate chips. He made a few changes to personalize the recipe and started to give out his version of homemade cookies as a sort of calling card. His clients and business associates liked them so much that Wally finally decided to quit show business and open a store. He did it with a Hollywood agent's flair. He opened on Sunset Boulevard, with two thousand invitations, a red carpet, and celebrities. With the same flair he put his picture on the bag, filled the bags with cookies, and started selling them to exclusive department stores and specialty shops. Ten years later, Famous Amos cookies were a $10 million business.

Ray Kroc was over fifty and selling milkshake mixers when he heard about a hamburger stand in California, owned by Dick and Mac McDonald, that was doing great business. He packed his car and headed to San Bernardino to check it out. What he saw was a sit-down restaurant that had a limited menu featuring a good hamburger recipe, and they were serving them faster than any place he'd ever seen. Figuring that if there were more places like this he could sell them a lot of milkshake mixers, Kroc pitched the McDonald brothers on the idea of opening some more McDonald's. They were interested but they didn't know who they could get to open the new restaurants. This time it was a recipe and a magic griddle, but it still needed the extra ingredient, imagination. On the spot, Ray Kroc offered to go into business with them and open the restaurants himself. According to the signs on the Golden Arches, Ray Kroc's imagination has paid off in billions of hamburgers sold.

In 1982 Howard Schultz went to work as the director of marketing for a small coffee importer-wholesaler called Starbucks which had only one location, in Seattle's Pike Place Market. While he was on a trip to Italy, Schultz got the *idea that the coffee-bar culture he saw in Milan could be transposed to the downtown Seattle scene. He convinced the company to try it. His coffee-house idea was such a success that Schultz went out and raised the money to buy the company. Five years after he'd joined Starbucks he was CEO of a company that had seventeen locations. Fifteen years later Schultz's coffee-house culture was on every corner of America and there were more than seven thousand Starbucks worldwide.*

As a final example of imagination, we offer Paul Newman's salad dressing. Now, it would seem that it doesn't take much imagination for a big celebrity to put his name on a product, and that's what Newman thought too. But when he and his partner, A. E. Hotchner, pitched their salad dressing idea to companies that specialize in marketing foods, nobody was interested unless they would personally put up about one million dollars for the first year's operations. According to Newman and Hotchner's book, Shameless Exploitation, *they found out that almost all celebrity products in the food business have been disastrous failures and now nobody would touch them.*

So when it came to marketing salad dressing, even Paul Newman's big name wasn't the magic they needed. And unless they were willing to put up a ridiculous amount, money wasn't the magic either. The magic would have to be in the imaginative way they would convince the right people to help them, and in having the perseverance to stick with it until they succeeded. And just like most everyone with an idea, they were told they were crazy to try it. They were turned down by bottling companies that wouldn't do small runs and they were rejected by distributors who wouldn't take a chance on another celebrity product.

In the end it was one supermarket owner, Stew Leonard, who helped hook them up with the right suppliers. But even that wouldn't have been enough if Stew Leonard hadn't had enough imagination to see the possibilities and agree to put Newman's Own Salad Dressing on the shelves in his store. Fifteen years later Newman's Own Brands was a $100 million company (which gives all profits to charity).

NOTES & COMMENTS

What I Would Do If I Had a Million Dollars

The following story proves the truth of that old saying "Where there's a will, there's a way." It was told to me by that beloved educator and clergyman Frank W. Gunsaulus, who began his preaching career in the stockyards region of Chicago.

While Dr. Gunsaulus was going through college, he observed many defects in our educational system. Defects that he believed he could correct, if he were the head of a college.

He made up his mind to organize a new college in which he could carry out his ideas, without being handicapped by orthodox methods of education.

He needed a million dollars to put the project across! Where was he to lay his hands on so large a sum of money? That was the question that absorbed most of this ambitious young preacher's thought. But he couldn't seem to make any progress.

Every night he took that thought to bed with him. He got up with it in the morning. He took it with him everywhere he went. He turned it over and over in his mind until it became a consuming obsession with him.

Being a philosopher as well as a preacher, Dr. Gunsaulus recognized, as do all who succeed in life, that definiteness of purpose is the starting point from which one must begin. He recognized, too, that definiteness of purpose takes on life and power when backed by a burning desire to translate that purpose into its material equivalent.

He knew all these great truths, yet he did not know where or how to lay his hands on a million dollars. The normal thing would have been to give up and quit, saying, "Ah, well, my idea is a good one, but I can't do anything with it because I can't raise the million dollars." That is exactly what the majority of people would have said, but it is not what Dr. Gunsaulus said. What he said, and what he did, are so important that I will now introduce him and let him speak for himself:

"One Saturday afternoon I sat in my room thinking of ways and means of raising the money to carry out my plans. For nearly two years I had been thinking, but I had done nothing but think. The time had come for action!

"I made up my mind, then and there, that I would get the necessary million dollars within a week. How? I was not concerned about that. The main thing of importance was the decision to get the money within a specified time. I want to tell you that the moment I reached a definite decision to get the money within a specified time, a strange feeling of assurance came over me such as I had never before experienced. Something inside me seemed to say, 'Why didn't you reach that decision a long time ago? The money was waiting for you all the time!'

"Things began to happen in a hurry. I called the newspapers and announced I would preach a sermon the following morning entitled 'What I Would Do If I Had a Million Dollars.'

"I went to work on the sermon immediately, but I must tell you frankly that the task was not difficult, because I had been preparing that sermon for almost two years.

"Long before midnight I had finished writing the sermon. I went to bed and slept with a feeling of confidence, for I could see myself already in possession of the million dollars.

"Next morning I arose early, went into the bathroom, read the sermon, then knelt on my knees and asked that my sermon might come to the attention of someone who would supply the needed money.

"While I was praying I again had that feeling of assurance that the money would be forthcoming. In my excitement, I walked out without my sermon and did not discover the oversight until I was in my pulpit and about ready to begin delivering it.

"It was too late to go back for my notes, and what a blessing that I couldn't go back! Instead, my own subconscious mind yielded the material I needed. When I arose to begin my sermon, I closed my eyes and spoke, with all my heart and soul, of my dreams. I not only talked to my audience, but I fancy I talked also to God. I told what I would do with a million dollars if that amount were placed in my hands. I described the plan I had in mind for organizing a great educational institution, where young people would learn to do practical things and at the same time develop their minds.

"When I had finished and sat down, a man slowly arose from his seat, about three rows from the rear, and made his way toward the pulpit. I wondered what he was going to do. He came into the pulpit, extended his hand, and said, "Reverend, I liked your sermon. I believe you can do everything you said you would, if you had a million dollars. To prove that I believe in you and your sermon, if you will come to my office tomorrow morning, I will give you the million dollars. My name is Philip D. Armour."

Young Gunsaulus went to Mr. Armour's office and the million dollars was presented to him. With that money he founded the Armour Institute of Technology, now known as Illinois Institute of Technology.

The million dollars that launched the Armour Institute came as a result of an idea. Behind the idea was a desire that young Gunsaulus had been nursing in his mind for almost two years.

Observe this important fact: he got the money within thirty-six hours after he reached a definite decision in his own mind to get it— and decided upon a definite plan for getting it!

There was nothing new or unique about young Gunsaulus' vaguely thinking about a million dollars and weakly hoping for it. Others have had similar thoughts. But there was something very unique and different about the decision he reached on that memorable Saturday, when he put vagueness into the background and definitely said, "I will get that money within a week!"

The principle through which Dr. Gunsaulus got his million dollars is still alive. It is available to you. This universal law is as workable today as it was when the young preacher made use of it so successfully.

COMMENTARY

The Armour Institute of Technology opened in 1893, offering courses in engi-neering, chemistry, architecture, and library science, and in 1940 became the Illinois Institute of Technology when the Armour Institute merged with the Lewis Institute, a Chicago college that had opened in 1895 and offered liberal arts as well as science and engineering courses. In 1949 the Institute of Design, founded in 1937, also merged with IIT, followed in 1969 by the Chicago-Kent College of Law and the Stuart School of Business, and in 1986 by the Midwest College of Engineering. Today there are several campuses in downtown Chicago. IIT has been called the alma mater of accomplishments.

HOW TO TRANSMUTE IDEAS INTO CASH

Asa Candler and Dr. Frank Gunsaulus had one characteristic in common. Both knew the astounding truth that ideas can be transmuted into cash through the power of definite purpose, plus definite plans.

If you are one of those who believe that hard work and honesty alone will bring riches, you can forget it! It is not true. Riches, when they come in huge quantities, are never the result of hard work alone. Riches come, if they come at all, in response to definite demands based upon the application of definite principles, and not by chance or luck.

Generally speaking, an idea is a thought that prompts you to action because it appeals to your imagination. All master salespeople know that ideas can be sold where merchandise cannot. Ordinary salespeople do not know this. That is why they are "ordinary."

A publisher of low-priced books made a discovery that has been worth much to publishers. He learned that many people buy titles, and

NOTES & COMMENTS

not the contents, of books. By merely changing the name of one book that was not moving, his sales of that book jumped upward more than a million copies. The inside of the book was not changed in any way. He merely ripped off the cover and put on a new cover with a title that had "box-office" appeal.

That, as simple as it may seem, was an idea. It was imagination.

COMMENTARY

For those readers who think that replacing the cover of a book is just too simple, or that they couldn't do it anyway because they're not book publishers, the editors would point out that if you had had that simple idea before the publisher did, he probably would have been glad to sell you those failed books at pennies on the dollar. Then you could have been the one to change the cover, and suddenly you would have been the publisher of a bestseller. However, the idea of replacing the covers wouldn't have meant a thing if you didn't also have ideas about how to market and promote that flashy new cover. And that is Hill's point. Coca-Cola was a recipe, a creative idea, but it would have stayed just a recipe if Asa Candler hadn't also had other creative ideas to market it and the faith in himself to carry through on those ideas.

Spence Silver was a chemist working for 3M when, by accident, he created a glue that wasn't very sticky. Needless to say, 3M was not much interested in glue that didn't stick, and Silver's invention was shelved as a failure. But Silver liked his glue, so for five years he kept demonstrating it to anyone who would listen. Nobody did, until Arthur Fry, who worked in the tape division at 3M, found that when he was at choir practice he kept losing his place in the hymnal because the pieces of paper he used to mark his place slipped down or fell out of the book. However, with a little of Silver's not-very-sticky glue on the slips of paper, they stayed where he wanted them and then peeled off easily when he was done. That was the eureka moment. They had just invented the world's best bookmark: Post-its.

But that's not the end of the story, or the end of the imaginative ideas that were needed to make Post-its happen. Fry would also need perseverance. First he had to convince the engineers to solve production problems, and to do it he knocked a hole in his basement wall so he could install a prototype of the production equipment. He stuck with it, and finally, two years later, 3M gave the project to their marketing department. The marketing experts put together ads and brochures selling this "sticky notepad" idea, and rolled it out in a four-city test. The results were a disaster. Nobody "got" it, so nobody bought it. Who would pay money for scratch paper?

The Post-it project was about to be scrapped when Geoffrey Nicholson and Joseph Ramey added their imaginations. Like Silver and Fry, Nicholson and Ramey had faith in the idea because they saw how people in their own office fell in love with these little sticky pieces of paper once they started working with them. So Nicholson and Ramey went to Richmond, Virginia, one of the four test cities that had failed, and they went up and down the business district, going into offices and giving pads of Post-its to receptionists, secretaries, and anyone else who would listen.

Whereas 3M's conventional marketing machinery had failed, giving Post-its to the people who would actually use them did the trick. Once those Richmond officeworkers started to use Post-its, it didn't seem like a bad idea at all to pay for scratch paper. They "got" it, and they bought it. The Richmond test turned from failure to success, and soon Post-its were sticking to everything around the world.

Here is another simple idea that imagination turned into success. This story began with a man whose problem was just the opposite of Spence Silver's. This man had something that stuck too well. George de Mestrel was a Swiss mountaineer who went hunting one day with his dog. When they got home they were both covered with burrs. The burrs were so difficult to remove that de Mestrel put them under a magnifying glass to learn why. He saw that they were covered with tiny hooks which attached themselves to fur and fabric. That was when the flash hit. If burrs stuck where you didn't want them, why couldn't you put tiny hooks on things so they would stick where you did want them?

Like everyone else mentioned in this book, de Mestrel had an imaginative idea. But that was just the beginning. He also had the faith in himself to

NOTES & COMMENTS

keep going when people laughed at his idea, which many did, until he eventually found a French textile plant that would help him do what he wanted. However, even when they finally worked out a way to use cotton fabric to make what they called "locking tape," they couldn't afford to mass-produce it. And that's when de Mestrel accidentally discovered that when you sew nylon under infrared light, it naturally made little hooks. Now that they could manufacture it economically, all they needed was a name. One side was fuzzy like velvet and the other side was crochet, the French word for hook. Take half "vel" and half "cro," combine it with imagination, the result is Velcro, and a Swiss mountaineer becomes a business tycoon.

The Sony Corporation once tried to make a very small stereo tape recorder that would work with standard-size cassettes, but they couldn't do it. They could make a small playback machine but, at the time, the electronics needed to also make it a recording machine just couldn't be made small enough. They concluded that the design was a failure.

Then one day Sony's honorary chairman, Masaru Ibuka, walked into the laboratory and saw that a few of the engineers were using the prototypes of the failed tape recorder to listen to music tapes. They didn't seem to care that it couldn't record, they just liked to be able to walk around listening to their favorite music.

Then came the imaginative idea that made all the difference. Ibuka remembered that another division was working on lightweight headphones. That was the flash. Ibuka's imagination made the connection that the rest of the engineers' had not. In Ibuka's view, they hadn't made a failed "recorder," they'd created a successful "private stereo listener." They added the headphones, named it the Walkman, and it revolutionized both the music business and the electronics industry.

Clarence Saunders was a grocery clerk in a small southern retail store. One day he was standing with a tray in his hands, waiting his turn in a cafeteria. He had never earned more than twenty dollars a week before then and no one had ever noticed anything about him that indicated unusual ability, but something took place in his mind, as he stood in the line of waiting people, that put his Imagination to work. That was when he came up with the idea that this same self-serve concept would also work at the grocery store.

Clarence Saunders took the idea to his boss. Naturally, his boss told him he was crazy. So Saunders quit his job, went out and did what he needed to do to raise the money, and he opened the first self-serve grocery store. He called it Piggly-Wiggly, and Clarence Saunders, the twenty-dollar-a-week grocery clerk, rapidly became the multimillion-dollar chain-store groceryman of America.

Sylvan Goldman was the owner of a number of Piggly-Wiggly stores in Oklahoma, and like any good businessman, he spent a lot of time watching his customers go up and down the aisles putting their choices into their baskets or net shopping bags. One night, while trying to figure how to get his customers to buy more at one time, he found himself staring at a basket sitting on the seat of a wooden folding chair. Eureka! He called in his mechanic, Fred Young, they put some wheels on the bottom of the legs, added another basket below the seat, and the shopping cart was born.

As this edition is being readied for publication there are about 35 million shopping carts in America, and approximately 1.25 million new carts are sold each year.

Thomas Stemberg, whom we also mentioned earlier, was another supermarket executive who watched his customers as they shopped. By this time shopping carts were well established in supermarkets, and it was because his customers were pushing shopping carts up and down the aisles that he got his flash of inspiration. He was so sure of his idea that he convinced another supermarket executive, Leo Kahn, to join him. Together they took the supermarket concept and applied it to selling office supplies, and in 1986 they opened their first store in Brighton, Massachusetts. They called it Staples.

In 1989 they took the company public, and ten years later there were more than 1,000 Staples stores, with revenues exceeding $7 billion.

NOTES & COMMENTS

We'll end this commentary with another set of connected stories which make the point that sometimes the most imaginative part of marketing is in the timing.

If you were to go shopping in the late 1800s it usually meant bartering with a merchant who would then have to get the goods from storage shelves kept behind the counter. In the 1870s fixed pricing was just starting to be used by storekeepers. Merchants were trying the idea by setting out a table of merchandise that was all priced the same, usually five cents.

Frank Winfield Woolworth was a clerk in a general store and he convinced the storeowner to let him try the five-cent-table idea. Although it worked, the owner wasn't impressed. So Woolworth borrowed $350 from his boss, and in 1879 opened his first Five Cents Store in Utica, New York. It was an entire store full of goods where everything cost a nickel. A year later he had four stores, and the fourth one, in Lancaster, Pennsylvania, was the first that he named F. W. Woolworth's Five and Ten Cents Store. Twenty years later he had 238 stores. By the time of his death in 1919, there were over 1,000 F. W. Woolworth locations, he had established the first nationwide chain of general-merchandise stores, and he had built the tallest building in New York City as his headquarters.

The Woolworth company stayed true to the original idea and didn't carry any merchandise that cost more than a dime until 1932 when the top price was raised to twenty cents. But, as times changed, the fixed-price was dropped, the merchandise became more varied, and the company kept growing until it had over 8,000 stores worldwide, selling everything from notions to appliances and furniture.

Then in the 1960s and 1970s something started to happen. The mood of America was changing but the Woolworth stores weren't. And that was when Sam Walton opened the first Wal-Mart in Rogers, Arkansas, in 1962.

Walton got into the retail business after the Second World War when his father-in-law loaned him the money to buy a franchised Butler Brothers store in Bentonville, Arkansas. By 1962 Sam and his brother Bud owned 16 variety stores in Arkansas, Missouri, and Kansas. It was in these stores that Sam Walton first started adding the magic ingredient of imagination. In addition to his flair for promotion, Sam tried new approaches to the way household goods and general merchandise could be sold at retail. He insisted on clean, well-lighted interiors and he introduced the concept of self-service, with aisles wide enough for shopping carts and checkout counters at the front of the store. He also started buying direct from manufacturers, and he created profit-sharing plans that kept his family of employees loyal, hardworking, and neighborly.

In 1962 he incorporated those and other imaginative ideas when he opened his first store that he called Wal-Mart. The basic magic was that he sold brand-name merchandise at discount prices, but there was also magic in the way he kept a friendly hometown feel to his store even though it was what is now called a big-box store.

Sam Walton's Wal-Mart store was a success. So he just kept building and opening more of them. First in small towns and rural areas, then in larger towns, then big cities, and it wasn't long before he had a national chain. By 1992 when Sam Walton died, there were more than 1,700 Wal-Mart stores, it was the biggest retailer in the country, it employed more than 600,000 people, and Sam Walton was the richest man in America. In 2003 the stores numbered more than 3,200 in the U.S. and more than 1,100 in foreign countries, the company employed more than 1,300,000 people worldwide, and served more than one million customers a week.

Along the way, Woolworth's and other older retailers such as Kresge's tried to get on the bandwagon with their Woolco and Kmart stores, but they couldn't seem to get it right. They had given up their old five-and-dime identity to become higher-priced general retailers, and when Wal-Mart came along and redefined that part of the market, the others seemed to have run out of the kind of imagination they'd had in the beginning.

Now, here's the twist to the story. David Gold was running a liquor store that he had inherited from his father. He noticed that whenever he put out a display of goods priced at 99 cents, the merchandise would sell out faster than any other discounted price. He decided that he would open a store called The 99¢ Only Store, where everything would be priced at 99 cents.

NOTES & COMMENTS

Sound familiar? Frank Woolworth's imaginative idea from 1879, which had been dropped at his namesake chain by the 1940s and 1950s, had just gotten a fresh shot of imagination from David Gold in 1982.

As usual, friends and family told him he was crazy, but David Gold went out to find suppliers who would sell him discontinued merchandise or over-produced products at a price low enough that he could offer them to the public at 99 cents. He found them. And they even had brand-name products of everything from hardware to pantihose, cleaning products, motor oil, kitchen-ware, cosmetics, electronics, toys, canned goods, frozen foods, cookies, fresh fruit, even gourmet foods—more than 5,000 items that he could sell for 99 cents and still make a profit!

David Gold opened his first well-lighted, brightly colored, green-and-fuchsia, wide-aisle store in Inglewood, California, in 1982. By 2003 he had 142 stores in California, Nevada, and Arizona, and he was listed on the Forbes 400 as having earned a personal fortune estimated at more than $650 million.

As Napoleon Hill wrote in Law of Success *about the creation of Piggly-Wiggly, "Where in this story do you see the slightest indication of something that you could not duplicate? The plan, which made millions of dollars for its originator, was a very simple idea that anyone could have adopted, yet considerable Imagination was required to put the idea to work in a practical sort of way. The more simple and easily adapted an idea is, the greater is its value, as no one is looking for ideas that are involved with great detail or are in any way complicated."*

There is no standard price on ideas. The creator of ideas sets his or her own price, and, if they are smart, they get it.

The story of practically every great fortune starts with the day when a creator of ideas and a seller of ideas got together and worked in harmony. Carnegie surrounded himself with men who could do what he could not do, men who created ideas and men who put ideas into operation, and that was what made him and the others fabulously rich.

Millions of people go through life hoping for favorable "breaks." Perhaps a favorable break can get you an opportunity, but the safest plan is not to depend upon luck. It was a favorable "break" that gave me the biggest opportunity of my life—but more than twenty years of determined effort had to be devoted to that opportunity before it became an asset.

The break consisted of my good fortune in meeting and gaining the cooperation of Andrew Carnegie. On that occasion Carnegie planted in my mind the idea of organizing the principles of achievement into a philosophy of success. Millions of people have profited by the discoveries made in the years of research, and fortunes have been accumulated through the application of the philosophy. The beginning was simple. It was an idea that anyone might have developed.

The favorable break came through Carnegie, but what about the determination, definiteness of purpose, and the desire to attain the goal, and the persistent effort of all those years of research? It was no ordinary desire that survived disappointment, discouragement, temporary defeat, criticism, and the constant reminding that I was wasting my time. It was a burning desire! An obsession!

When the idea was first planted in my mind by Mr. Carnegie, it was coaxed, nursed, and enticed to remain alive. Gradually, the idea became a giant under its own power, and it coaxed, nursed, and drove me. Ideas are like that. First you give life and action and guidance to ideas, then they take on a power of their own and sweep aside all opposition.

Ideas are intangible forces, but they have more power than the physical brains that give birth to them. They have the power to live on, after the brain that creates them has returned to dust.

TELL THE WORLD

WHAT YOU INTEND TO DO,

BUT FIRST

SHOW IT.

ORGANIZED PLANNING

THE CRYSTALLIZATION OF DESIRE INTO ACTION

The Sixth Step Toward Riches

You have learned that everything we create or acquire begins in the form of desire. Desire is taken on the first lap of its journey, from the abstract to the concrete, in the workshop of the imagination, where plans for its transition are created and organized.

In chapter 3, Desire, you were instructed to take six definite, practical steps to begin translating your desire for money into its monetary equivalent. One of the steps you must take is the formation of a definite, practical plan, or plans, through which this transformation may be made.

Following are the basic instructions for making practical plans:

- Ally yourself with a group of as many people as you may need for the creation and carrying out of your plan or plans for the accumulation of money—making use of the Master Mind principle. Compliance with this instruction is absolutely essential. Do not neglect it.

NOTES & COMMENTS

[The Master Mind alliance is built of two or more minds working actively together in perfect harmony toward a common goal. This concept was introduced in chapter 6, Specialized Knowledge, and is described in more detail in chapter 11, The Power of the Master Mind.]

- Before forming your Master Mind alliance, decide what advantages and benefits you may offer the individual members of your group in return for their cooperation. No one will work indefinitely without some form of compensation. No intelligent person should request or expect another to work without adequate compensation, although this may not always be in the form of money.

- Arrange to meet with the members of your Master Mind group at least twice a week, and more often if possible, until you have jointly perfected the necessary plan or plans for the accumulation of money.

- Maintain perfect harmony between yourself and every member of your Master Mind group. If you fail to carry out this instruction to the letter, you may expect to meet with failure. The Master Mind principle cannot work where perfect harmony does not prevail.

Keep in mind these facts:

- You are engaged in an undertaking of major importance to you. To be sure of success, you must have plans that are faultless.

- You must have the advantage of the experience, education, native ability, and imagination of other minds. This is the way it has been done by every person who has accumulated a great fortune.

No individual has sufficient experience, education, natural ability, and knowledge to ensure the accumulation of a great fortune without the cooperation of other people. Every plan you adopt for making money should be the joint creation of yourself and every other member of your Master Mind group. You may originate your own plans, either in whole or in part, but see that those plans are checked, and approved, by the members of your Master Mind alliance.

IF YOUR FIRST PLAN FAILS—TRY ANOTHER!

If the first plan that you adopt does not work successfully, replace it with a new plan. If this new plan fails to work, replace it with still another, and so on, until you find a plan that does work. Right here is the point at which the majority of people meet with failure, because of their lack of persistence in creating new plans to take the place of those that fail.

The most intelligent person living cannot succeed in accumulating money—or in any other undertaking—without plans that are practical and workable. Just keep this fact in mind and remember, when your plans fail, that temporary defeat is not permanent failure. It may only mean that your plans have not been sound. Build other plans. Start all over again.

Temporary defeat should mean only one thing: the certain knowledge that there is something wrong with your plan. Millions of people go through life in misery and poverty because they lack a sound plan through which to accumulate a fortune.

Your achievement can only be as good as the plans you make.

You are never whipped, until you quit—in your own mind.

James J. Hill, who was the greatest railroad builder of them all, met with temporary defeat when he first tried to raise the capital needed to build the Great Northern Railroad from the East to the West, but he turned defeat into victory through new plans.

Henry Ford met with temporary defeat not only at the beginning of his automobile career but even after he had gone a long way toward the top. But he, too, created new plans and went marching on to financial victory.

We see people who have accumulated great fortunes, but we often recognize only their triumph and we overlook the temporary defeats that they had to surmount before "arriving."

No follower of this philosophy can reasonably expect to accumulate a fortune without experiencing "temporary defeat." When defeat comes, accept it as a signal that your plans are not sound, rebuild those plans, and set sail once more toward your goal. If you give up before your goal has been reached, you are a "quitter." A quitter never wins—and a winner never quits. Write this sentence on a piece of paper, in letters an inch high, and place it where you will see it every night before you go to sleep and every morning before you go to work.

When you begin to select members for your Master Mind group, choose those who do not take defeat seriously.

Some people foolishly believe that only money can make money. This is not true. Desire, transmuted into its monetary equivalent through the principles in this book, is the way money is "made." Money, of itself, is nothing but inert matter. It cannot move, think, or talk, but it can "hear" when someone who desires it calls it to come!

Intelligent planning is essential for success in any undertaking designed to accumulate riches. Following are detailed instructions to those who must begin the accumulation of riches by selling personal services.

It should encourage you to know that practically all the great fortunes began either from selling personal services or from the sale of ideas. When you think about it, what else except ideas and personal services can you give in return for riches if you don't have products or property?

LEADERS AND FOLLOWERS

Broadly speaking, there are two types of people in the world. One type is known as leaders and the other as followers. Decide at the outset whether you intend to become a leader in your chosen calling, or remain a follower. The difference in compensation is vast. The follower cannot expect to make as much as a leader, although some followers make the mistake of thinking they should.

It is no disgrace to be a follower. On the other hand, it is no credit to remain a follower. Most great leaders began as followers. They became great leaders because they were intelligent followers. With few exceptions, the person who cannot follow a leader intelligently cannot become an efficient leader. The person who can follow a leader most efficiently is usually the person who develops into leadership most rapidly. An intelligent follower has many advantages, including the opportunity to acquire knowledge from the leader.

The Major Attributes of Leadership

The following are important factors of leadership:

1. *Unwavering courage* based upon knowledge of yourself and your occupation. No follower wishes to be dominated by a leader who lacks self-confidence and courage. Certainly no intelligent follower will be dominated by such a leader for very long.

2. *Self-control.* The person who cannot control themself can never control others. Self-control sets a strong example for your followers, which the more intelligent followers will emulate.

3. *A keen sense of justice.* Without a sense of fairness and justice, no leader can command and retain the respect of their followers.

4. *Definiteness of decision.* Those who waver in decisions show that they are not sure of themselves, and therefore cannot lead others successfully.

5. *Definiteness of plans.* Successful leaders must plan their work, and work their plans. Leaders who move by guesswork, without practical, definite plans, are like a ship without a rudder. Sooner or later they will land on the rocks.

6. *The habit of doing more than paid for.* One of the penalties of leadership is the necessity of the leaders to willingly do more than they require of their followers.

7. *A pleasing personality.* Leadership calls for respect. Followers will not respect a leader who does not grade high on all of the factors of a pleasing personality.

8. *Sympathy and understanding.* Successful leaders must be in sympathy with their followers. Moreover, they must understand them and their problems.

9. *Mastery of detail.* Successful leadership calls for mastery of the details of the leader's position.

10. *Willingness to assume full responsibility.* Successful leaders must be willing to assume responsibility for the mistakes and the shortcomings of their followers. If a leader tries to shift this responsibility, that leader will not remain the leader. If one of your followers makes a mistake, or is incompetent, you must consider that it is you who failed.

11. *Cooperation.* The successful leader must understand and apply the principle of cooperative effort and be able to induce followers to do the same. Leadership calls for power, and power calls for cooperation.

There are two forms of leadership. The first, and by far the most effective, is leadership by consent of and with the sympathy of the followers. The second is leadership by force, without the consent and sympathy of the followers.

History is filled with evidences that leadership by force cannot endure. The downfall and disappearance of dictators and kings is significant. It means that people will not follow forced leadership indefinitely.

Napoleon, Mussolini, Hitler were examples of leadership by force. Their leadership passed. *[The following may also be added to the list: Idi Amin, Francisco Franco, Saddam Hussein, Ferdinand Marcos, Slobodan Milosevic, Juan Peron, General Augusto Pinochet, Pol Pot, General Suharto, the Taliban leaders in Afghanistan, Marshal (Josip Broz) Tito, Joseph Stalin, and subsequent leaders of the Soviet Union, East Germany, and the other countries in the communist bloc].* Those that remain see their power eroding and slipping away. Leadership by consent of the followers is the only leadership that can endure.

People may follow forced leadership temporarily, but they will not do so willingly.

Successful leaders will embrace the eleven factors of leadership described in this chapter, as well as some other factors. Those who make these attributes the basis of their leadership will find abundant opportunity to lead in any walk of life.

The Ten Major Causes of Failure in Leadership

The following are the major faults of leaders who fail. It is just as essential for you to know what not to do as it is to know what to do.

1. *Inability to organize details.* Efficient leadership calls for the ability to organize and master details. No genuine leader is ever "too busy" to do anything that may be required in the capacity as leader. Whether a leader or follower, when you admit that you are "too

busy" to change your plans, or to give attention to any emergency, you are admitting your inefficiency. The successful leader must be the master of all details connected with the position. That means, of course, that you must acquire the habit of relegating details to capable lieutenants.

2. *Unwillingness to render humble service.* Truly great leaders are willing, when occasion demands, to perform any sort of labor that they would ask another to perform. "The greatest among ye shall be the servant of all" is a truth that all able leaders observe and respect.

3. *Expectation of pay for what they "know,"* instead of what they do with what they know. The world does not pay you for what you "know." It pays you for what you do, or what you induce others to do.

4. *Fear of competition from followers.* Leaders who fear that one of their followers may take their position are practically sure to realize that fear sooner or later. Able leaders train understudies to whom they may delegate any of the details of their position. Only in this way can leaders multiply themselves and be at many places, and give attention to many things, at one time. It is an eternal truth that leaders receive more pay for their ability to get others to perform than they could possibly earn by their own efforts. An efficient leader may, through knowledge of the job, and a magnetic personality, greatly increase the efficiency of others and get them to render more service and better service than they could render without the leader's guidance.

5. *Lack of imagination.* Without imagination, the leader is incapable of meeting emergencies or of creating plans by which to guide followers efficiently.

6. *Selfishness.* Leaders who claim all the honor for the work of their followers are sure to be met by resentment. The really great leader claims none of the honors. Great leaders are content to see the honors, when there are any, go to their followers, because the great leaders know that most people will work harder for commendation and recognition than they will for money alone.

7. *Intemperance.* Followers do not respect an intemperate leader. Moreover, intemperance in any form destroys the endurance and the vitality of those who indulge in it.

8. *Disloyalty.* Perhaps this should have come at the head of the list. Leaders who are not loyal to their duty, and to those both above and below them, cannot maintain their leadership for long. Disloyalty marks you as being less than the dust of the earth, and it will bring the contempt it deserves. Lack of loyalty is one of the major causes of failure in every walk of life.

9. *Emphasis of the "authority" of leadership.* The efficient leader leads by encouraging, and not by trying to instill fear in the hearts of those who follow. Leaders who try to impress their followers with their "authority" come within the category of leadership through force. If you are a real leader, you will have no need to advertise that fact. It is apparent in your conduct—by your sympathy, understanding, fairness, and a demonstration that you know your job.

10. *Emphasis of title.* Competent leaders require no "title" to give them the respect of their followers. Leaders who make too much of their titles generally have little else to emphasize. The doors to the office of the real leader are open to all, and free from formality or ostentation.

These are among the most common causes of failure in leadership. Any one of these faults is sufficient to cause failure. Study the list carefully if you aspire to leadership, and make sure that you are free of these faults.

COMMENTARY

Warren Bennis, a professor who teaches management and organization, said: "A manager is someone who does things right. A leader is someone who does the right thing."

Admiral Grace Hopper was the ranking female Navy officer when she was interviewed for 60 Minutes. She said: "You manage things. You lead people."

WHEN AND HOW TO APPLY FOR A POSITION

The information described here is the net result of many years of experience during which thousands of men and women were helped to market their services effectively.

COMMENTARY

The Internet, email, and faxed résumés have radically changed the way employers search for new employees, and the way that most people apply for jobs. However, Think and Grow Rich was never intended for "most people"; it was written for those who want to stand out. If you are such a person, the editors of this updated edition strongly advise that you give serious thought to each of the following suggestions about how to apply for a position and how to prepare a résumé. If you are tempted to think the suggestions are too obvious, simplistic, or out of date, we assure you they are not. In those instances where it is appropriate to update the material, we have added commentary.

1. *Employment agencies.* Care must be taken to select only reputable companies that can show adequate records of achievement of satisfactory results.

[As anyone in the job market knows, today employment agencies range from companies that supply temporary office help to headhunters who connect high-level executives with companies seeking experienced management talent. If you are seeking a mid- to upper-level position, the old adage that you get what you pay for is particularly true.]

2. *Advertising in newspapers, trade journals, magazines.* Classified advertising may produce satisfactory results for those applying for entry-level, clerical, or salaried positions. For those seeking executive positions, a well-written and well-designed display ad, though more expensive, may be more desirable. The copy should be prepared by an expert who understands how to inject sufficient selling qualities to produce replies.

    [For individuals, the display-ad approach is not very common in the contemporary job market. But for that reason, if you are sure of the position you want, a well-written and well-designed ad selling yourself, and placed in the right trade paper or industry journal, might be just the thing to get the attention you want. However, if you attempt this approach, be prepared that it will be an expensive experiment. In effect, you will have gone into the advertising business, and it is a rule of thumb in advertising that a single ad rarely sells anything; it usually requires multiple exposures before the buyer (the potential employer) is motivated to buy (hire) a product (you).]

3. *Personal letters of application.* These should be directed to particular firms or individuals that could need the kind of service or experience you have to offer. Letters should be neatly typed, always, and signed by hand. You should include a complete résumé or outline of your qualifications. Both the letter of application and the résumé should be prepared by an expert.

    [In the contemporary job market, sending a letter of application when no job has been advertised can, in fact, be a very successful approach. But this is only for those who truly know what they want and will take the time to prepare a convincing presentation.

NOTES & COMMENTS

NOTES & COMMENTS

Managers in a position to hire always have an eye out for good prospective employees. If they receive a well-constructed and intriguing presentation that clearly states you are interested in a position whenever one is available, it will not be thrown away. And the first thing good managers do when a position comes open is go to their files. When that happens, if your presentation made a good and convincing impression, it will be there.

The only question is, are you willing to make yourself available when they are ready for you? If you are just blanketing everybody with a stock letter in hopes of getting a job, it very likely won't work. This approach is not for someone looking for a job. This approach is only for those who really want a specific career.]

4. *Application in person.* In some instances it may be more effective if the applicant personally offers his or her services to prospective employers, in which event a complete written statement of qualifications for the position should be presented, as prospective employers will often wish to discuss your record with associates.

   [Asking for an interview when no job has been advertised is an even stronger statement that you know what you want and you are serious about working in a particular industry. If you pursue this approach, keep in mind that you are asking someone to give you their time. Some managers will not be receptive because it does not fit into their company's business practice, and some managers will just find it an annoyance. This approach will work for you only if you are confident that you can make an outstanding impression in person. If you make a strong, positive impression, it will be remembered when an opening is available.]

5. *Application through personal acquaintances.* When possible, the applicant should approach prospective employers through some mutual acquaintance. This method is particularly advantageous in the case of those who seek executive connections and do not wish to appear to be "peddling" themselves.

NOTES & COMMENTS

Information to Be Supplied in a Written Résumé

A good résumé should be prepared as carefully as a lawyer would prepare the brief for a case to be tried in court. Unless the applicant is experienced in the preparation of such briefs, an expert should be consulted for this purpose. When successful businesses want to advertise, they hire specialists who understand the psychology of advertising to sell their products. If you are "selling" your personal services, you should do the same.

COMMENTARY

The job market in America has never been as bad as it was when Napoleon Hill wrote the preceding paragraph. Because of the Great Depression, many adults had never had any kind of steady job let alone sought a career position, and there were few places to learn how to do it. Since that time many excellent books have been published on the subject, and companies that offer professional help in preparing résumés have become very common. However, neither books nor copywriters are magic. It all begins with what you have to offer.

The editors of this edition suggest that you start to assemble your presentation using the guidelines that appear below. Once you have a first draft, you should then review at least one of the books on the subject to see what suggestions are offered that might help you sell yourself better than you have already done. Then, depending how satisfied you are, you might also want to seek advice from a professional who specializes in such presentations.

We offer two notes of caution: First, make sure that your presentation does not look like something turned out by a résumé mill. Having received many résumés over the years, the editors warn you that some professionals use the same stock phrases, buzzwords, and formats for every client, and this can be a dead giveaway that someone else prepared your résumé, or that you have simply copied from a book. Your intention should be to make yours stand out.

The second word of caution is don't go overboard in trying to stand out. There is a balance between catching an employer's attention and looking like you are trying too hard.

NOTES & COMMENTS

For instance, if you are a New York marketing executive applying to a Los Angeles company, sending your application with a bag of fresh bagels by next-morning FedEx would probably make a good impression, whereas sending a dartboard with your picture in the center might be viewed as just a little too cute and a little too much. Clever is good, but professional is a must. Never be so clever that you don't look professional.

Following are a set of guidelines for preparing your résumé. Because part of your search for a position will involve responding to ads for job openings, and because it has become common to respond by faxing applications and résumés, Napoleon Hill's guidelines should be used to prepare two separate presentations: As Hill suggests below, you should prepare an elaborate presentation to be used when mailed or presented in person. But you should also prepare a second, shorter version that is designed specifically to be faxed. Take care to make your fax version complete and interesting, but it should be no more than three pages.

The following information should appear in your presentation:

1. *Education.* State briefly, but definitely, what schooling you have had and in what subjects you specialized in school, giving the reasons for that specialization.

     [Never exaggerate. This is very serious advice and it applies not only to education but also the next two categories, experience and references. Smart employers will check in all three areas.

     Labor laws have become so demanding that employers filling responsible positions are very cautious about whom they hire in the first place. There are rules about such things as the difference between salaried and hourly employment, sexual harassment, what constitutes grounds for dismissal, what questions can and cannot be asked in job interviews, and a host of other things that leave the employer open to potential lawsuits. Consequently, smart employers, the kind you want to work for, will check your education, experience, and references.

Also, bear in mind, you are providing information that will follow you for the rest of your career. If you keep up with the news, you know that in recent times even executives headed for the top have been dismissed, military men have resigned in disgrace, politicians have been removed from office, and professors have been forced to resign, all because someone looked into their background and found that they had exaggerated their qualifications.]

2. *Experience.* If you have had experience in connection with positions similar to the one you seek, describe it fully. Give the names and addresses of former employers. Be sure to clearly point out any special experience you may have had that would equip you to fill the position you seek.

3. *References.* Practically every business firm wants to know as much as possible about the background of prospective employees who seek positions of responsibility. Attach copies of letters from former employers, from teachers under whom you studied, and from prominent people whose judgment may be relied upon.

4. *Photograph of yourself.* Include a recent, professional photograph of yourself as a part of your presentation.

    [In the contemporary job market, this is not a common practice at all. However, from personal experience, the editors of this edition know it can be advantageous. We have received only one such job application, but unquestionably it was the photograph that prompted us to ask the applicant to come in for an interview.

    If you are confident that your appearance makes a good, professional impression, you may want to consider this unusual approach. There is the danger that you may be seen as vain or self-centered, but it could also be the thing that gives you an edge.]

5. *Apply for a specific position.* Never apply for "just a job." That indicates you lack specialized qualifications.

6. *State your qualifications for the particular position for which you apply.* Give full details why you believe you are qualified for the particular position you seek. This is the most important detail of your application. It will determine, more than anything else, what consideration you receive.

7. *Offer to go to work on probation.* This may appear to be a radical suggestion, but experience has proved that it seldom fails to win at least a trial. If you are sure of your qualifications, a trial is all you need. Incidentally, such an offer indicates that you have confidence in your ability to fill the position you seek. It is most convincing. Make it clear that your offer is based on your confidence in your ability to fill the position, your confidence in your prospective employer's decision to employ you after the trial period, and your determination to have the position.

> *[As you will learn in chapter 10 when you read the story of Napoleon Hill's application to Rufus Ayers, Hill gives this advice based on his personal experience. Unfortunately, this is an instance where times may have changed so much that the approach is rarely applicable. In today's environment, modern labor laws and business practice may prevent an employer from taking you up on your offer, but many companies do have internship programs that allow an employer to "test-drive" employees to see how they might fit in.]*

8. *Knowledge of your prospective employer's business.* Before applying for a position, do sufficient research to familiarize yourself thoroughly with that business, and indicate the knowledge you have acquired in this field. This will be impressive because it indicates that you have imagination, and a real interest in the position you seek.

> *[When you do this, and you certainly should, bear in mind that you will be talking with people who really* know *the business. Even by researching extensively, at best you will only know* about *their business. If you try to appear too knowledgeable or familiar, it may backfire and reveal that you*

have only a superficial view of the business. Unless you are already working in the particular industry and have insights based on experience, do not be presumptuous. Use your knowledge to indicate that you have taken the time to educate yourself, and that you really are interested, but don't try to tell a prospective employer how you would run the business.]

Remember that it is not the lawyer who knows the most law, but the one who best prepares his case, who wins. If your "case" is properly prepared and presented, your victory will have been more than half won at the outset.

Do not be afraid of making your presentation too long. Employers are just as much interested in purchasing the services of well-qualified applicants as you are in securing employment. In fact, the success of most successful employers is due to their ability to select well-qualified lieutenants. They want all the information available.

[As noted above, when faxing a résumé it should be no more than three pages, and should state that you will be pleased to provide a more detailed résumé if requested.]

Remember another thing: neatness in the preparation of your résumé and application will indicate that you are a painstaking person. Successful salespeople groom themselves with care. They understand that first impressions are lasting. Your presentation is your sales rep. Give it a good suit of clothes so it will stand out in bold contrast to anything else your prospective employer ever saw. If the position you seek is worth having, it is worth going after with care. More important, if you sell yourself in a manner that shows off your individuality, you probably will receive more money from the very start than you would if you applied for employment in the usual, conventional way.

When your résumé package has been completed, you should prepare individual and personalized copies for each company or person to whom it will be presented. This personal touch is sure to command attention. Have it neatly typed, proofread, printed, and properly bound on the finest paper you can obtain. Your photograph should be mounted and included on one of the pages. Prepare a separate binding with the proper company name inserted, if it is to be shown to more than one company.

If you seek employment through an employment agency, have the agent use copies of your presentation in marketing your services. This will help to gain preference for you, both with the agent and the prospective employers.

I have helped to prepare presentations for clients that were so striking and out of the ordinary that they resulted in the employment of the applicant without a personal interview. If you want similar results, follow the instructions to the letter, improving upon them however your imagination suggests.

COMMENTARY

Today, every office supply store offers a wide variety of paper stock, folders, binders, and presentation materials that can be put together in a way that is both unique and professional-looking. With all of those possibilities available, if you simply present standard sheets of papers stapled in the corner, the response will very likely be standard too.

If you apply a little creativity you should have no trouble preparing a presentation that is tailored to the company to which you are applying, appropriate for the position you seek, and reflective of your personality and style.

HOW TO GET THE EXACT POSITION YOU DESIRE

Everyone enjoys doing the kind of work for which he or she is best suited. An artist loves to work with paints, a craftsman with his or her hands, a writer loves to write. Those with less definite talents have their preferences for certain fields of business and industry. If America does anything well, it offers a full range of occupations.

1. Decide exactly what kind of a job you want. If the job doesn't already exist, perhaps you can create it.

2. Choose the company or individual for whom you wish to work.

3. Study your prospective employer as to policies, personnel, and chances for advancement.

4. By analysis of yourself, your talents, and your capabilities, figure what you can offer. Plan specific ways and means of giving advantages, services, developments, or ideas that you believe you can successfully deliver.

5. Forget about "a job." Forget whether or not there is an opening. Forget the usual routine of "have you got a job for me?" Concentrate on what you can give.

6. Once you have your plan in mind put it on paper in neat form and in full detail.

7. Present it to the proper person with authority and the rest will come automatically. Every company is looking for people who can give something of value, whether it is ideas, services, or "connections." Every company has room for the person who has a definite plan of action that is to the advantage of that company.

This procedure may take a few days or weeks of extra time, but the difference in income, in advancement, and in gaining recognition will save years of hard work at small pay. It has many advantages, the main one being that it will often save you from one to five years of your time in reaching a chosen goal.

Every person who starts, or "gets in," halfway up the ladder does so by deliberate and careful planning.

NOTES & COMMENTS

NOTES & COMMENTS

The New Way of Marketing Services

Men and women who market their services must recognize the change that has taken place in connection with the relationship between employer and employee. The future relationship should be more in the nature of a partnership consisting of the employer, the employee, and the public they serve.

In the past, employers and employees have bartered among themselves, not considering that in reality they were bargaining at the expense of the third party, the public they served. Both the employer and the employee should consider themselves as fellow employees whose business it will be to serve the public efficiently.

COMMENTARY

In the preceding paragraph and the following section, Napoleon Hill once again demonstrates his foresight into the future direction of American business. As you will recognize, the point he makes by citing the coal and gas companies would at a later time be equally applicable to the telephone monopolies, and later still to computer software and Internet companies, and to cable-television suppliers when competitors started to offer satellite TV. This snapshot of how and why business has changed should provide you with a blueprint for the attitude you must adopt and the way you must conduct yourself if you are going to attain the success you are seeking.

During the Depression, I spent several months in the anthracite coal region of Pennsylvania, studying conditions that all but destroyed the coal industry. The coal operators and the unions drove hard bargains in negotiating their labor contracts. The cost of the "bargaining" was passed on to the customer by adding to the price of the coal. However, in the end they discovered their actions had worked against them. What their delays and high prices had actually accomplished was to open the market to their competitors. Inadvertently, they

NOTES & COMMENTS

had built up a wonderful business for the manufacturers of oil-burning stoves and furnaces, as well as for the producers of oil.

A similar experience happened to the gas companies. We can all remember the time when the gas-meter reader pounded on the door hard enough to break the panels. When the door was opened, he pushed his way in, uninvited, with a scowl on his face that plainly said, "What-the-hell-did-you-keep-me-waiting-for?" All that has undergone a change. The meter man now conducts himself as a gentleman who is "delighted-to-be-at-your-service-sir." Before the gas companies learned that their scowling meter men were offending customers, their competitors, the polite salesmen of oil burners, came along and did a land-office business.

These illustrations are mentioned here to show that we are where we are, and what we are, because of our own conduct. If there is a principle of cause and effect that controls business, finance, and transportation, this same principle controls individuals and determines their economic status.

"Courtesy" and "service" are the watchwords of merchandising today, and they apply to the person who is marketing personal services even more directly than to the employer. In the final analysis, you are employed by the customer. If you fail to serve well, both you and your employer will pay for it by the loss of the privilege of serving.

What Is Your "QQS" Rating?

In the preceding, the causes of success in marketing services effectively and permanently have been clearly described. Unless those causes are studied, analyzed, understood, and applied, no one can market services effectively and permanently. Every man or woman must be their own sales force of their personal services. The quality and the quantity of service rendered, and the spirit in which it is rendered, determine the price and the duration of employment.

NOTES & COMMENTS

To market your personal services effectively (which means a permanent market, at a satisfactory price, under pleasant conditions) you must adopt and follow the "QQS" formula. QQS means that Quality, plus Quantity, plus the proper Spirit of cooperation, equals perfect salesmanship of service. Remember the "QQS" formula, but do more—apply it as a habit!

Analyze the formula to make sure you understand exactly what it means.

- *Quality* of service means the performance of every detail, in connection with your position, in the most efficient manner possible, with the object of greater efficiency always in mind.

- *Quantity* of service means the habit of rendering all the service of which you are capable, at all times, with the purpose of increasing the amount of service rendered as you develop greater skill through practice and experience. Emphasis is again placed on the word *habit.*

- *Spirit* of service means the habit of agreeable, harmonious conduct, which will induce cooperation from associates and fellow employees.

Adequate quality and adequate quantity of service is not sufficient to maintain a permanent market for your services. The spirit in which you deliver service is a strong determining factor in connection with both the price you receive and the duration of your employment.

Andrew Carnegie stressed this point in his description of the factors that lead to success in the marketing of personal services. He emphasized again and again the necessity for harmonious conduct. He stressed the fact that he would not retain any man, no matter how great a quantity or how efficient the quality of his work, unless he worked in a spirit of harmony. Mr. Carnegie insisted upon his people working with each other in an agreeable manner. To prove that he placed a high value on this quality, he helped many who met his standards to become very wealthy. Those who did not conform had to make room for others who did.

The importance of a pleasing personality has been stressed because it is so important in rendering service in the proper spirit. If you have a personality that pleases, and you render service in a spirit of harmony, these assets often make up for what you may lack in both the quality and the quantity of service you render. Nothing, however, can be successfully substituted for pleasing conduct.

The Capital Value of Your Services

The person whose income is derived entirely from the sale of personal services is a merchant, just like the person who sells hard goods, and such a person is subject to exactly the same rules of conduct as the merchant who sells merchandise.

I emphasize this because many people who live by the sale of personal services make the mistake of considering themselves free from the rules of conduct and the responsibilities attached to those who are engaged in marketing commodities.

The day of the "go-getter" has been supplanted by the "go-giver."

The actual capitalized value of your brainpower may be determined by the amount of income you can produce by marketing your services. A fair estimate of the capital value of your brainpower may be made by using the following assumptions: Money (the amount of capital) can be borrowed from a bank at a certain rate of interest. Money is worth no more than brains, and it is often worth much less. Therefore, if your brainpower is as valuable as money, in effect, you should be "lending" your brainpower (your amount of capital) at least at the same rate that banks charge to lend money. This means that what you earn in a year (your income) is comparable to what a bank earns from a loan in a year (the interest they charge).

NOTES & COMMENTS

You can then calculate the capital value of your brainpower using this formula: Divide 100 by the current rate of interest that banks charge for lending money. Then multiply the result by the amount of your annual income.

As an example, assume that the current interest rate is 5 percent. Assume your annual income is $50,000. The formula would be as follows: 100 divided by 5 equals 20, and 20 multiplied by $50,000 equals $1,000,000. Therefore, if you lend out your brainpower (your capital) at the same rate as the bank lends money (5 percent interest), your brainpower is worth $1,000,000.

Competent "brains," if effectively marketed, represent a much more desirable form of capital than the money that is required to conduct a business dealing in commodities. This is true because "brains" are a form of capital that cannot be permanently depreciated by economic depressions, nor can this form of capital be stolen or spent. Moreover, the money that is essential for the conduct of business is as worthless as a sand dune, until it has been mixed with efficient "brains."

THE THIRTY-ONE MAJOR CAUSES OF FAILURE

Life's greatest tragedy consists of men and women who earnestly try, and fail. The tragedy lies in the overwhelmingly large majority of people who fail, as compared with the few who succeed.

I have had the privilege of analyzing several thousand men and women, 98 percent of whom were classed as "failures."

My analysis proved that there are thirteen major principles through which people accumulate fortunes (each of the thirteen principles of success has its own chapter in this book), and there are thirty-one major reasons for failure. The thirty-one causes of failure are listed below. As you go through the list, measure yourself point by point. It will help you to discover how many of these causes of failure stand between you and success.

1. *Unfavorable hereditary background.* There is little, if anything, that can be done for people who are born with a deficiency in brain-power. This is the only one of the thirty-one causes of failure that may not be easily corrected by any individual. My philosophy can offer only one method of bridging this weakness—through the aid of the Master Mind.

2. *Lack of a well-defined purpose in life.* There is no hope of success for the person who does not have a central purpose or definite goal at which to aim. Ninety-eight out of every hundred of those whom I have analyzed had no such aim. Perhaps this was the major cause of their failure.

3. *Lack of ambition to aim above mediocrity.* I can offer no hope for those who are so indifferent they do not want to get ahead in life, and are not willing to pay the price.

4. *Insufficient education.* This is a handicap that may be overcome with comparative ease. Experience has proven that the best-educated people are often those who are self-made or self-educated. It takes more than a college degree to make you a person of education. Any person who is educated has learned to get whatever they want in life without violating the rights of others. Education consists not so much of knowledge, but of knowledge effectively and persistently applied. You are paid not merely for what you know, but for what you do with what you know.

5. *Lack of self-discipline.* Discipline comes through self-control. This means that you must control all negative qualities. Before you can control conditions, you must first control yourself. Self-mastery is the hardest job you will ever tackle. If you do not conquer

yourself, you will be conquered by yourself. By stepping in front of a mirror, you may see both your best friend and your greatest enemy.

6. *Ill health.* No person may enjoy outstanding success without good health. Many of the causes of ill health are subject to mastery and control. These, in the main, are:

   - Overeating of foods not conducive to health.

   - Wrong habits of thought, or negative thinking.

   - Wrong use of, and overindulgence in, sex.

   - Lack of proper physical exercise.

   - An inadequate supply of fresh air, due to improper breathing.

7. *Unfavorable environmental influences during childhood.* "As the twig is bent, so shall the tree grow." Most people who have criminal tendencies acquire them as the result of bad environment and improper associates during their childhood or youth.

8. *Procrastination.* This is one of the most common causes of failure. Procrastination stands within the shadow of every human being, waiting its opportunity to spoil your chances of success. Most of us go through life as failures because we are waiting for "the time to be right" to start doing something worthwhile. Do not wait. The time will never be "just right." Start where you stand, work with whatever tools you have at your command, and you will acquire better tools as you go along.

9. *Lack of persistence.* Most of us are good "starters" but poor "finishers" of everything we begin. People are prone to give up at the first signs of defeat. There is no substitute for persistence. The person who makes persistence his or her watchword discovers that "failure"

finally becomes tired and makes its departure. Failure cannot cope with persistence.

10. *Negative personality.* There is no hope of success for the person who repels people through a negative personality. Success comes through the application of power, and power is attained through the cooperative efforts of other people. A negative personality will not induce cooperation.

11. *Lack of control of sexual urges.* Sexual energy is the most powerful of all the stimuli that move people into action. Because it is the most powerful of the emotions, if it is controlled it can be converted into other creative channels.

12. *Uncontrolled desire for "something for nothing."* The gambling instinct drives millions of people to failure. Evidence of this may be found in the Wall Street stock market crash of 1929, during which millions of people tried to make money by gambling on stock margins.

COMMENTARY

For those who are not familiar with the stock market and buying "on margin," the following is a simplified explanation of what caused the crash of '29. The first thing to understand is that prior to the Great Depression there was widespread optimism about the expanding economy. Businesses were booming, and the people who had invested in those companies were making fortunes almost overnight. When the average person saw how much money was being made, they wanted to get in on it. And there was a way for them to do it.

Even average people who didn't have enough ready cash to buy stocks could do so because brokers allowed customers to purchase stocks "on margin"—by making what amounted to a down payment. However, part of the

NOTES & COMMENTS

purchase agreement stated that when the brokers "called in" the margin accounts, which they could do at any time, the customers would have to come up with the rest of the cash immediately to pay the balance owing on the original purchase price.

That is why Hill used the term "gambling" when he referred to the stock market. These average people weren't investing in companies, they were betting on the future rise in value. The idea in the average person's mind was that they would only have to scrape together enough to pay the margin, which was a small percentage of the full cost. Then when the price of the stock went up they would sell, which would give them more than enough money to pay the broker the balance owing on the purchase price, and they could pocket the difference.

This worked fine as long as stock prices continued to rise. But when the stock market crashed the stockbrokers called in the margins, and the people who had bought at prices they really couldn't afford suddenly found that they had to come up with the cash. And that was why so many average people got wiped out in the crash of '29. They gambled money they didn't have, by buying on margin.

13. *Lack of a well-defined power of decision.* Those who succeed reach decisions promptly and change them very slowly. Those who fail reach decisions very slowly and change them frequently, and quickly. Indecision and procrastination are twins. Where one is found, the other is also usually found. Kill off this pair before they completely tie you to the treadmill of failure.

14. *One or more of the six basic fears* (fear of poverty, criticism, ill health, loss of love, old age, and death). You will find an in-depth analysis of these six basic fears in the final chapter. They must be mastered before you can market your services effectively.

15. *Wrong selection of a mate in marriage.* This is a most common cause of failure. The relationship of marriage brings people intimately

into contact. Unless this relationship is harmonious, failure is likely to follow. Moreover, it will be a form of failure that destroys ambition.

16. *Overcaution.* The person who takes no chances generally has to take whatever is left when others are through choosing. Overcaution is as bad as undercaution. Both are extremes to be guarded against. Life itself is filled with the element of chance.

17. *Wrong selection of associates in business.* This is one of the most common causes of failure in business. In marketing personal services, you should use great care to select an employer who will be an inspiration and who is intelligent and successful. We emulate those with whom we associate most closely. Pick an employer who is worth emulating.

18. *Superstition and prejudice.* Superstition is a form of fear. It is also a sign of ignorance. Successful people keep open minds and are afraid of nothing.

19. *Wrong selection of a vocation.* You cannot have outstanding success in work that you do not like. The most essential step in the marketing of personal services is that of selecting an occupation into which you can throw yourself wholeheartedly. Although money or circumstances may require you to do something you don't like for a time, no one can stop you from developing plans to make your goal in life a reality.

COMMENTARY

Most contemporary experts agree with Napoleon Hill's statement that finding the work you love is of key importance in achieving success that is truly rewarding. This concept coincides so well with modern attitudes that it has inspired a number of books including Feel the Fear and Do It Anyway *by*

NOTES & COMMENTS

NOTES & COMMENTS

Susan Jeffers, Wishcraft *by Barbara Sher, and* Do What You Love, The Money Will Follow *by Marsha Sinetar. All three books became bestsellers by expanding upon that single concept.*

20. *Lack of concentration of effort.* The jack-of-all-trades seldom is good at any. Concentrate all of your efforts on one definite chief aim.

21. *The habit of indiscriminate spending.* You cannot succeed if you are eternally in fear of poverty. Form the habit of systematic saving by putting aside a definite percentage of your income. Money in the bank gives you a very safe foundation of courage when bargaining for the sale of personal services. Without money, you must take what you are offered, and be glad to get it.

22. *Lack of enthusiasm.* Without enthusiasm you cannot be convincing. Moreover, enthusiasm is contagious, and the person who has it (under control) is generally welcome in any group of people.

23. *Intolerance.* The person with a closed mind on any subject seldom gets ahead. Intolerance means that you have stopped acquiring knowledge. The most damaging forms of intolerance are those connected with religious, racial, and political differences of opinion.

24. *Intemperance.* The most damaging forms of intemperance are connected with overeating, alcohol, drugs, and sexual activities. Overindulgence in any of these can be fatal to success.

25. *Inability to cooperate with others.* More people lose their positions, and their big opportunities in life, because of this fault than for all other reasons combined. It is a fault that no well-informed businessperson or leader will tolerate.

26. *Possession of power that was not acquired through self-effort* (sons and daughters of wealthy parents, and others who inherit money that they did not earn). Power in the hands of one who did not acquire it gradually is often fatal to success. Quick riches are more dangerous than poverty.

27. *Intentional dishonesty.* There is no substitute for honesty. You may be temporarily dishonest, because of circumstances over which you have no control, without permanent damage. But there is no hope for you if you are dishonest by choice. Sooner or later your deeds will catch up with you, and you will pay by loss of reputation and perhaps even loss of liberty.

28. *Egotism and vanity.* These qualities serve as red lights that warn others to keep away. They are fatal to success.

29. *Guessing instead of thinking.* Most people are too indifferent or lazy to acquire facts with which to think accurately. They prefer to act on "opinions" created by guesswork or snap judgments.

30. *Lack of capital.* This is a common cause of failure among those who start out in business for the first time. You must have a sufficient reserve of capital to absorb the shock of your mistakes and to carry you over until you have established a reputation.

31. Here, name any particular cause of failure from which *you* have suffered that has not been included in the foregoing list.

Contained in these thirty-one major causes of failure is the description of practically every person who tries and fails. It will be helpful if you get someone who knows you well to go over this list with you and help you to analyze yourself by each of these causes of failure. Most people cannot see themselves as others see them. You may be one who cannot.

DO YOU KNOW YOUR OWN WORTH?

The oldest of admonitions is "Know thyself!" If you market merchandise successfully, you must know the merchandise. The same is true in marketing personal services. You should know all of your weaknesses in order to bridge them or eliminate them entirely. You should know your strengths in order to call attention to them when selling your services. You can know yourself only through accurate analysis.

There is a story about a young man applying for job, who was making a good impression until the manager asked him what salary he expected. He replied that he had no fixed sum in mind (lack of a definite aim). The manager then said, "We will pay you all you are worth, after we try you out for a week."

"I can't accept that," the applicant replied, "I'm already getting more than that where I'm now employed."

It may seem funny, but it makes a serious point. Before you even begin to negotiate for a better salary in your present position, or begin to seek employment elsewhere, be sure that you are worth more than you now receive.

It is one thing to want money—everyone wants more—but it is something entirely different to be worth more. Many people mistake their wants for their just dues. Your financial wants have nothing whatever to do with your worth. Your value is established entirely by your ability to render useful service or your capacity to induce others to render such service.

Take Inventory of Yourself

Annual self-analysis is essential in the effective marketing of personal services, just like you would take an annual inventory if you were in merchandising. Moreover, your yearly analysis should show a decrease in your faults and an increase in your virtues. You go ahead, stand still, or go backward in life. Your objective should be to go ahead.

Annual self-analysis will disclose whether advancement has been made and, if so, how much. It will also disclose any backward steps you may have taken. The effective marketing of personal services requires you to move forward even if the progress is slow.

This self-analysis should be made at the end of each year, so you can include in your New Year's resolutions any improvements that the analysis indicates should be made. Take this inventory by asking yourself the following questions, and by checking your answers with the aid of someone who will not permit you to deceive yourself.

Self-Analysis Questionnaire

1. Have I attained the goal that I established as my objective for this year? (You should work with a definite yearly objective to be attained as a part of your major life objective.)

2. Have I delivered service of the best possible quality of which I was capable, or could I have improved any part of this service?

3. Have I delivered service in the greatest possible quantity of which I was capable?

4. Has the spirit of my conduct been harmonious and cooperative at all times?

5. Have I permitted the habit of procrastination to decrease my efficiency and, if so, to what extent?

6. Have I improved my personality and, if so, in what ways?

7. Have I been persistent in following my plans through to completion?

8. Have I reached decisions promptly and definitely on all occasions?

9. Have I permitted any of the six basic fears to decrease my efficiency?

10. Have I been either overcautious or undercautious?

NOTES & COMMENTS

11. Has my relationship with my associates in work been pleasant, or unpleasant? If it has been unpleasant, has the fault been partly or wholly mine?

12. Have I dissipated any of my energy through lack of concentration of effort?

13. Have I been open-minded and tolerant in connection with all subjects?

14. In what ways have I improved my ability to render service?

15. Have I been intemperate in any of my personal habits?

16. Have I expressed, either openly or secretly, any form of egotism?

17. Has my conduct toward my associates been such that they respect me?

18. Have my opinions and decisions been based upon guesswork, or accuracy of analysis and thought?

19. Have I followed the habit of budgeting my time, my expenses, and my income, and have I been conservative in these budgets?

20. How much time have I devoted to unprofitable effort, which I might have used to better advantage?

21. How may I rebudget my time and change my habits so I will be more efficient during the coming year?

22. Have I been guilty of any conduct that was not approved by my own conscience?

23. In what ways have I rendered more service and better service than I was paid to render?

24. Have I been unfair to anyone and, if so, in what way?

25. If I had been the purchaser of my own services for the year, would I be satisfied with my purchase?

26. Am I in the right vocation and, if not, why not?

27. Has the purchaser of my services been satisfied with the service I have rendered and, if not, why not?

28. What is my present rating on the fundamental principles of success? (Make this rating fairly and frankly, and have it checked by someone who is courageous enough to do it accurately.)

After you have finished reading through to the end of this book at least once, and you are sure you have assimilated the information in this chapter, you will be ready to create a practical plan for marketing your personal services. In this chapter you should have found adequate descriptions of every principle essential in planning the sale of personal services. These include the major attributes of leadership, the most common causes of failure in leadership, a description of the fields of opportunity for leadership, the main causes of failure in all walks of life, and the important questions that should be used in self-analysis.

This extensive and detailed presentation has been included because it will be needed by you if you are going to earn your riches by marketing your personal services. Those who have lost their fortunes, and those who are just beginning to earn money, have nothing but personal services to offer in return for riches; therefore it is essential that you have real, practical information that you'll need to market your services to best advantage.

Complete assimilation and understanding of the information will help you to market your services, and it will help you to become more analytical and capable of judging people. The information will be priceless to you if you work in an executive position where you select employees.

NOTES & COMMENTS

WHERE AND HOW TO FIND OPPORTUNITIES TO ACCUMULATE RICHES

Now that we have analyzed the principles by which riches may be accumulated, you naturally ask, "Where can I find the opportunities to apply these principles?" Very well, let us take inventory and see what the United States of America offers the person seeking riches.

To begin with, remember that we live in a country where every law-abiding citizen enjoys freedom of thought and freedom of deed unequaled anywhere in the world. Most of us have never taken inventory of the advantages of this freedom. We have never compared our unlimited freedom with the curtailed freedom in other countries.

Here we have freedom of thought; freedom in the choice and enjoyment of education; freedom in religion; freedom in politics; freedom in the choice of a business, profession, or occupation; freedom to accumulate and own all the property we can accumulate; freedom to choose our place of residence; freedom in marriage; freedom through equal opportunity to all races; freedom of travel from one state to another; freedom in our choice of foods; and freedom to aim for any station in life for which we have prepared ourselves, even for the presidency of the United States.

We have other forms of freedom, but this list gives an overview of the most important freedoms that offer you the opportunity to *think and grow rich.* The United States is the only country guaranteeing to every citizen, whether native-born or naturalized, so broad and varied a list of freedoms.

Next, let us recount some of the blessings that our widespread freedom has placed within our hands. Take the average American family of average income and sum up the benefits available to every member of the family, in this land of opportunity and plenty!

- *Food.* Next to freedom of thought and deed comes food, clothing, and shelter—the three basic necessities of life. Because of our universal freedom, the average American family has available at its door the choicest selection of food to be found anywhere in the world, and at prices within its financial range.

- *Shelter.* This family lives in a comfortable apartment or house, complete with light, heat, water, and many conveniences. The toast they had for breakfast was toasted in an electric toaster, which cost but a few dollars; the apartment is cleaned with a vacuum cleaner that is run by electricity. Hot and cold water is available, at all times, in the kitchen and the bathroom. The food is kept cool in a refrigerator, clothes are washed and dried, dishes are cleaned, and numerous labor-saving devices are run on power obtained by putting a plug into a wall socket. The family receives entertainment and information from all over the world, twenty-four hours a day, if they want it, by merely flipping a switch on their radio *[or television or computer]*.

    There are other conveniences but the foregoing list will give a fair idea of some of the concrete evidences of the freedoms that we in America enjoy.

- *Clothing.* Anywhere in the United States, the family with average clothing requirements can dress very comfortably at a cost that is only a small portion of their earnings.

Only the three basic necessities of food, clothing, and shelter have been mentioned. The average American also has other options and advantages that are available in return for reasonable effort.

The average American has security of property rights not found in any other country in the world. We can place any surplus money in a bank with the assurance that our government will protect it, and make good to us if the bank fails. Anyone wanting to travel from one state to another needs no passport, and no one's permission. You may go when you please, and you may travel by car, train, bus, airplane, ship, or any other method that you can afford.

NOTES & COMMENTS

The "Miracle" That Has Provided These Blessings

We often hear politicians proclaiming the freedom of America when they solicit votes, but they seldom take the time or trouble to analyze the source of this "freedom." Having no axe to grind, no grudge to express, and no ulterior motives, I will give you a frank analysis of that mysterious, abstract, greatly misunderstood "something" that gives to every citizen of America more blessings, more opportunities to accumulate wealth, and more freedom of every nature than may be found in any other country.

I have the right to analyze the source and nature of this unseen power because I know, and have known for more than half a century, many of the men who organized that power and many who are now responsible for its maintenance.

The name of this mysterious benefactor of mankind is *capital.*

Capital consists not only of money but also of highly organized, intelligent groups of individuals who plan ways and means of using money efficiently for the good of the public, as well as profitably to themselves.

These groups consist of scientists, educators, chemists, inventors, business analysts, publicists, transportation experts, accountants, lawyers, doctors, and other men and women who have highly specialized knowledge in all fields of industry and business. They pioneer, experiment, and blaze trails in new fields of endeavor. They support colleges, hospitals, schools, build good roads, publish newspapers, pay most of the cost of government, and take care of the many details essential to human progress. Stated briefly, the capitalists are the brains of civilization because they supply the entire fabric of which all education, enlightenment, and human progress consists.

Money without brains is always dangerous. Properly used, it is the most important essential of civilization.

To give you an idea of how important organized capital is, try to imagine that it is your job to provide and prepare a simple family breakfast, but you have to do it without the aid of capital.

To supply the tea, you would have to make a trip to China or India. Unless you are an excellent swimmer, you would become rather tired before making the round trip. Then, too, another problem would confront you. What would you use for money, even if you had the physical endurance to swim the ocean?

To supply sugar, you would have to take another swim, to the Caribbean Islands, or a long walk to the sugar-beet section of Utah. But even then you might come back without the sugar, because organized effort and money are necessary to produce sugar, to say nothing of what is required to refine, transport, and deliver it to the breakfast table anywhere in the United States.

Eggs you could obtain easily enough from nearby farms, but you might have a very long walk to Florida or California and back before you could serve grapefruit juice.

You would have another long walk, to Kansas or one of the other wheat-growing states, when you went after wheat bread.

Dry cereal would have to be omitted from the menu, because it would not be available except through the labor of a trained group of workers and suitable machinery, all of which call for capital.

After resting, you could take off for another little swim down to South America, where you would pick up a couple of bananas. On your return you could take a short walk to the nearest farm having a dairy and pick up some butter and cream. Then your family would be ready to sit down and enjoy breakfast.

Seems absurd, doesn't it? Well, the procedure described would be the only possible way these simple items of food could be delivered if we had no capitalistic system.

NOTES & COMMENTS

The Capital Cornerstone of Our Lives

The sum of money required for the building and maintenance of the planes, trucks, trains, and cargo ships used in the delivery of that simple breakfast is so huge that it staggers the imagination. It runs into billions of dollars, not to mention the armies of trained employees required to run all those planes, trucks, ships, and trains. But transportation is only a part of the requirements of modern civilization in capitalistic America. Before there can be anything to haul, something must be grown from the ground, or manufactured and prepared for market. This calls for more billions of dollars for equipment, machinery, packaging, marketing, and to pay the wages of millions of men and women.

Transportation systems do not spring up from the earth and function automatically. They come in response to the call of civilization. They come through the labor and ingenuity and organizing ability of people who have imagination, faith, enthusiasm, decision, and persistence. These men and women are known as capitalists. They are motivated by the desire to build, construct, achieve, render useful service, earn profits, and accumulate riches. And because they render service without which there would be no civilization, they earn for themselves great riches.

Just to keep the record simple and understandable, I will add that these capitalists are the same men and women who are often denounced as the "greedy establishment" or "Wall Street."

I am not attempting to present a case for or against any group or any system of economics. The purpose of this book—a purpose to which I have faithfully devoted more than half a century—is to present, to anyone who wants the knowledge, the most dependable philosophy through which individuals may accumulate riches in whatever amounts they desire.

The reasons I have analyzed the economic advantages of the capitalistic system are:

1. To point out that all who seek riches must recognize and adapt themselves to the system that controls all approaches to fortunes, large or small.

2. To present the side of the picture opposite to the one portrayed by politicians and demagogues *[and the media]* who often refer to organized capital as if it were something poisonous.

This is a capitalistic country. It was developed through the use of capital. We who claim the right to partake of the blessings of freedom and opportunity, we who seek to accumulate riches here, should know that neither riches nor opportunity would be available to us if organized capital had not provided these benefits.

There is only one dependable method of accumulating and legally holding riches, and that is by rendering useful service. No system has ever been created by which anyone can legally acquire riches through mere force of numbers, or without giving in return an equivalent value of one form or another.

Your Opportunities in the Midst of Riches

America provides all the freedom and all the opportunity to accumulate riches that any honest person may require. When you go hunting for game, you select hunting grounds where game is plentiful. When you are seeking riches, the same rule naturally applies.

If it is riches you are seeking, do not overlook the possibilities of a country whose citizens are so rich that women, alone, spend billions of dollars each year for cosmetics and other beauty products.

Do not be in too big a hurry to get away from a country whose men willingly, even eagerly, hand over more billions of dollars annually for football, basketball, baseball, and all the related products that go with these and other sporting events.

Only a few of the luxuries and nonessentials have been mentioned, but remember that the business of producing and marketing these few

NOTES & COMMENTS

products gives regular employment to many millions of men and women, who receive for their services many millions of dollars monthly, and spend it freely for both the luxuries and the necessities.

Especially remember that behind all this exchange of merchandise and personal services is an abundance of opportunity to accumulate riches. Here our American freedom comes to your aid. There is nothing to stop you or anyone from engaging in any portion of the effort necessary to carry on these businesses. If you have superior talent, training, experience, you may accumulate riches in large amounts. Those not so fortunate may accumulate smaller amounts. Anyone may earn a living in return for a very nominal amount of labor.

So there you are! Opportunity has spread its wares before you. Step up to the front, select what you want, create your plan, put the plan into action, and follow through with persistence. Capitalistic America will do the rest. You can depend on this much: capitalistic America ensures every person the opportunity to render useful service and to collect riches in proportion to the value of the service.

The "system" denies no one this right, but it does not and cannot promise something for nothing. The system, itself, is irrevocably controlled by the law of economics, which neither recognizes nor tolerates, for long, getting without giving.

CONCEIT IS A FOG

THAT ENVELOPS A MAN'S

REAL CHARACTER BEYOND

HIS OWN RECOGNITION.

IT WEAKENS HIS NATIVE ABILITY

AND STRENGTHENS ALL

HIS INCONSISTENCIES.

DECISION

THE MASTERY OF PROCRASTINATION

The Seventh Step Toward Riches

Analysis of over twenty-five thousand men and women who had experienced failure reveals that lack of decision was near the head of the list of the thirty-one major causes of failure.

Procrastination, the opposite of decision, is a common enemy which practically every person must conquer.

You will have an opportunity to test your capacity to reach quick and definite decisions when you finish reading this book and begin to put the principles into action.

My analysis of several hundred people who had accumulated fortunes well beyond the million-dollar mark disclosed the fact that every one of them had the habit of reaching decisions promptly, and of changing these decisions slowly. People who fail to accumulate money, without exception, have the habit of reaching decisions, if at all, very slowly, and of changing these decisions quickly and often.

NOTES & COMMENTS

One of Henry Ford's most outstanding qualities was his habit of reaching decisions quickly and definitely, and changing them slowly. This quality was so pronounced in Mr. Ford that it gave him the reputation of being obstinate. It was this quality that prompted Mr. Ford to continue to manufacture his famous Model T (the world's ugliest car) when all of his advisers, and many of the purchasers of the car, were urging him to change it.

Perhaps Mr. Ford delayed too long in making the change, but the other side of the story is that Mr. Ford's firmness of decision yielded a huge fortune, before the change in model became necessary. Some say that Mr. Ford's definiteness of decision was just obstinacy, but even this quality is preferable to slowness in reaching decisions and quickness in changing them.

COMMENTARY

Henry Ford's consistency, or definiteness of decision, extended also to the color of the Model T, fifteen million of which, in nineteen years of production from 1908 to 1927, were made only in black.

Shortly after its introduction, Napoleon Hill met with Ford to talk about the principles of success. According to Hill, in Michael Ritt's book A Lifetime of Riches: The Biography of Napoleon Hill, *Henry Ford was "cold, indifferent, unenthusiastic, and spoke only when forced to," unless he was talking about "his car." Early on, few people other than Carnegie could foresee the success Ford would achieve, which Hill later attributed to Ford's self-control and concentrated effort. At Hill's first meeting with him in 1911, Ford was interested only in talking about the Model T. After Ford took him for a "spin around the factory," Hill bought one for $680.*

MAKING YOUR OWN DECISIONS

The majority of people who fail to accumulate the money they need are, generally, easily influenced by the opinions of others. They permit gossip, rumors, other people's opinions, and the news reporters to do their thinking for them. Opinions are the cheapest commodities on earth. Everyone has a flock of opinions they are ready to tell anyone who will listen. If you are too influenced by other people's opinions when you reach decisions, you will not succeed in any undertaking, much less in that of transmuting your own desire into money.

If you are influenced by the opinions of others, you will have no desire of your own.

Keep your own counsel. Rely on yourself to reach your own decisions when you begin to put these principles into practice, and follow through on your decisions. Take no one into your confidence, except the members of your Master Mind group, and be very sure that you choose for your group only those who will be in complete sympathy and harmony with your purpose.

Close friends and relatives, while not meaning to do so, often handicap one through "opinions" and sometimes through ridicule, thinking they are being humorous. Thousands of men and women carry inferiority complexes with them all through life because some well-meaning but ignorant person destroyed their confidence through opinions or ridicule.

You have a brain and mind of your own. Use it, and reach your own decisions. If you need facts or information from others to help you reach decisions, acquire the facts or information you need quietly, without disclosing your purpose.

It is characteristic of people who have a smattering of knowledge to try to give the impression that they know more than they do. Such people generally do too much talking, and too little listening. Keep your eyes and ears open—and your mouth closed—if you wish to acquire the habit of prompt decision. Those who talk too much do little else. If you talk more than you listen, you may miss some important piece of knowledge that might have been very useful to you. By talking too much you may also disclose your plans and purposes to

NOTES & COMMENTS

people who will take great delight in defeating you, because they envy you.

Remember, every time you open your mouth in the presence of a person who really has knowledge, you tip your hand and show that person your exact stock of knowledge or you tip your hand to your lack of it! The mark of genuine wisdom is modesty and silence.

Keep in mind that every person is, like you, seeking the opportunity to accumulate money. If you talk about your plans too freely, you may be surprised when you learn that some other person has beat you to it by using the plans you bragged about.

Let one of your first decisions be to keep a closed mouth and open ears and eyes.

As a reminder to yourself, copy the following epigram in large letters and place it where you will see it daily: "Tell the world what you intend to do, but first show it."

This is the equivalent of saying that "deeds, and not words, are what count most."

The value of decisions depends upon the courage required to render them. The great decisions that served as the foundation of civilization were reached by assuming great risks, which often meant the chance of death.

Lincoln's decision to issue his famous Proclamation of Emancipation, which gave freedom to African Americans, was rendered with full understanding that his act would turn thousands of friends and political supporters against him.

When the rulers of Athens gave Socrates the choice of disclaiming his teachings or being sentenced to death, Socrates' decision to drink the cup of poison, rather than compromise in his personal belief, was a decision of courage. It turned time ahead a thousand years, and gave to people then unborn the right to freedom of thought and of speech.

FIFTY-SIX WHO RISKED THE GALLOWS

The greatest decision of all time, as far as any American citizen is concerned, was reached in Philadelphia on July 4, 1776, when fifty-six men signed their names to a document that they well knew would bring freedom to all Americans, or leave every one of the fifty-six hanging from a gallows!

You have heard of this famous document, the Declaration of Independence, but have you taken from it the great lesson in personal achievement it so plainly taught?

We all remember the date of this momentous decision, but few of us realize what courage that decision required. We remember our history, as it was taught; we remember dates, and the names of the men who fought; we remember Valley Forge, and Yorktown; we remember George Washington, and Lord Cornwallis. But we know little of the real forces behind these names, dates, and places. We know even less of that intangible power that ensured freedom long before Washington's armies reached Yorktown.

It is nothing short of tragedy that the writers of history have missed, entirely, even the slightest reference to the irresistible power that gave birth and freedom to the nation destined to set up new standards of independence for all the peoples of the earth. I say it is a tragedy because it is the same power that must be used by every individual who overcomes the difficulties of life and forces life to pay the price asked.

Let us briefly review the events that gave birth to this power. The story begins with an incident in Boston on March 5, 1770. British soldiers were patrolling the streets, openly threatening the citizens by their presence. The colonists resented armed men marching in their midst. They began to express their resentment openly, hurling stones as well as epithets at the marching soldiers, until the commanding officer gave orders: "Fix bayonets. . . . Charge!"

The battle was on. It resulted in the death and injury of many. The incident aroused such resentment that the Provincial Assembly (made up of prominent colonists) called a meeting for the purpose of taking definite action. Two of the members of that Assembly were John Hancock and Samuel Adams. They spoke up courageously and declared that a move must be made to eject all British soldiers from Boston.

Remember this—a decision, in the minds of two men, might properly be called the beginning of the freedom that we of the United States now enjoy. Remember, too, that the decision of these two men called for faith, and courage, because it was dangerous.

Before the Assembly adjourned, Samuel Adams was appointed to call on Hutchinson, the governor of the province, and demand the withdrawal of the British troops.

The request was granted and the troops were removed from Boston, but the incident was not closed. It had caused a situation that was destined to change the entire trend of civilization.

Richard Henry Lee became an important factor in this story because he and Samuel Adams corresponded frequently, sharing freely their fears and their hopes concerning the welfare of the people of their provinces. From this practice, Adams conceived the idea that a mutual exchange of letters between the thirteen colonies might help to bring about the coordination of effort so badly needed in connection with the solution of their problems. In March of 1772, two years after the clash with the soldiers in Boston, Adams presented this idea to the Assembly. He made a motion that a correspondence committee be established among the colonies, with definitely appointed correspondents in each colony, "for the purpose of friendly cooperation for the betterment of the colonies of British America."

It was the beginning of the organization of the far-flung power that was destined to give freedom to you and to me. A Master Mind group had already been organized. It consisted of Adams, Lee, and Hancock.

The Committee of Correspondence was organized. The citizens of the colonies had been waging disorganized warfare against the British soldiers, through incidents similar to the Boston riot, but nothing of benefit had been accomplished. Their individual grievances had not been consolidated under one Master Mind. No group of individuals had put their hearts, minds, souls, and bodies together in one definite decision to settle their difficulty with the British once and for all—until Adams, Hancock, and Lee got together.

Meanwhile, the British were not idle. They, too, were doing some planning and "Master-Minding." And they had the advantage of having behind them money and organized soldiery.

A Decision That Changed History

The Crown appointed Gage to supplant Hutchinson as the governor of Massachusetts. One of the new governor's first acts was to send a messenger to call on Samuel Adams for the purpose of endeavoring to stop his opposition—by fear.

You will best understand the spirit of what happened from this quotation of the conversation between Colonel Fenton (the messenger sent by Gage) and Adams.

Colonel Fenton: "I have been authorized by Governor Gage to assure you, Mr. Adams, that the governor has been empowered to confer upon you such benefits as would be satisfactory *[endeavor to win Adams by promise of bribes]*, upon the condition that you engage to cease in your opposition to the measures of the government. It is the governor's advice to you, sir, not to incur the further displeasure of His Majesty. Your conduct has been such as makes you liable to penalties of an Act of Henry VIII, by which persons can be sent to England for trial for treason, or misprision of treason, at the discretion of a governor of a province. But, by changing your political course, you will not only receive great personal advantages, but you will make your peace with the King."

Samuel Adams had the choice of two decisions. He could cease his opposition, and receive personal bribes, or he could continue, and run the risk of being hanged!

Clearly, the time had come when Adams was forced to reach, instantly, a decision that could have cost his life. Adams insisted upon Colonel Fenton's word of honor that the colonel would deliver to the governor the answer exactly as Adams would give it to him.

Adams' answer: "Then you may tell Governor Gage that I trust I have long since made my peace with the King of Kings. No personal consideration shall induce me to abandon the righteous cause of my country. And tell Governor Gage it is the advice of Samuel Adams to him, no longer to insult the feelings of an exasperated people."

When Governor Gage received Adams' caustic reply, he flew into a rage and issued a proclamation that read, "I do, hereby, in His Majesty's name, offer and promise his most gracious pardon to all persons who shall forthwith lay down their arms and return to the duties of peaceable subjects, excepting only from the benefit of such pardon, Samuel Adams and John Hancock, whose offences are of too flagitious a nature to admit of any other consideration but that of condign punishment."

Adams and Hancock were on the spot. The threat of the irate governor forced the two men to reach another decision, equally as dangerous. They hurriedly called a secret meeting of their staunchest followers. After the meeting had been called to order, Adams locked the door, placed the key in his pocket, and informed all present that it was imperative that a congress of the colonists be organized, and that no man should leave the room until the decision for such a congress had been reached.

Great excitement followed. Some weighed the possible consequences of such radicalism. Some expressed grave doubt as to the

NOTES & COMMENTS

wisdom of so definite a decision in defiance of the Crown. Locked in that room were two men immune to fear, blind to the possibility of failure: Hancock and Adams. Through the influence of their minds, the others were induced to agree that, through the Correspondence Committee, arrangements should be made for a meeting of the First Continental Congress, to be held in Philadelphia, September 5, 1774.

Remember this date. It is more important than July 4, 1776. If there had been no decision to hold a Continental Congress, there could have been no signing of the Declaration of Independence.

Before the first meeting of the new Congress, another leader, in a different section of the country, was deep in the throes of publishing a "Summary View of the Rights of British America." He was Thomas Jefferson, of the province of Virginia, whose relationship to Lord Dunmore (representative of the Crown in Virginia) was as strained as that of Hancock's and Adams' with their governor.

Shortly after his famous Summary of Rights was published, Jefferson was informed that he was subject to prosecution for high treason against His Majesty's government. Inspired by the threat, one of Jefferson's colleagues, Patrick Henry, boldly spoke his mind, concluding his remarks with a sentence that shall remain forever a classic: "If this be treason, then make the most of it."

It was such men as these who, without power, without authority, without military strength, without money, sat in solemn consideration of the destiny of the colonies, beginning at the opening of the First Continental Congress and continuing at intervals for two years—until on June 7, 1776, Richard Henry Lee arose, addressed the Chair, and to the startled Assembly made this motion:

"Gentlemen, I make the motion that these United Colonies are, and of right ought to be, free and independent states, that they be absolved from all allegiance to the British Crown, and that all political connection between them and the state of Great Britain is, and ought to be, totally dissolved."

The Most Momentous Decision Ever Placed on Paper

Lee's astounding motion was discussed fervently, and at such length that he began to lose patience. Finally, after days of argument, he again took the floor, and declared in a clear, firm voice, "Mr. President, we have discussed this issue for days. It is the only course for us to follow. Why then, sir, do we longer delay? Why still deliberate? Let this happy day give birth to an American Republic. Let her arise, not to devastate and to conquer, but to reestablish the reign of peace, and of law."

Before his motion was finally voted upon, Lee was called back to Virginia because of serious family illness. But before leaving, he placed his cause in the hands of his friend Thomas Jefferson, who promised to fight until favorable action was taken. Shortly thereafter, the president of the Congress (Hancock) appointed Jefferson as chairman of a committee to draw up a Declaration of Independence.

Long and hard the committee labored on a document that would mean, when accepted by the Congress, that every man who signed it would be signing his own death warrant, should the colonies lose in the fight with Great Britain that was sure to follow.

The document was drawn, and on June 28 the original draft was read before the Congress. For several days it was discussed, altered, and made ready. On July 4, 1776, Thomas Jefferson stood before the Assembly and fearlessly read the most momentous decision ever placed on paper.

"When in the course of human events it becomes necessary for one people to dissolve the political bands which have connected them with another, and to assume among the powers of the earth, the separate and equal station to which the laws of nature and of nature's God entitle them, a decent respect to the opinions of mankind requires that they should declare the causes which impel them to the separation. . . ."

When Jefferson finished, the document was voted upon, accepted, and signed by the fifty-six men, every one staking his own life upon his decision to write his name. By that decision came into existence a nation destined to bring to mankind forever the privilege of making decisions.

Analyze the events that led to the Declaration of Independence, and be convinced that this nation, which now holds a position of commanding respect and power among all nations of the world, was born of a decision created by a Master Mind consisting of fifty-six men. Note well the fact that it was their decision that ensured the success of Washington's armies, because the spirit of that decision was in the heart of every soldier who fought with him, and served as a spiritual power, which recognizes no such thing as failure.

Note also (with great personal benefit) that the power that gave this nation its freedom is the same power that must be used by every individual who becomes self-determining. This power is made up of the principles described in this book. It will not be difficult to detect, in the story of the Declaration of Independence, at least six of these principles: desire, decision, faith, persistence, the Master Mind, and organized planning.

KNOW WHAT YOU WANT AND YOU WILL GENERALLY GET IT

Throughout this philosophy you will find the suggestion that thought, backed by strong desire, will transmute itself into its physical equivalent. The story of the founding of America, and the story of the organization of the United States Steel Corporation, are perfect examples of the method by which thought makes this astounding transformation.

In your search for the secret of the method, do not look for a miracle, because you will not find it. You will find only the eternal laws of nature. These laws are available to every person who has the faith and the courage to use them. They may be used to bring freedom to a nation, or to accumulate riches.

Those who reach decisions promptly, and definitely, know what they want and generally get it. The leaders in every walk of life decide quickly, and firmly. That is the major reason why they are leaders. The world has a habit of making room for the people whose words and actions show that they know where they are going.

Indecision is a habit that usually begins when a person is young. It becomes more and more of a habit as the youth goes through grade school, high school, and even through college, without definiteness of purpose.

The habit of indecision goes with the student into the occupation he or she chooses. Generally, a young person just out of school seeks any job that can be found. Young people take the first job they can find because they have fallen into the habit of indecision. The vast majority of people working today are in the positions they hold because they lacked the definiteness of decision to plan a definite position, and the knowledge of how to choose an employer.

Definiteness of decision always requires courage. Sometimes very great courage. The fifty-six men who signed the Declaration of Independence staked their lives on the decision to affix their signatures to that document. The person who reaches a definite decision to go after a specific job, and make life pay the price he or she asks, does not stake his or her life on that decision; they stake their economic freedom. Financial independence, riches, and desirable business positions are not within reach of the person who neglects or refuses to expect, plan, and demand these things. The person who desires riches in the same spirit that Samuel Adams desired freedom for the colonies is sure to accumulate wealth.

NO MAN ACHIEVES

GREAT SUCCESS

WHO IS UNWILLING

TO MAKE PERSONAL SACRIFICES.

PERSISTENCE

THE SUSTAINED EFFORT NECESSARY TO INDUCE FAITH

The Eighth Step Toward Riches

Persistence is an essential factor in the procedure of transmuting desire into its monetary equivalent. The basis of persistence is the power of will.

Willpower and desire, when properly combined, make an irresistible pair. Those who accumulate great fortunes are sometimes called cold-blooded or ruthless. Frequently it is simply because their critics don't understand that what they have is a strong desire backed up by willpower, which they mix with persistence. It is the combination that ensures the attainment of their objectives.

The majority of people are ready to throw their aims and purposes overboard and give up at the first sign of opposition or misfortune. A few carry on despite all opposition, until they attain their goal.

There may be no heroic connotation to the word *persistence*, but persistence does for your character what carbon does to iron—it hardens it to steel.

NOTES & COMMENTS

The building of a fortune will involve the application of the entire thirteen factors of this philosophy. These principles must be understood, and they must be applied with persistence by all who accumulate money.

YOUR TEST OF PERSISTENCE

If you are reading this book with the intention of seriously applying the knowledge, the first test of your persistence will come when you begin to follow the six steps described in the third chapter, Desire. Unless you are one of the few people who already have a definite goal, and a definite plan for its attainment, you may read the instructions but you will never actually apply them in your daily life.

Lack of persistence is one of the major causes of failure. Moreover, my experience with thousands of people has proved that lack of persistence is a weakness common to the majority of people. However, it is a weakness that may be overcome by effort. The ease with which lack of persistence may be conquered will depend entirely upon the intensity of your desire.

The starting point of all achievement is desire. Keep this constantly in mind. Weak desires bring weak results, just as a small amount of fire makes a small amount of heat. If you are lacking in persistence, this weakness may be remedied by building a stronger fire under your desires.

Continue reading through to the end of this book, then go back to chapter 3 and start immediately to carry out the instructions for using the six steps. The eagerness with which you follow these instructions will indicate clearly how much or how little you really desire to accumulate money. If you find that you are indifferent, you may be sure that you have not yet acquired the "money consciousness" that you must possess before you can be sure of accumulating a fortune.

Fortunes gravitate to those whose minds have been prepared to attract them, just as surely as water gravitates to the ocean.

If you are weak in persistence, focus on the instructions in chapter 11—Power of the Master Mind. Surround yourself with a Master Mind group, and through the cooperation of the members of this group, you can develop persistence. You will find additional instructions for the development of persistence in chapter 5, Autosuggestion, and in chapter 13, The Subconscious Mind. Follow the instructions in these chapters until you build up habits that convey to your subconscious mind a clear picture of the object of your desire. From that point on, you will not be handicapped by lack of persistence.

Your subconscious mind works continuously, while you are awake and while you are asleep.

Are You "Money Conscious" or "Poverty Conscious"?

Occasional effort to apply the rules will be of no value to you. To get results, you must apply all of the rules until they become a fixed habit with you. In no other way can you develop the necessary "money consciousness."

Just as money is attracted to those who have deliberately set their mind on it, poverty is attracted to those whose mind is open to it. And although money consciousness must be developed intentionally, poverty consciousness develops without conscious application of habits favorable to it. Poverty consciousness will seize the mind that is not occupied with money consciousness.

If you understand the point of the preceding paragraph, you will understand the importance of persistence in the accumulation of a fortune. Without persistence, you will be defeated even before you start. With persistence, you will win.

If you have ever had a nightmare, you will realize the value of persistence. You are lying in bed, half-awake, with a feeling that you are about to smother. You are unable to turn over, or to move a

NOTES & COMMENTS

muscle. You realize that you must begin to regain control over your muscles. Through persistent effort of willpower, you finally manage to move the fingers of one hand. By continuing to move your fingers, you extend your control to the muscles of one arm until you can lift it. Then you gain control of the other arm. You finally gain control over the muscles of one leg, and then extend it to the other leg. Then—with one supreme effort of will—you regain complete control over your muscular system and "snap" out of your nightmare. You did it step by step.

You may find it necessary to "snap" yourself out of your mental inertia in a similar way, first by moving slowly, then increasing your speed, until you gain complete control over your will. Be persistent no matter how slowly you may have to move at first. With persistence will come success.

"Snap Out Of" Mental Inertia

If you select your Master Mind group with care, you will have in it at least one person who will aid you in the development of persistence. Some people who have accumulated great fortunes did so because of necessity. They developed the habit of persistence because circumstances forced them to become persistent.

Those who have cultivated the habit of persistence seem to enjoy insurance against failure. No matter how many times they are defeated, they finally arrive up toward the top of the ladder. Sometimes it appears that there is a hidden guide whose duty is to test us through all sorts of discouraging experiences. Those who pick themselves up after defeat and keep on trying finally arrive, and the world says, "I knew you could do it!" The hidden guide lets no one enjoy great achievement without passing the persistence test. Those who can't take it simply do not make the grade.

Those who can "take it" are rewarded for their persistence, and in return they get the goal they are pursuing. But that is not all! They receive something infinitely more important than material compensation—the knowledge that "every failure brings with it the seed of an equivalent advantage."

PERSIST PAST YOUR FAILURES

The people who learn from experience the importance of persistence will not accept defeat as being anything more than temporary. They are the ones whose desires are so persistently applied that defeat is finally changed into victory.

We see that an overwhelmingly large number of people go down in defeat, never to rise again. We also see the few who take the punishment of defeat as an urge to greater effort. But what we do not see, what most of us never suspect of existing, is the silent but irresistible power that comes to the rescue of those who fight on in the face of discouragement. If we speak of this power at all, we call it persistence and let it go at that. One thing is sure: if you do not have persistence, you will not achieve noteworthy success in any calling.

As I am writing these lines, I can look out the window and see, less than a block away, the great mysterious Broadway, the "Graveyard of Dead Hopes" and the "Front Porch of Opportunity." From all over the world, people have come to Broadway seeking fame, fortune, power, love, or whatever it is that human beings call success. Once in a great while someone steps out from the long procession of seekers, and the world hears that another person has conquered Broadway. But Broadway is not easily nor quickly conquered. Broadway acknowledges talent, recognizes genius, and pays off in money only after a person has refused to quit. The secret is always inseparably attached to one word: *persistence.*

NOTES & COMMENTS

_____

_____

_____

_____

_____

_____

_____

_____

_____

_____

_____

_____

_____

_____

_____

_____

_____

_____

_____

_____

_____

_____

COMMENTARY

Today we think of making it on Broadway in terms of the theater, but here Napoleon Hill uses Broadway as a metaphor for the New York arts, publishing, and entertainment industries in general. In the original edition of Think and Grow Rich, *Hill used this introduction to tell of Fannie Hurst, one of the best-selling authors of the day, who pounded the streets of New York for four years and received thirty-six rejection slips from one publisher alone before her persistence paid off and she finally got published.*

Although Napoleon Hill chose Fannie Hurst to illustrate his point about overcoming poverty and adversity, he knew all about both from personal experience. Hill's own story is one of very humble beginnings and devastating failures that would have defeated most people. It was only through his extraordinary persistence that the original edition of the book you hold in your hands was published, and for that reason the editors of this edition have included this brief biography of Napoleon Hill.

The following is adapted from A Lifetime of Riches: The Biography of Napoleon Hill, *written by Michael J. Ritt Jr. and Kirk Landers, and also draws upon Napoleon Hill's first bestseller, his four-volume masterwork,* Law of Success. *In it, Hill told of the seven turning points in his own life, and those reprinted excerpts are in the same font as the regular text of this book.*

Born into poverty in the backwoods of Virginia, young Nap, as he was called, was the local gun-toting troublemaker. He would probably have ended up a criminal had his widowed father not met and married Martha Ramey Banner. Nap's new stepmother set out to change the family's mountain ways, and she started by trading Napoleon a typewriter for his six-shooter pistol. She told him, "If you become as good with a typewriter as you are with that gun, you may become rich and famous and known throughout the world." Her faith and encouragement turned young Nap around, and by the age of fifteen he was submitting stories to the local newspapers and doing everything he could to get himself out of his meager circumstance.

After completing high school and one year at a business college, he wrote an audacious letter to Rufus Ayers, one of the most powerful men in the coal industry. Hill wrote to apply for a job, but he said that he didn't want a salary. In fact, he said he would pay Ayers! Hill proposed that Ayers could charge him whatever he wanted on a monthly basis, but if at the end of three months Hill had proved his worth, he then would expect Ayers to pay him a salary of the same monthly amount. Ayers admired Hill's style and hired him— with pay.

FIRST TURNING POINT

After finishing a course at a business college I took a job as stenographer and bookkeeper. As a result of having practiced the habit of performing more work and better work than that for which I was paid, I advanced rapidly until I was assuming responsibilities and receiving a salary far out of proportion to my age.

Hill also proved to be so trustworthy and honest that Ayers promoted him to replace the manager—making this nineteen-year-old the youngest manager of a mine, and in charge of three hundred and fifty men.

Then Fate reached out and gave me a gentle nudge. My employer lost his fortune and I lost my position. This was my first real defeat, and even though it came about as a result of causes beyond my control, I didn't learn a lesson from it until many years later.

SECOND TURNING POINT

My next position was that of sales manager for a large lumber manufacturer in the South. My advancement was rapid, and I did so well that my employer took me into partnership with him. We began to make money and I began to see myself on top of the world again.

NOTES & COMMENTS

Like a stroke of lightning out of a clear sky, the 1907 panic swept down, and overnight it rendered me an enduring service by destroying our business and relieving me of every dollar that I had.

The panic Hill refers to began in the summer of 1907 when a number of banks and stock brokerages declared bankruptcy. Word spread to the general public and it created a "run on the banks" as depositors lined up to demand they be given the money they had on deposit. Banks called in loans to meet the demand for cash, but those borrowers couldn't find buyers for their goods or property so they couldn't pay back their loans. When the banks couldn't get back the money they had loaned, they repossessed the homes or businesses that the borrowers had put up as collateral. Businesses were closed, farmers were evicted from their land, jobs were lost, so even more banks were forced to close, and it just kept getting worse.

America was caught in a downward spiral that was reversed only when the major Wall Street bankers and financial executives, who were themselves in danger of losing their businesses, stepped in to shore up the troubled banks.

It was in large part because of the bank panic of 1907 that legislation was enacted in 1913 to create the Federal Reserve System.

THIRD TURNING POINT

This was my first serious defeat. I mistook it, then, for failure. But it was not, and before I complete this lesson I will tell you why it was not.

It required the 1907 panic, and the defeat that it brought me, to redirect my efforts from the lumber business to the study of law. I entered law school with the firm belief that I would emerge doubly prepared to catch up with the end of the rainbow and claim my pot of gold.

Napoleon Hill had planned to put himself and his brother through law school by writing articles for Bob Taylor's Magazine, *and it was through the magazine that he arranged the fateful meeting with Andrew Carnegie described at the beginning of this book. As was noted there, when Carnegie proposed the idea of writing the philosophy of success, he told Hill that he would have to earn his own way.*

I attended law school at night and worked as an automobile salesman during the day. Because of the job, I saw the need for trained automobile mechanics. I opened an educational department in the manufacturing plant and began to train ordinary machinists in automobile assembly and repair work. The school prospered, paying me over a thousand dollars a month in net profits.

My banker knew that I was prospering, therefore he loaned me money with which to expand. A peculiar trait of bankers is that they will loan us money without any hesitation when we are prosperous.

My banker loaned me money until I was hopelessly in his debt, then he took over my business as calmly as if it had belonged to him. Which it did.

From an income of more than a thousand dollars a month, I was suddenly reduced to poverty.

For the third time Hill had experienced defeat, but he was not beaten. He got another job, and all the while continued to work on the Carnegie project.

FOURTH TURNING POINT *[1912]*

Because my wife's family had influence, I secured the appointment as assistant to the chief counsel for one of the largest coal companies in the world. I was among friends and relatives, and I had a position that I could keep for as long as I wished, without exerting myself. What more did I need? Nothing, I was beginning to say to myself.

Then without consultation with my friends, and without warning, I resigned. This was the first turning point that was of my own selection. It was not forced upon me. I quit that position because the work was too easy and I was performing it with too little effort.

This move proved to be the next most important turning point of my life, although it was followed by ten years of effort that brought almost every conceivable grief the human heart can experience.

I selected Chicago as my new field of endeavor. I made up my mind that if I could gain recognition in Chicago, in any honorable sort of work, it would prove that I had something that might be developed into real ability.

FIFTH TURNING POINT

My first position in Chicago was that of advertising manager for a large correspondence school. I did so well that the president of the school induced me to resign my position and go into the candy manufacturing business with him. We organized the Betsy Ross Candy Company and I became its first president. The business grew rapidly, and soon we had a chain of stores in eighteen different cities.

They did so well in fact, Hill's partners decided they wanted to take over the business. They had Hill arrested on a false charge and then offered to withdraw the charge if he would turn over to them his interest in the business. Outraged at the suggestion, Hill refused.

When the case went to court, his partners failed to appear for the hearing. Hill sued them for malicious damage to his character. The judge's ruling completely vindicated Hill, and allowed him the option to have his partners thrown in jail.

Being arrested seemed, at the time, a terrible disgrace, even though the charge was false. It was not a pleasant experience, and I would not wish to go through a similar experience again, but I must admit that it was worth all the grief it cost me, because it gave me the opportunity to find out that revenge was not a part of my makeup.

SIXTH TURNING POINT

This turning point came shortly after my dreams of success in the candy business had been shattered, when I turned my efforts to teaching advertising and salesmanship as a department of one of the colleges in the Midwest.

My school prospered from the very beginning. I had a resident class and also a correspondence school through which I was teaching students in nearly every English-speaking country.

It was 1917, and in April of that year President Woodrow Wilson declared the United States would enter the war against Germany. Hill contacted the president, whom he had previously met through Andrew Carnegie, and offered his services to help the war effort. Hill was given the position of creating public relations materials and helping to sell war bonds. When not operating his school, he threw himself into his war work, for which he insisted that he be paid only one dollar a year.

Then came the second military draft and it practically destroyed my school, as it caught most of those who were enrolled as students. At one stroke I charged off more than $75,000 in tuition fees.

NOTES & COMMENTS

Once more I was penniless!

Despite the fact that he had to scrape just to get by, Napoleon Hill continued to work for President Wilson, and he continued to refuse to accept any compensation.

Though Hill had a family to support, and the ridicule of his relatives put a tremendous strain on relations, he also continued to work on the Carnegie project. Hill later said:

> Believe me, there were times when, between the needling of my relatives and the hardships I endured, it was not easy to maintain a positive mental attitude and persevere. Sometimes, in barren hotel rooms, I almost believed my family was right. The thing that kept me going was my conviction that one day I would not only successfully complete my work but also be proud of myself when it was finished.

SEVENTH TURNING POINT

To describe the seventh of the turning points of my life, I must go back to November 11, 1918—Armistice Day, the end of the world war. The war had left me without a penny, as I have already said, but I was happy to know that the slaughter had ceased and reason was about to reclaim civilization.

The time had come for another turning point!

I sat down at my typewriter and, to my astonishment, my hands began to play a tune on the keyboard. I had never written so rapidly or so easily before. I did not plan or think about what I was writing—I just wrote whatever came into my mind.

What Hill wrote was a long essay in which he described a new idealism, based on the Golden Rule, which he thought could emerge from the war. He declared that he would help spread the word, and promised that somehow he was going to find the money to launch a new magazine to be called Hill's Golden Rule.

He took his essay to George Williams, a Chicago printer he had met while working at the White House, and by early January of 1919 Hill's Golden Rule *magazine was on the newsstands.*

The first issue was forty-eight pages. In the beginning, with no money to pay anyone else, Hill wrote and edited every word himself, changing his writing style for each article as well as using a variety of pen names. Additional staff was hired later, which soon led to problems on the inside and on the outside, and Williams attempted to buy out Hill's share of the business. However, when Hill realized that one stipulation of the buyout prevented him from any involvement in a competing publication, in October of 1920 he simply left.

By April of 1921 he had raised the money for a new publication, Napoleon Hill's Magazine, *the foundation of which was again the Golden Rule, but it also expanded into presenting many of the principles of success that would become the basis of Hill's later books. The magazine's acceptance and success also led to Hill's success as a speaker and motivator, which led to even greater success for the magazine.*

At the same time, Napoleon Hill was working with one of the inmates of a penitentiary to develop a correspondence course which he took to the prisons to encourage prisoner rehabilitation. Most everything Hill did during this time was successful, and the success of the prison program was significant. But the greed of two members of the board of directors, one of whom was the prison chaplain, eventually led in 1923 to the demise of not only the educational rehabilitation programs but also the magazine and numerous other successful offshoot ventures.

"The bleak irony," as Michael Ritt notes in A Lifetime of Riches, *was that "few enterprises in the 1920s could have been more idealistic or humanitarian in concept . . . yet in seeking to stir goodness in men's souls these enterprises had stirred mean-spirited men to a blood lust that destroyed everything."*

Without his magazine, Hill went back to teaching and lecturing, which led to an introduction to a crusading newspaper publisher, Don Mellet, who offered to help Hill publish the results of his work on the Carnegie project.

At this same time Mellett learned that Prohibition gangsters were selling narcotics and bootleg liquor to schoolchildren in Canton, and members of the local police force were being bribed to do nothing about it. Mellett was outraged and wrote an exposé in his Canton Daily News, *while Hill contacted the governor to implement a state investigation of the corrupt police department.*

A week before Hill and Mellett were to have finalized the financing for the publication of Hill's book, Don Mellett was ambushed outside his home and assassinated by a gangster and a renegade cop.

They tried to kill Hill too, but through pure luck he escaped and fled to the Smoky Mountains, where he remained holed up in a backwoods shack for most of a year. Destitute and in fear for his life, he lapsed into a state of deep depression.

Then, in one extraordinary night of self-analysis, he willed himself out of his depression and resolved to finish the challenge Carnegie had posed almost twenty years earlier. Hill went to Philadelphia, convinced a publisher to put up the money, then worked night and day for almost four months to finish the manuscript. In March of 1928 Hill published the results of his efforts— a multivolume masterwork entitled Law of Success. *No one had ever seen anything like it. It was a phenomenon. A runaway bestseller.*

A little over a year later, while Hill was finally enjoying the fruits of his long labors, the stock market crash of '29 hit. The bottom fell out of everything. Including the market for books.

Although he never gave up on his vision, like the rest of America, Hill struggled through the Depression. He lectured, he wrote, and he taught in every way he could, but it was very hard to preach personal achievement to a country that had lost faith in itself. Napoleon Hill made it his personal mission to turn the tide by creating a variety of self-help programs, but it became disappointingly apparent that it was going to take more than one man to do it.

When Franklin Delano Roosevelt was elected president he reached out to Hill. Though Napoleon Hill was an avowed capitalist, he believed enough in the ultimate goal of FDR's policies that he committed himself to helping the new administration. Throughout the Depression years he became a close confidant of the president's, helping to guide Roosevelt in his efforts to revitalize America. It is said that it was Hill who gave FDR the famous line "We have nothing to fear but fear itself." And though Hill was dead broke, just as he had done for President Wilson, he refused to accept more than one dollar a year for his efforts.

In 1937, as America was finally beginning to see glimmerings of hope that the Great Depression might end, Hill convinced his publisher that America now needed a book to help shake off the mental and emotional stigma of those terrible times. He was right. They released Think and Grow Rich to such resounding success that it sold well over a million copies even before the Depression ended. At this writing it has sold more than 60 million copies worldwide, and to this day it still sells more than a million copies a year in its various editions.

TAKE YOUR OWN "PERSISTENCE INVENTORY"

Persistence is a state of mind, therefore it can be cultivated. Like all states of mind, persistence is based upon definite causes, among them these:

- *Definiteness of purpose.* Knowing what you want is the first and most important step toward the development of persistence. A strong motive will force you to surmount difficulties.

- *Desire.* It is comparatively easy to acquire and maintain persistence in pursuing the object of intense desire.

NOTES & COMMENTS

- *Self-reliance.* Belief in your ability to carry out a plan encourages you to follow the plan through with persistence. (Self-reliance can be developed through the principle described in chapter 5, Autosuggestion.)

- *Definiteness of plans.* Organized plans, even ones that may be weak or impractical, encourage persistence.

- *Accurate knowledge.* Knowing that your plans are sound, based upon experience or observation, encourages persistence; "guessing" instead of "knowing" destroys persistence.

- *Cooperation.* Sympathy, understanding, and cooperation with others tend to develop persistence.

- *Willpower.* The habit of concentrating your thoughts on making plans to attain your definite purpose leads to persistence.

- *Habit.* Persistence is the direct result of habit. The mind absorbs and becomes a part of the daily experiences upon which it feeds. Fear, the worst of all enemies, can be overcome by forcing yourself to perform and repeat acts of courage. Everyone who has seen active service in war knows this.

Take inventory of yourself and determine what you are lacking in this essential quality of persistence. Measure yourself, point by point, and see how many of the previous eight factors of persistence you lack. The analysis may lead to discoveries that will give you a new understanding of yourself and what *you* need to get ahead.

The following is a list of the real enemies that stand between you and achievement. These are not only the "symptoms" indicating weakness of persistence, but also the deeply seated subconscious causes of this weakness. Study the list carefully, and face yourself squarely if you really wish to know who you are and what you are capable of doing. These are the weaknesses that must be mastered by anyone who really wants to accumulate riches:

1. Failure to recognize and to define clearly exactly what you want.

2. Procrastination, with or without cause. (Usually backed up with a long list of alibis and excuses.)

3. Lack of interest in acquiring specialized knowledge.

4. Indecision, and the habit of "passing the buck" instead of facing issues squarely. (Also backed by alibis and excuses.)

5. The habit of relying upon excuses instead of making definite plans to solve your problems.

6. Self-satisfaction. There is little remedy for this, and no hope for those who suffer from it.

7. Indifference, usually reflected in your readiness to compromise rather than meet opposition and fight it.

8. The habit of blaming others for your mistakes, and accepting circumstances as being unavoidable.

9. Weakness of desire because you neglected to choose motives that will push you to take action.

10. Willingness to quit at the first sign of defeat. (Based upon one or more of the six basic fears.)

11. Lack of organized plans that you have written out so they can be analyzed.

12. The habit of neglecting to act on ideas, or to grasp opportunity when it presents itself.

13. Wishing instead of willing.

14. The habit of compromising with poverty instead of aiming at riches. A general lack of ambition to be, to do, or to own.

15. Searching for all the shortcuts to riches, trying to get without giving a fair equivalent. Usually reflected in the habit of gambling, or trying to drive unfair bargains.

16. Fear of criticism, resulting in failure to create plans and put them into action, because of what other people might think, do, or say. This is one of your most dangerous enemies, because it often exists in your subconscious mind and you may not even know it is there. (See the Six Basic Fears in the last chapter.)

IF YOU FEAR CRITICISM

Following is an examination of the symptoms of the fear of criticism. The majority of people permit relatives, friends, and the public at large to influence them so that they cannot live their own lives because they fear criticism.

Many people make mistakes in marriage but stay married, then go through life miserable and unhappy, because they fear criticism. Anyone who has submitted to this form of fear knows the irreparable damage it does by destroying one's ambition and the desire to achieve.

Millions of people neglect to go back and get an education after having left school, because they fear criticism.

Countless numbers of men and women permit relatives to wreck their lives in the name of family duty, because they fear criticism. Duty does not require you to submit to the destruction of your personal ambitions and the right to live your own life in your own way.

People refuse to take chances in business, because they fear the criticism that may follow if they fail. The fear of criticism in such cases is stronger than the desire for success.

Too many people refuse to set high goals for themselves, because they fear the criticism of relatives and friends who may say, "Don't aim so high, people will think you are crazy."

When Andrew Carnegie suggested that I devote twenty years to the organization of a philosophy of individual achievement, my first impulse was fear of what people might say. His suggestion was far greater than anything I had ever conceived for myself. My first instinct was to create excuses, all of them traceable to the fear of criticism. Something inside of me said, "You can't do it—the job is too big and requires too much time—what will your relatives think of you?—how will you earn a living?—no one has ever organized a philosophy of success, what right have you to believe you can do it?—who are you, anyway, to aim so high?—remember your humble birth—what do you know about philosophy?—people will think you are crazy (and they did)—why hasn't some other person done this before now?"

These and many other questions flashed into my mind. It seemed as if the whole world had suddenly turned its attention to me with the purpose of ridiculing me into giving up all desire to carry out Mr. Carnegie's suggestion.

Later in life, after having analyzed thousands of people, I discovered that most ideas are stillborn. To grow, ideas need the breath of life injected into them through definite plans of immediate action. The time to nurse an idea is at the time of its birth. Every minute it lives gives it a better chance of surviving. The fear of criticism is what kills most ideas that never reach the planning and action stage.

"BREAKS" CAN BE MADE TO ORDER

Many people believe that success is the result of "lucky breaks." There may be something to that, but if you depend upon luck you will almost surely be disappointed. The only "break" anyone can afford

NOTES & COMMENTS

to rely on is a self-made "break." These come through the application of persistence. The starting point is definiteness of purpose.

COMMENTARY

In 1999, Marc Myers, editor of one of the country's most influential self-help newsletters, Bottom Line/Personal, *wrote a book entitled* How to Make Luck: 7 Secrets Lucky People Use to Succeed. *In it he tells of a study that was done by the psychology department at the University of Hertfordshire near London. They assembled a group of people, half of whom either thought themselves lucky or were considered by others to be lucky. The other half of the group believed they were unlucky. They were all brought to campus to watch a computerized random coin toss. Each person watched as a cartoon elf came on screen and flipped a coin. Each was asked to call heads or tails.*

The results of the experiment proved that the "unlucky" group guessed right approximately the same number of times as the "lucky" group. In follow-up interviews the researchers concluded that the only difference between so-called lucky and unlucky people was that the "lucky" people tended to remember the good things that had happened in their lives, and those that thought they were unlucky tended to dwell on the bad things. The scientific fact is that luck, in terms of calling a coin toss, spinning a wheel, or turning a card is completely random and there is nothing we can do about it. All we can control is what we say and do. Everything else that happens to us depends upon the actions of others and the random world in which we live.

Then why do some people seem to be so lucky and get all the lucky breaks?

Myers says it is because, unlike luck, lucky breaks are something you can control. And lucky people, whether they know it or not, have taken specific steps to make their good luck. You can influence lucky breaks in two ways: you have to intentionally put yourself in luck's way, and you must make people want to help you—because they believe that you deserve their help.

Once you have let the world know you are ready for a break, luck is largely a matter of being introduced to opportunities by people who "open doors" for us. Myers calls these people "gatekeepers." Gatekeepers offer help not only out of goodwill but also because they hope you will help them in return when you are in a position to do so. People who are lucky make it a point to impress their gatekeepers so that they will be the first to come to mind when opportunities arise.

Your gatekeepers must believe that you deserve a break and that it is worth it to them to give you one. One of the best ways to do that is simply to behave and act lucky. If you act like a loser, people think you are a loser. If you perceive yourself as lucky, it will be easier for others to see you that way. And if you are believed to be a lucky person your chances of receiving lucky opportunities will increase, partly because others hope some of your luck will rub off on them.

This is the biggest secret lucky people know. They know that when they seem lucky, more people want to help them. There are people waiting to make a difference in your life if you show them you are willing to make an effort and that you are enthusiastic. Marc Myers' book is devoted to explaining ways to do that.

As Hill says, "The only lucky break anyone can afford to rely upon is a self-made break. These come through the application of persistence. The starting point is definiteness of purpose."

If you stopped the first hundred people you meet on the street, and asked them what they want most in life, ninety-eight of them would not be able to tell you. If you press them for an answer, some will say security, many will say money, a few will say happiness, and others will say fame and power. Some might tell you they want social recognition, ease in living, the ability to sing, dance, or write; but none of them will be able to give you the slightest indication of a plan by which they hope to attain these vaguely expressed wishes. Riches do not respond to wishes. They respond only to definite plans, backed by definite desires, through constant persistence.

HOW TO DEVELOP PERSISTENCE

There are four simple steps that lead to the habit of persistence. They call for no great amount of intelligence, no particular amount of education, and little time or effort. These necessary steps are:

1. A definite purpose backed by a burning desire for its fulfillment.

2. A definite plan, expressed in continuous action.

3. A mind closed tightly against all negative and discouraging influences, including negative suggestions of relatives, friends, and acquaintances.

4. A friendly alliance with one or more persons who will encourage you to follow through with both plan and purpose.

These four steps are essential for success in all walks of life. An important purpose of the thirteen principles of this philosophy is to enable you to take those four steps as a matter of habit.

They are steps by which you may control your economic destiny.

They are steps that lead to freedom and independence of thought.

They are steps that lead to riches, in small or great quantities.

They are steps that lead the way to power, fame, and worldly recognition.

They are four steps that guarantee favorable "breaks."

They are steps that convert dreams into physical realities.

They are steps that lead also to the mastery of fear, discouragement, indifference.

There is a magnificent reward for anyone who learns to take these four steps. It is the privilege of writing your own ticket and of making life yield whatever price is asked.

HOW TO MASTER DIFFICULTIES

What mystical power gives people of persistence the capacity to master difficulties? Does the quality of persistence set up in your mind some form of spiritual, mental, or chemical activity that gives you access to supernatural forces? Does Infinite Intelligence throw itself on the side of the person who still fights on when the whole world seems to be against them?

These and many other similar questions were in my mind as I watched Henry Ford start from scratch and build an industrial empire, with little more than persistence. Or Thomas A. Edison who, with less than three months of schooling, became the world's leading inventor. He turned his persistence into sound-recording and play-back machines, motion-picture cameras and projectors, and the incandescent light, to say nothing of half a hundred other useful inventions.

I had the opportunity to analyze both Mr. Edison and Mr. Ford, up close and personal, year by year, over a long period of time. So I speak from actual knowledge when I say that I found no quality except persistence, in either of them, that even remotely suggested the major source of their stupendous achievements.

If you make an impartial study of the prophets, philosophers, and religious leaders of the past you will come to the inevitable conclusion that persistence, concentration of effort, and definiteness of purpose were the major sources of their achievements.

Consider, for example, the fascinating story of Mohammed. Analyze his life, compare him with men of achievement in this modern age of industry and finance, and observe how they all have one outstanding trait in common: persistence. If you want to understand more about the power of persistence and how it works, I strongly suggest that you read a biography of Mohammed.

NOTES & COMMENTS

COMMENTARY

At the beginning of the twenty-first century there was an increased interest in Islam due to the attacks on the World Trade Center and the subsequent War on Terror. Consequently, the modern reader will have no difficulty finding a number of very good books about Mohammed.

At the time that Hill was writing the first edition of Think and Grow Rich, *one of the best biographies of Mohammed was written by Essad Bey, who was born in Baku, Azerbaijan, the son of a Jewish businessman named Nussimbaum. Later, he changed his name when he converted to Islam. During the Russian Revolution he fled his home for Berlin where he lived until the rise of Hitler again forced him to move, first to Austria and then finally to Italy. It is believed by some that this man known as Essad Bey also wrote under another pen name, Kurban Said, and was in fact the author of the acclaimed Azerbaijani novel,* Ali and Nino.

That Napoleon Hill was very impressed with this particular biography of Mohammed is clear from his recommendation which follows.

I strongly suggest that you read a biography of Mohammed, especially the one by Essad Bey. This brief review of that book, which appeared in the *Herald-Tribune*, will provide a preview of the rare treat in store for those who take the time to read the entire story of one of the most astounding examples of the power of persistence known to civilization.

THE LAST GREAT PROPHET

Reviewed by Thomas Sugrue

Mohammed was a prophet, but he never performed a miracle. He was not a mystic; he had no formal schooling; he did not begin his mission until he was forty. When he announced that he was the Messenger of God, bringing word of the true religion, he was ridiculed and labeled a lunatic. Children tripped him and women threw filth upon him. He was banished from his native city, Mecca, and his followers were stripped of their worldly goods and sent into the desert after him. When he had been preaching ten years he had nothing to show for it but banishment, poverty and ridicule. Yet before another ten years had passed, he was dictator of all Arabia, ruler of Mecca, and the head of a new world religion which was to sweep to the Danube and the Pyrenees before exhausting the impetus he gave it. That impetus was threefold: the power of words, the efficacy of prayer, and man's kinship with God.

His career never made sense. Mohammed was born to impoverished members of a leading family of Mecca. Because Mecca, the crossroads of the world, home of the magic stone called the Caaba, great city of trade and the center of trade routes, was unsanitary, its children were sent to be raised in the desert by Bedouins. Mohammed was thus nurtured, drawing strength and health from the milk of nomad, vicarious mothers. He tended sheep and soon hired out to a rich widow as leader of her caravans. He traveled to all parts of the Eastern World, talked with many men of diverse beliefs and observed the decline of Christianity into warring sects. When he was twenty-eight, Khadija, the widow, looked upon him with favor, and married him. Her father would have objected to such a marriage, so she got him drunk and held him up while he gave the paternal blessing. For the next twelve years Mohammed lived as a rich and respected and very shrewd trader. Then he took to wandering in the desert, and one day he returned with the first verse of the Koran and told Khadija that the archangel Gabriel had appeared to him and said that he was to be the Messenger of God.

The Koran, the revealed word of God, was the closest thing to a miracle in Mohammed's life. He had not been a poet; he had no gift of words. Yet the verses of the Koran,

NOTES & COMMENTS

as he received them and recited them to the faithful, were better than any verses which the professional poets of the tribes could produce. This, to the Arabs, was a miracle. To them the gift of words was the greatest gift, the poet was all-powerful. In addition the Koran said that all men were equal before God, that the world should be a democratic state—Islam. It was this political heresy, plus Mohammed's desire to destroy all the 360 idols in the courtyard of the Caaba, which brought about his banishment. The idols brought the desert tribes to Mecca, and that meant trade. So the businessmen of Mecca, the capitalists, of which he had been one, set upon Mohammed. Then he retreated to the desert and demanded sovereignty over the world.

The rise of Islam began. Out of the desert came a flame which would not be extinguished—a democratic army fighting as a unit and prepared to die without wincing. Mohammed had invited the Jews and Christians to join him; for he was not building a new religion. He was calling all who believed in one God to join in a single faith. If the Jews and Christians had accepted his invitation Islam would have conquered the world. They didn't. They would not even accept Mohammed's innovation of humane warfare. When the armies of the prophet entered Jerusalem not a single person was killed because of his faith. When the crusaders entered the city, centuries later, not a Moslem man, woman, or child was spared. But the Christians did accept one Moslem idea—the place of learning, the university.

THE LADDER OF SUCCESS

IS NEVER CROWDED

AT THE TOP.

POWER OF THE MASTER MIND

THE DRIVING FORCE

The Ninth Step Toward Riches

11

Power is essential for success in the accumulation of money. Plans are useless without sufficient power to turn them into action. This chapter will describe the method by which an individual may attain and apply power.

Power may be defined as "organized and intelligently directed knowledge." Power, as the term is used here, refers to organized effort, sufficient to enable an individual to transmute desire into its monetary equivalent. Organized effort is produced through the coordination of effort of two or more people, who work toward a definite end, in a spirit of harmony.

Power is required to accumulate money. Power is necessary to keep the money after it has been accumulated.

How can power be acquired? If power is "organized knowledge," let us examine the sources of knowledge:

NOTES & COMMENTS

- *Infinite Intelligence.* This source of knowledge may be accessed with the aid of creative imagination, through the subconscious mind, as described in the previous chapters on faith, autosuggestion, and imagination, and as will be elaborated on in chapter 13, The Subconscious Mind, and chapter 14, The Brain.

- *Accumulated experience.* The accumulated experience of humanity may be found in any well-equipped public library. An important part of this accumulated experience is taught in public schools and colleges, where it has been classified and organized.

  [The computer revolution and the Internet have had a profound effect on the quantity of information available and on the ease of access and ability to organize that information.]

- *Experiment and research.* In the field of science, and in practically every other walk of life, people are gathering, classifying, and organizing new facts daily. This is the source to which you must turn when knowledge is not available through "accumulated experience." Here, too, the creative imagination must often be used.

  [Today, because of the computer revolution and the Internet, publishing and dissemination of information happens so quickly that there is almost no lag time between experiment or research and the integration of those results into available knowledge.]

Knowledge may be acquired from any of the foregoing sources. It may be converted into power by organizing it into definite plans and by putting those plans into action.

If you examine the three sources of knowledge you will see how difficult it would be if you had to depend upon just your own efforts to assemble all the knowledge you need and turn it into definite plans of action. If your plans are big and comprehensive, generally you will have to get others to cooperate with you if you are going to organize your knowledge so that you can turn your plans into power.

GAINING POWER THROUGH THE MASTER MIND

The Master Mind may be defined as "coordination of knowledge and effort, in a spirit of harmony, between two or more people, for the attainment of a definite purpose."

No individual may have great power without utilizing the Master Mind. In chapter 8, Organized Planning, I commented on how to create plans for translating desire into its monetary equivalent. If you carry out these instructions with persistence and intelligence, and use discrimination in choosing your Master Mind group, your objective will have been halfway reached, even before you begin to recognize it.

COMMENTARY

In the following section Hill describes the two kinds of power that an individual can access by assembling a Master Mind alliance and working with that group. The first kind of power that he mentions is economic power, which needs no comment from the editors. However, to describe the second kind of power, for want of a better term Hill uses the word psychic. Because this word has taken on connotations that Hill never intended, this concept deserves clarification before you read on.

As is obvious throughout this book, Napoleon Hill was a very practical man. His use of the word psychic in this chapter has nothing to do with séances, fortunetelling, magic, or any other aspect of the paranormal. The word psychic is defined as "of or pertaining to the human mind," and Hill uses the term to describe something pertaining to the mind that everyone reading this book has experienced. It is that feeling you get when you are working together with other people, everyone is very focused on the same goal, and it is going so well that you seem to be in tune with each other. When that happens, you not only work better with the others but it also seems that your own work and ideas are better and are operating on a higher plane than usual.

NOTES & COMMENTS

So you may better understand the potential power available to you through a properly chosen Master Mind group, I will explain the two characteristics of the Master Mind principle. One kind of power is economic, and the other psychic.

- *Economic power.* The economic feature is obvious. Economic advantages may be created by any person who surrounds themself with the advice, counsel, and personal cooperation of a group of people who are willing to lend him or her wholehearted aid, in a spirit of perfect harmony. This form of cooperative alliance has been the basis of nearly every great fortune. Your understanding of this great truth may definitely determine your financial status.

- *Psychic power.* What I refer to as the psychic phase of the Master Mind principle is a little more difficult to comprehend. You will get a better sense of the meaning from this statement: "No two minds ever come together without creating a third, invisible, intangible force, which may be likened to a third mind." The human mind is a form of energy. When the minds of two people are coordinated in a spirit of harmony, the energy of each mind seems to "pick up on" the energy of the other mind, which constitutes the "psychic" phase of the Master Mind.

The Master Mind principle, or rather the economic feature of it, was first called to my attention by Andrew Carnegie. Discovery of this principle was responsible for the choice of my life's work.

Mr. Carnegie's Master Mind group consisted of a staff of approximately fifty people with whom he surrounded himself for the purpose of manufacturing and marketing steel. He knew little of the technical side of the steel business; his strength was his ability to get others to work together in perfect harmony toward achieving a common goal. Carnegie attributed his entire fortune to the power he accumulated through this Master Mind alliance.

If you analyze the record of anyone who has accumulated a great fortune, and many of those who have accumulated modest fortunes, you will find that they have either consciously or unconsciously employed the Master Mind principle.

Great power can be accumulated through no other principle!

How to Multiply Your Brainpower

The human brain may be compared to an electric battery. It is a fact that a group of batteries will provide more energy than a single battery. It is also a fact that the amount of energy provided by each individual battery depends upon the number and capacity of the cells it contains.

The brain functions in a similar fashion. Some brains are more efficient than others.

A group of brains coordinated (or connected) in a spirit of harmony will provide more thought-energy than a single brain, just as a group of electric batteries will provide more energy than a single battery.

Through this metaphor, you can see that the Master Mind principle holds the secret of the power wielded by those who surround themselves with others of great brainpower.

The following will further define the so-called psychic phase of the Master Mind principle: When a group of individual minds are coordinated and function in harmony, the increased energy created through that alliance becomes available to every individual mind in the group.

Henry Ford began his business career under the handicap of poverty, illiteracy, and ignorance. Within the inconceivably short period of ten years Mr. Ford mastered these three handicaps, and within twenty-five years he made himself one of the richest men in America.

How did he do it? Here is an important clue: Mr. Ford's most rapid strides became noticeable from the time he became a personal friend of the famed inventor Thomas A. Edison. In the story of Ford's success, this is just the first indication of what the influence of one mind upon another can accomplish. Follow his story further, and you will have even more evidence that power may be produced through friendly alliance of minds. It is a fact that Mr. Ford's most outstanding achievements became even more pronounced later, after he formed the acquaintances of Harvey Firestone, John Burroughs, and Luther Burbank (each a man of great mental capacity).

People take on the nature and the habits and the power of thought of those with whom they associate in a spirit of sympathy and harmony. Through his association with Edison, Burbank, Burroughs, and Firestone, Mr. Ford added to his own brainpower the intelligence, experience, knowledge, and spiritual forces of these four men. Henry Ford used the Master Mind principle in exactly the way it is described in this book.

This principle is available to you.

I have already mentioned Mahatma Gandhi. Let me review the method by which he attained his stupendous power. It may be explained in a few words. He came by power through inducing over two hundred million people to coordinate, with mind and body, in a spirit of harmony, for a definite purpose.

In brief, Gandhi accomplished a miracle, for it is a miracle when two hundred million people can be induced—not forced—to cooperate in a spirit of harmony. If you doubt that this is a miracle, try to get even two people to cooperate in a spirit of harmony for any length of time.

Every person who manages a business knows how difficult it is to get employees to work together in a spirit even remotely resembling harmony.

COMMENTARY

The first step in putting together your Master Mind alliance is to clearly know your desire. Your desire will tell you what you need. It could be a small group, just two or three people, as was the case with Steven Jobs and Steve Wozniak when they formed Apple; Bill Gates and Paul Allen launching Microsoft; or Steven Spielberg, Jeffrey Katzenberg, and David Geffen creating DreamWorks SKG. Or it could be a large group, such as the Master Mind alliance of thirty regional directors of Century 21 Real Estate, which founder Arthur Barlette firmly believes was essential to the company's success. Napoleon Hill suggests that in most cases it should be a dozen people or less, and generally the smaller the better.

Choosing the people means finding those who not only share your vision but who will also share their ideas, information, and contacts with you. They will let you use the full strength of their experience, training, and knowledge as if it were your own. And they will do it in a spirit of perfect harmony.

The question that immediately comes to every reader's mind is, "Where do I find people who will help me to that degree?" Napoleon Hill cannot answer that question for you, but he does tell you what to look for. Where you look is up to you. And if you really do have the desire to succeed, you will start looking and you won't give up until you find the right people.

Napoleon Hill's description of the Master Mind that appears below is augmented with additional material from articles and speeches he wrote after the publication of Think and Grow Rich. *These were compiled for publication by Hill's friend, mentor, and business associate, W. Clement Stone, and appear in two books,* Napoleon Hill's Keys to Success *and* Believe and Achieve.

Finding Your Master Mind Members

Ally yourself with a group of as many people as you may need in order to assemble a Master Mind that will assist you in creating and carrying out your plan or plans for the accumulation of money. Compliance with this instruction is absolutely essential.

NOTES & COMMENTS

Choose to associate with people who share common values, goals, and interests, yet who each have a strong desire to contribute to the overall effort. Trial and error will be part of the process, but there are two qualities to keep foremost in your mind.

The first is ability to do the job. Do not select people for your alliance merely because you know them and like them. Such people are valuable to you because they improve the quality of your life, but they are not necessarily suited to a Master Mind alliance. Your best friend may not be the most knowledgeable marketing professional, but perhaps he or she can introduce you to someone who is.

The second quality is the ability to work in a spirit of harmony with others. There must be a complete meeting of minds, without any reservations. Personal ambition must be subordinate to the achievement of the purpose of the alliance. This includes your own.

You must also insist upon confidentiality. Some people can give away an idea simply because they love to talk. You don't need them in your group.

Attune yourself to every member of the group. Try to imagine how you would react in a given situation if you were in his or her shoes.

Pay attention to body language. Sometimes facial expressions and movements say far more about what a person feels than the words that come out of his or her mouth.

Be sensitive to what is not being said. Sometimes what is left out is far more important than what is included.

Don't try to force the group along too quickly. Allow for those who want to test ideas by playing devil's advocate.

Compensating Your Master Mind

Before forming your Master Mind alliance, decide what advantages and benefits you may offer the individual members of your group in return for their cooperation. No one will work indefinitely without some form of compensation. No intelligent person should request or expect another to work without adequate compensation.

Wealth will obviously have the most appeal to your members. Be fair and generous in your offer.

Recognition and self-expression may be just as important as money to some of your members.

Remember that in such partnerships the principle of going the extra mile (doing more and better than paid for) is especially important. As the leader you should set an example for the others to follow.

Each member must agree at the outset on the contribution each will make, and on the division of benefits and profits. Otherwise, be assured that dissension will arise, you will have wasted everyone's time, you will ruin friendships, and your venture will be destroyed.

Meeting with Your Master Mind

Arrange to meet with the members of your Master Mind group at least twice a week, and more often if possible, until you have jointly perfected the necessary plan or plans for the accumulation of money.

The first meeting will be involved in sorting out strengths and weaknesses, and in fine-tuning your plans.

Your alliance must be active to do any good. Establish specific responsibilities and action steps to be taken.

As your Master Mind matures and harmony grows among the members, you will find that the meetings create a flow of ideas into every member's mind.

Don't let the meetings become so regular and formalized that they inhibit phone calls and other less formal contact.

Master Mind Maintenance

Maintain perfect harmony between yourself and every member of your Master Mind group. If you fail to carry out this instruction to the letter, you may expect to meet with failure. The Master Mind principle cannot work where perfect harmony does not prevail.

Create a nonthreatening environment. Explore all ideas with equal interest and concern for the originator's feelings.

Everyone must deal with everyone else on a completely ethical basis. No member should seek unfair advantage at the expense of others.

As the leader you must inspire confidence in your members by your dedication to your desire—which is the object of the group. The members must know with certainty that you are reliable, trustworthy, and loyal.

When you are finally ready to present the results of your efforts to investors, buyers, or the public, you may face your greatest leadership challenge in maintaining the harmony of your Master Mind. The group's efforts will now be judged by outsiders, and facing judgment takes courage and persistence. The courage of separate individuals is nothing compared with that of a united team. The more you are able to maintain harmony, the greater the power. And the greater the power, the more resistance you can overcome.

Marriage and the Master Mind

A Master Mind alliance with the person you love most deeply is of untold importance. If you are married and have not built your relationship on the same principles of harmony that are crucial to any alliance, you may have some reselling to do with your spouse. Set aside time each day to talk about what you want to achieve and how you are going about it. Rely on your definiteness of purpose to build your persuasive abilities to convince your partner of the benefits of the work you are doing. It is very unlikely that your work will not affect your husband or wife in some significant way, and you absolutely must not drag your partner unwillingly into any adventure.

Build your Master Mind alliance into your marriage from the start, and it will steady and support you through the darkest moments. In fact, your whole family should be incorporated into your alliance. Lack of harmony at home can easily spill over elsewhere. A united family is a great team.

The Master Mind and Infinite Intelligence

The list of sources from which you can get power is headed by Infinite Intelligence. When two or more people coordinate in a spirit of harmony, and work toward a definite objective, they place themselves in position to absorb power directly from that great universal storehouse that I refer to as Infinite Intelligence. This is the greatest of all sources of power. It is the source to which geniuses and great leaders turn (whether they may be conscious of the fact or not).

In chapter 13, The Subconscious Mind, and chapter 14, The Brain, the methods for accessing Infinite Intelligence will be described in greater detail.

This is not a course on religion. Neither the principle of Infinite Intelligence nor any other principle in this book should be interpreted as interfering with, endorsing, or rejecting any person's religious beliefs. This book is confined, exclusively, to instructing the reader how to transmute the definite purpose of desire for money into its monetary equivalent.

Read, and really think about what you are reading. Soon the entire subject will unfold and you will see it in perspective. At this point you are only seeing the detail of the individual chapters.

COMMENTARY

This chapter would not be complete without commenting on a Master Mind that came into being almost fifteen years after the first publication of Think and Grow Rich—*Napoleon Hill's own Master Mind alliance with multimillionaire businessman and philanthropist, W. Clement Stone.*

NOTES & COMMENTS

NOTES & COMMENTS

On May 2, 1951, at the age of 67, Napoleon Hill and his wife, Annie Lou, agreed it was time for Napoleon to think about retiring. They decided to begin by cutting back on his speaking engagements after he completed the lectures that were already on his calendar, including one he was scheduled to give a few weeks later in Chicago. Unbeknownst to them, at that event W. Clement Stone had prearranged to sit at the head table next to Napoleon Hill.

Like Hill, Stone had been born into poverty. At the age of six he started selling newspapers to help pay the rent, and by thirteen he owned his own stand. By sixteen he was selling insurance and by twenty he'd managed to scrape together $100, which he used to start his own insurance agency. Stone was a consummate salesman and motivator, and his company was growing very nicely. Then in 1938 he read Think and Grow Rich *and was so inspired by it that he bought a copy for every one of his employees, and continued to do so for each new person who joined his company. Over the years this amounted to thousands of copies.*

When Stone was introduced to Hill, he told him about all the copies he had purchased of Think and Grow Rich, *and said that he firmly believed it was Hill's book that had transformed his sales force and turned his company from modest to extraordinary success.*

Napoleon Hill and W. Clement Stone found that they were in such complete accord that by the end of their first meeting Hill had decided to postpone his retirement and join with Stone in a venture dedicated to "creating a better world for this and future generations." Within a year they launched Napoleon Hill Associates; they published new books by Hill including How to Raise Your Own Salary *and* The Master Key to Riches; *they reissued Hill's earlier bestsellers; and they co-authored a new bestseller,* Success Through a Positive Mental Attitude. *They also launched* Success Unlimited *magazine, created* PMA Science of Success *home-study courses, made television programs, radio shows, a documentary film—*A New Sound in Paris, *which showed the amazing changes that happened when the entire town of Paris, Missouri, adopted the Napoleon Hill philosophy—and they both crisscrossed America speaking,* *teaching, giving interviews, and spreading the philosophy to as many people as possible.*

In addition to his work with Napoleon Hill Associates, Hill also consulted to W. Clement Stone's company, Combined Insurance Company of America. Hill designed and implemented a new training program for the sales force which was so successful he astounded the business world by helping Stone grow his company from $30 million in assets to $100 million in less than ten years. When W. Clement Stone passed away in 2002, his company, now known as AON Corporation, had revenues of $2 billion a year. W. Clement Stone had personally given more than $275 million to various charitable and philanthropic organizations.

There has perhaps never been a greater example of "coordination of knowledge and effort, in a spirit of harmony, between two or more people for the attainment of a definite purpose." The sheer volume of work and scope of influence achieved in a ten-year period by Napoleon Hill and W. Clement Stone leaves little question as to the power and importance of a Master Mind alliance.

THE POWER OF POSITIVE EMOTIONS

Money is shy and elusive. It must be wooed and won by methods not unlike those used by a determined lover. And the power you use in the wooing of money is not greatly different from what you use to attract the one you love. It is the power of positive emotion. That power, when successfully used in the pursuit of money, must be mixed with faith. It must be mixed with desire. It must be mixed with persistence. It must be applied through a plan, and that plan must be set into action.

When money comes in large quantities, it flows to the one who accumulates it as easily as water flows downhill. There exists a great, unseen stream of power, which may be compared to a river that

NOTES & COMMENTS

flows in two directions. One side flows in one direction, carrying all who get into that side of the stream onward and upward to wealth. The other side flows in the opposite direction, carrying all who are unfortunate enough to get into it (and can't pull themselves out) downward to misery and poverty.

Everyone who has accumulated a great fortune has recognized the existence of this stream of life. It consists of one's thinking process. Positive emotions form the side of the stream that carries you to fortune. Negative emotions form the side that carries you down to poverty.

This is a point of great importance to the person who is following this book with the object of accumulating a fortune.

If you are caught in the side of the stream of power that leads to poverty, this book will serve as an oar by which you may propel yourself over into the other side of the stream. But it can serve you only through application and use. Merely reading and passing judgment on it, either one way or another, will be of no benefit to you.

Poverty and riches can change places. But when riches take the place of poverty, the change only happens through well-conceived and carefully executed plans. The same is not true of poverty. Poverty needs no plan. It needs no one to help it, because it is bold and ruthless. Riches are shy and timid. They have to be "attracted."

MORE GOLD HAS BEEN MINED

FROM THE THOUGHTS OF MEN

THAN HAS EVER BEEN TAKEN

FROM THE EARTH.

SEXUALITY

CHARISMA AND CREATIVITY

The Tenth Step Toward Riches

COMMENTARY

What motivates human beings is the subject of continuing scientific research and philosophical debate. There is general agreement that the prime motivators are the basic human needs for food and water, shelter and clothing, and safety. Beyond these basic life-sustaining needs, however, there are other factors that motivate people to action. It is the definition of the other factors, and their order of importance, that continues to be open to interpretation.

Probably the most widely known theory is psychologist Abraham Maslow's Hierarchy of Human Needs, which lists eight levels of motivational forces starting with the basic physiological and safety needs, then ascends through belonging and love, esteem, understanding, aesthetics, self-actualization, and transcendence. Other psychologists and sociologists have defined and arranged the categories differently, but in almost all cases there is agreement that after the primary life-sustaining needs are met, sex and love are the next most important motivating forces.

NOTES & COMMENTS

Napoleon Hill also compiled a hierarchy of what he referred to as mind stimuli. Like Maslow and other researchers, Hill identified sex and love as the most powerful non-life-sustaining factors in human motivation. But his focus was not on sex and love as they pertain to procreation. Hill was intrigued by the theory that if sex and love are such powerful forces in driving humans to action, there might be a correlation to outstanding achievement or material success. And if such a relationship exists, can the motivating force be intentionally channeled to this purpose?

In the original edition of the following chapter, Hill used terms such as "sex emotion" and "sex energy" in his analysis of these motivating forces as they relate to attitude and personality. In this context the use of the word sex was not meant to have the physical connotation that it often has today. Today these concepts would be conveyed by words such as "sexuality," "passion," or "charisma." In this edition, where appropriate, the editors have opted for the modern usage of these and similar terms.

CHARISMA

The world is ruled, and the destiny of civilization is established, by the human emotions. People are influenced more by feelings than by reason. Your creativity is set into action entirely by emotions, and not by cold reason.

The human mind responds to stimuli, through which it may be "keyed up" in such a way that it takes on characteristics such as enthusiasm, creative imagination, and intense desire. The stimuli to which the mind responds most freely are:

1. The desire for sexual expression

2. Love

3. A burning desire for fame, power, or financial gain; money

4. Music

5. Close friendship and/or admiration

6. A Master Mind alliance based upon the harmony of two or more people who ally themselves for advancement

7. Mutual suffering, such as that experienced by people who are persecuted

8. Autosuggestion

9. Fear

10. Alcohol and drugs

The desire for sexual expression comes at the head of the list of stimuli that "step up" the mind and start the "wheels" of physical action. The emotions associated with the human sexual drive bring into being a state of mind. When motivated by this desire, people often show courage, willpower, persistence, imagination, and creative ability that they don't normally have. So strong and impelling is the desire for sexual expression that people freely run the risk of life and reputation because of it.

A river may be dammed and its water controlled for a time, but eventually it will force an outlet. The same is true of the emotions related to sexual expression. It may be submerged and controlled for a time, but its very nature causes it to be ever seeking means of expression.

The desire for sexual expression is inborn and natural. The desire cannot, and should not, be submerged or eliminated, but it can be given other outlets that enrich the body, mind, and spirit. When harnessed and redirected, this motivating force has been used as a powerful creative force in literature, art, and other pursuits, including the accumulation of riches.

A teacher, who has trained more than thirty thousand salespeople, came to the conclusion that individuals who are most confident

NOTES & COMMENTS

sexually are the most efficient salespeople. The explanation is that the factor of personality known as "personal magnetism" is a manifestation of sexual energy.

COMMENTARY

There have been numerous psychological and sociological studies about the relationship between sexuality and success that tend to support Hill's observation. Because physical characteristics are the most quantifiable aspects of sexuality, most research studies focus on gender, attractiveness, body size, and age, and they measure indicators such as first impressions, expectation of performance, perception of performance, and social interaction. These studies generally conclude that when comparing individuals of equal competence, for men the perception is that taller men will do better than short, a full head of hair will outperform balding, handsome or virile will beat out plain or older. For women the results are comparable. The perception is that attractive performs better than plain, slim or shapely scores higher than overweight, younger is expected to be superior to older.

These observations about physical sexuality may seem obvious, but they lead to a conclusion that is very significant. Obviously not all people who succeed are tall and virile or attractive and shapely. It is also a fact that the success of those who are short, balding, plump, or plain isn't always due to superior skill or luck. Clearly there is another kind of attractiveness that often supercedes physical appeal.

This other kind of attractiveness is connected to human sexuality, but it is not what would usually be referred to as "sexy." People who have this quality are often said to have "chemistry," "personality," "charm," or "appeal." Hill called this kind of attraction "personal magnetism." Today the more common term is charisma.

When employing salespeople, a good sales manager looks for personal magnetism or charisma as the first requirement. People who lack this kind of sexual energy will never become enthusiastic nor inspire others with enthusiasm. And enthusiasm is one of the most important requisites in salesmanship, no matter what you are selling.

The public speaker, preacher, lawyer, or salesperson who is lacking in charisma is a flop, as far as being able to influence others is concerned. That, plus the fact that most people are influenced through an appeal to their emotions, should easily convince you of the importance of charisma as a part of the salesperson's ability. Master salespeople attain mastery in selling because they either consciously or unconsciously transmute charisma (sexual energy) into sales enthusiasm.

That statement explains the actual, practical meaning of sexual transmutation.

The meaning of the word *transmute* is, in simple language, "the changing, or transferring, of one element or form of energy into another." The transmutation of sexual energy means switching the mind from thoughts of physical expression, to thoughts of some other nature.

Salespeople who know how to turn on charisma have acquired the art of sexual transmutation, whether they know it or not. The majority of salespeople who transmute their sexual energy do so without being aware of what they are doing, or how they are doing it.

You can cultivate and develop this quality in your dealings with others. Through cultivation and understanding, this vital motivating force may be drawn upon and used to great advantage in relationships between people. This energy may be communicated to others in the following ways:

1. *The handshake.* The touch of the hand indicates, instantly, the presence of charisma or the lack of it.

2. *The tone of voice.* Charisma, or sexual energy, is the factor with which the voice may be colored or made musical and charming.

3. *Posture and carriage of the body.* People with charisma move briskly, and with grace and ease.

4. *The vibrations of thought.* People with charisma project sexuality through their personality in a way that influences those around them.

5. *Clothing and style.* People who are charismatic are usually very careful about their personal appearance. They usually select clothing of a style becoming to their personality, physique, complexion, etc.

COMMENTARY

Having established a link between sexuality and success in the form of charisma, in the following section Napoleon Hill explores how sexuality might also be a motivating factor in success by enhancing creativity. To illustrate the connection, Hill draws upon the biographies of historical figures who exhibited both charisma and exceptional creativity.

In the time since Hill conducted his research, many women have risen to positions of power and influence. Their accomplishments have been well documented and are readily available in bookstores and libraries. However, when Hill was assembling his data, the majority of historical biographies available were about successful men. Further, the successful industrialists and political leaders he had personally studied during the previous thirty years were also men. Because of this limitation, Hill does not theorize about the role men might play in motivating the success of women. This issue is addressed in a later editorial comment.

CREATIVITY

It seemed quite significant to me when I made the discovery that practically every great leader I had the privilege of analyzing was a man whose achievements were largely inspired by a woman. In most instances the woman was a wife, of whom the public had heard little or nothing. In a few of the cases I studied, the source of inspiration was "the other woman."

The pages of history are filled with the records of great men whose achievements may be traced directly to the influence of women who aroused the creative faculties of their minds. Napoleon Bonaparte was one of these. When inspired by his first wife, Josephine, he was irresistible and invincible. When his "better judgment" or reasoning faculty prompted him to put Josephine aside, he began to decline. His defeat and exile to St. Helena were not far distant.

Abraham Lincoln was a notable example of a great leader who achieved his greatness through the discovery and use of his faculty of creative imagination. It is noted in practically every book written about Lincoln, that he discovered and began to use this faculty as the result of the love that he experienced when he met Anne Rutledge. This is more than an interesting historical fact; it is of significance in connection with the role sexuality plays in the study of the source of genius.

Following is a list of famous men of outstanding achievement:

George Washington

Napoleon Bonaparte

William Shakespeare

Abraham Lincoln

Ralph Waldo Emerson

Robert Burns

Thomas Jefferson

Elbert Hubbard

NOTES & COMMENTS

Elbert H. Gary

Woodrow Wilson

John H. Patterson

Andrew Jackson

Enrico Caruso

Wherever there was evidence available in connection with the lives of these men of achievement, it indicated most convincingly that each possessed a highly developed sexual nature. An analysis of the information taken from biographies and historical writings leads to the following conclusions:

1. Those of greatest achievement have a highly developed sexual nature but have learned the art of transmutation of sexual energy.

2. Those who have accumulated great fortunes and achieved outstanding recognition in literature, art, industry, architecture, and the professions were motivated by the influence of a mate or lover.

When driven by these emotions, people become gifted with a super power for action. If you understand this, you will also understand that sexual transmutation contains the secret of creative ability.

COMMENTARY

As noted previously, although Hill's analysis focused on men, today there is a wide range of biographies about women who have succeeded in every aspect of life including business, politics, religion, sports, entertainment, and the arts. Bearing in mind that biographical information is always subjective, the reader can now find ample material from which to draw a conclusion as to whether Hill's theory about sexuality as a motivating force is equally evident in women.

Napoleon Hill had to do an in-depth analysis of biographies in searching for indications that the subject's sexuality had a correlation to their success. Today we just turn on the television and we're inundated with intimate details about both men and women suggesting that the best and the brightest are apparently also the sexiest. Although scandals aren't usually cited as scientific proof, the exposés of some of the biggest entertainment and sports stars, high-profile CEOs of major companies, numerous politicians, and even a few presidents, all make at least a common-sense case for Hill's theory about the correlation between sexuality and success.

Obviously this does not mean that everyone who is highly sexed is a genius. People attain the status of a genius only when, and if, they stimulate their minds so that they can draw upon the forces available, through the creative faculty of the imagination. Although it is the most important of the stimuli or motivators, the mere possession of sexual energy is not sufficient to produce a genius. The energy must be transmuted from desire for physical contact into some other form of desire and action before it will lift one to the status of a genius.

GENIUS AND CREATIVE IMAGINATION

A definition of genius might be: "Someone who has discovered how to increase the intensity of thought to the point where that person can freely communicate with sources of knowledge not available through the ordinary rate of thought.

This definition should prompt some questions in the mind of anyone reading this book. The first question should be, "How may one communicate with sources of knowledge that are not available through ordinary thought?" The next question should be, "Are there known sources of knowledge that are available only to geniuses, and if so, what are these sources and exactly how may they be reached?"

NOTES & COMMENTS

In the following I will offer methods so that you can experiment and prove to yourself that this is true. By doing so, you will have the answer to both questions.

COMMENTARY

Humans perceive things through the five senses of sight, smell, taste, hearing, and touch. Another kind of perception, as when you "have a feeling" about something, was discussed in the chapters on desire, faith, and autosuggestion. This kind of perception is often referred to as the sixth sense, and in the following Hill explores the relationship between sexuality, motivation, creative imagination, and the sixth sense.

The reality of a "sixth sense" has been fairly well established. This sixth sense is *creative imagination*. The faculty of creative imagination is something the majority of people never use during an entire lifetime. And, if they do use it, it usually happens by mere accident. Only a small number of people deliberately use their creative imagination for a specific purpose. Those who do use this faculty voluntarily, and with understanding of its functions, are geniuses.

Creative imagination is the direct link between your finite mind and what I have termed Infinite Intelligence. All revelations, and all discoveries of basic or new principles in the field of invention, take place through the faculty of creative imagination.

When ideas, concepts, or hunches flash into your mind, they can only have come from one or more of the following sources:

1. From the mind of some other person who has just released the thought, idea, or concept, through conscious thought

2. Your subconscious mind, which stores every thought and impression that ever reached your brain through any of the five senses

3. From another person's subconscious storehouse

4. Infinite Intelligence

There are no other possible sources from which "inspired" ideas or "hunches" may be received.

When brain action has been stimulated, through one or more of the ten mind stimulants listed at the beginning of this chapter, it has the effect of lifting you far above the horizon of ordinary thought. It permits you to envision distance, scope, and quality of thoughts not available on the lower plane, such as when you are solving routine problems of business.

When you are lifted to a higher level of thought, through mind ✳ stimulation, it is as though you have taken off in an airplane. You can now see over and beyond the horizon that limits your vision when you are on the ground. Not only that, but while you are on this higher level of thought, you are not even aware of such things as the problems of gaining the three basic necessities of food, clothing, and shelter. You are in a world of thought in which the ordinary, work-a-day thoughts have been removed, just as the hills and valleys that obstruct your vision on the ground don't interfere when you are in an airplane.

While on this exalted plane of thought, the creative faculty of the mind is given freedom for action. The way has been cleared for the sixth sense to function. It becomes receptive to ideas that could not reach the individual under any other circumstances. The sixth sense is the faculty that marks the difference between a genius and an ordinary individual.

Developing Your Creative Imagination

A mind stimulant is any influence that will either temporarily or permanently increase the intensity of thought. The previously mentioned ten major stimulants are those most commonly resorted to. Through these sources you may commune with Infinite Intelligence, enter the storehouse of your subconscious mind, or perhaps even that of another person. That is all there is to genius.

The more you use your creative faculty, the more alert and receptive it becomes to factors originating outside your conscious mind. And the more this creative faculty is used, the more you will rely upon it for your thoughts and ideas. This faculty can be cultivated and developed only through use.

What we generally refer to as our "conscience" operates entirely through the faculty of the sixth sense.

The great artists, writers, musicians, and poets become great because they acquire the habit of relying upon the "still small voice" that speaks from within, through their creative imagination. Anyone with a keen imagination knows that some of their best ideas come through so-called "hunches."

One of the best-known public speakers admits that his speeches are only really great when he closes his eyes and begins to rely entirely upon the faculty of creative imagination. When asked why he closed his eyes just before the climax of his speech, he replied, "I do it because then I speak through ideas that come to me from within."

One of America's most successful and best-known financiers has the habit of closing his eyes for two or three minutes before making a decision. When asked why, he replied, "With my eyes closed, I am able to draw upon a source of superior intelligence."

Dr. Elmer R. Gates created more than two hundred useful patents through the process of cultivating and using his creative faculty. His method is both significant and interesting to anyone interested in attaining to the status of genius. Dr. Gates was one of the really great, though less publicized, scientists of the world.

In his laboratory he had what he called his "personal communication room." It was practically soundproof, and all light could be shut out. It had a small table on which he kept a pad of writing paper. In front of the table, on the wall, was a light switch. When Dr. Gates desired to draw upon the forces available to him through his creative imagination, he would go into this room, seat himself at the table, shut off the lights, and concentrate on the known factors of the invention he was working on. He would stay in that position until ideas began to "flash" into his mind in connection with the unknown factors of the invention.

On one occasion, ideas came through so fast that he was forced to write for almost three hours. When the thoughts stopped flowing, he examined his notes and found they contained a minute description of principles that had no parallel in the known data of the scientific world. Moreover, the answer to his problem was right there in those notes.

Dr. Gates earned his living by "sitting for ideas." He did it for individuals and corporations, and some of the most sensible people and largest traditional corporations in America paid him to do it.

The part of your mind that you generally use for reasoning may be faulty, because it is largely guided by your accumulated experience. Not all knowledge that you have learned through experience is accurate. Many times your "creative" ideas are much more reliable because they come from sources that are more reliable than those available to the reasoning faculty of the mind.

Methods Used by Geniuses Are Available to You

The major difference between the genius and the ordinary inventor is that the genius makes use of both the synthesized and the creative faculties of imagination. For example, the scientific inventor begins an invention by organizing and combining the known ideas, or principles accumulated through experience, through the synthesized faculty (the reasoning faculty). If this accumulated knowledge is found to be insufficient, the inventor then draws upon the sources of knowledge available through the creative faculty. The method by which the inventor does this varies with the individual, but this is the essence of the procedure:

1. The inventor stimulates his or her mind so that it functions on a higher-than-average plane, through one or more of the mind stimulants.

2. The inventor then concentrates on the known factors (the finished part) of the invention and creates in his or her mind a perfect picture of the unknown factors (the unfinished part of the invention). The inventor holds this picture in mind until it has been taken over by the subconscious mind, then relaxes by clearing his or her mind of all thought and waits for the answer to "flash" into mind.

Sometimes the results are both definite and immediate. At other times the results are negative, depending on the state of development of the sixth sense, or creative faculty.

Thomas Edison tried out more than ten thousand different combinations of ideas through the synthetic faculty of his imagination before he "tuned in" through the creative faculty and got the answer that perfected the incandescent light bulb. His experience was similar when he produced the phonograph.

COMMENTARY

Synchronicity, precognition, intuition, flashes of insight, hunches, gut feelings, symbolic dreams, these are all aspects of the phenomenon Napoleon Hill was describing in his two correlated terms, creative imagination and Infinite Intelligence. And the fact that Hill made a serious study of this function of the mind puts him in exceptional company.

The fathers of modern psychology, Sigmund Freud and Carl Jung, recognized and tried to explain this sixth sense. Jung's concept of the collective unconscious, which is the very basis of Jungian psychology, is in many ways identical to Hill's concept of Infinite Intelligence. Scientists from Archimedes to Newton to Einstein to the team of Watson and Crick who determined the structure of DNA, all conceded that intuition was instrumental in their discoveries. Duke University created a department for the sole purpose of studying these phenomena under scientific conditions.

Many scientists admit to using personalized techniques similar to Hill's method for accessing intuition and creativity. These include Friedrich Kekulé who discovered the molecular structure of benzene through a dream symbol, physiologist Otto Loewi who had a hunch followed by a dream that won him the Nobel prize for medicine, and, as mentioned above, James Watson's breakthrough in the structure of DNA.

Mozart, Shelley, Coleridge, Huxley, Descartes, Robert Louis Stevenson all claimed intuition played a role in their creations. William Blake learned the secret to a copper-engraving process from a dream. British prime minister Winston Churchill firmly believed a premonition saved him from being killed by a bomb during the blitz of London.

As was noted earlier, psychiatry, clinical hypnosis, and affirmations all had to overcome considerable skepticism before they were accepted. That is also true of those phenomena Hill terms Infinite Intelligence. However, in the 1970s and 80s the public's interest was piqued by well-researched books such as The Intuitive Edge *by Philip Goldberg,* Creative Dreaming *by Patricia Garfield, and* The Right-Brain Experience *by Marilee Zdenek. Though these anomalies of the mind still defy laboratory proof, contemporary researchers continue to publish tantalizing results.*

Nature has equipped the human brain and mind with internal stimulants that safely trigger the mind to tune in to fine and rare thoughts. No satisfactory substitute for Nature's stimulants has ever been found.

However, history is not lacking in examples of people who rose to the status of genius as the result of using artificial mind-stimulants. Edgar Allan Poe wrote *The Raven* while under the influence of alcohol, "dreaming dreams no mortal ever dared to dream before." Samuel Taylor Coleridge wrote *Kubla Khan* during an opium-induced dream, and Robert Burns wrote best when intoxicated. "For Auld Lang Syne, my dear, we'll take a cup of kindness yet, for Auld Lang Syne."

It is true that these and others who are known as geniuses relied upon artificial mind-stimulation, but a more important lesson to remember is how many of these people destroyed themselves through the use of those stimulants.

COMMENTARY

In more contemporary terms, Hill's point about the dangers of artificial mind-stimulants was never better made than it was in the television series Behind the Music *which began running on VH1 in the late 1990s. The series was meant to chronicle the lives of rock stars and celebrate their hits, but after viewing two or three of the shows, they all began to look the same: Young singer and band have a hit record, make millions of dollars, plunge into the sex-drugs-and-rock'n'roll lifestyle, everyone gets addicted, and they blow all of the money. By the end of the show at least one band member overdoses, the band breaks up, the singer hits the skids, meets someone who inspires him or her to go into rehab, the ex-star makes an antidrug TV spot and professes newfound faith and family values while announcing a comeback tour.*

Although the shows played like a bad parody of themselves, the fact that the stories were so similar, that so many talented singers and songwriters who depended on drugs ended up burning out, should be telling you something. Especially if you don't just want to succeed but want to keep and enjoy your success.

Every intelligent person knows that stimulation in excess, through alcohol or drugs, is a destructive form of intemperance. For some, overindulgence in sexual expression may become just as destructive. A sexually obsessed person is not essentially different from a person addicted to drugs or alcohol. Both have lost control over their faculties of reason and willpower.

Human sexuality is a mighty urge to action, but its forces are like a cyclone—almost impossible to completely control. When an individual is driven solely by emotions related to sexuality, that person may be capable of great achievement but their actions are often disorganized and destructive.

It is true that a person may pursue financial or business success by harnessing the driving force of sexual energy without self-control. But history is filled with evidence that such people likely have certain traits of character that rob them of the ability to either hold or enjoy their fortunes. Ignorance of this potential pitfall has cost thousands of people their happiness, even though they possessed riches.

From my analysis of over twenty-five thousand people, I found that those who succeed in an outstanding way often do not hit their stride until they are beyond the age of forty or fifty. This fact was so astounding that it prompted me to go into the study of its cause most carefully.

My investigation disclosed that the major reason why many people do not succeed early in life is their tendency to dissipate their energies through over indulgence. The majority of people never learn that sexual energy has possibilities other than physical expression. And many of those who make this discovery only do so after having wasted many years during the time when their sexual energy was at its height.

Most people come to the realization by accident, and many don't even know they have tapped into this power. They may recognize that their power of achievement has increased, but they have no idea what caused the change. They are just vaguely aware that nature begins to harmonize the emotions of love and sex, so that they may draw upon these great forces and apply them as stimuli to action.

THE IMPORTANCE OF LOVE

Love, romance, and sex are all emotions capable of driving people to heights of super achievement. When combined, these three emotions may lift you to an altitude of a genius.

Every person who has been moved by genuine love knows that it leaves enduring traces upon the human heart. The effect of love endures, because love is spiritual in nature. Those who cannot be stimulated to great heights of achievement by love, are hopeless—they are dead, though they may seem to live.

If you believe you are unfortunate because you have loved and lost, you are wrong. One who has loved truly can never lose entirely. Love is whimsical and temperamental. It comes when it pleases, and goes away without warning. Accept and enjoy it while it remains, but spend no time worrying about its departure. Worry will never bring it back.

Dismiss the thought that love only comes once. Love may come and go times without number, but there are no two love experiences that affect you in just the same way. There may be one love experience that leaves a deeper imprint on the heart than all the others, but all love experiences are beneficial except to the person who becomes resentful and cynical when love makes its departure.

Even the memories of love can lift you and stimulate your mind. Go back into your yesterdays, at times, and bathe your mind in the beautiful memories of past love. It will soften your worries and give you a source of escape from the unpleasant realities of life. And maybe, during this temporary retreat into the world of fantasy, your subconscious mind will yield to you ideas or plans that may change the entire financial or spiritual status of your life.

There should be no disappointment over love, and there would be none if people understood the difference between the emotions of love and sex. Love is an emotion of many shades and colors, but the most intense and burning of all is that experienced in the blending of the emotions of love and sex.

Marriages or committed relationships that are not blessed with love properly balanced with sex cannot be happy ones—and seldom endure. Love alone will not bring happiness, nor will sex alone. Love is spiritual. Sex is biological. No experience that touches the human heart with a spiritual force can possibly be harmful, except through ignorance or jealousy.

The presence of destructive emotions in the human mind may poison it in a way that destroys your sense of justice and fairness. Just as a chemist can take certain chemical elements—none of which are harmful in themselves—and by mixing them together create a deadly poison, in a similar manner the emotions of sex and jealousy, when mixed, may turn just as lethal.

Love is the emotion that serves as a safety valve and brings balance, reason, and constructive effort. Love is, without question, life's greatest experience. It can bring you into communion with Infinite Intelligence. When love guides the emotions it may lead you well on your way toward creative effort.

The road to genius consists of the development, control, and use of sex, love, and romance. Briefly, the process may be stated as follows:

Encourage the presence of the positive emotions as the dominating thoughts in your mind, and discourage all the destructive emotions. The mind is a creature of habit. It thrives on the dominating thoughts fed to it. Through your willpower you may discourage the presence of any emotion and encourage the presence of any other. Control of your mind, through the power of your will, is not difficult. Control comes from persistence and habit. The secret of control lies in understanding the process of transmutation. When any negative emotion presents itself in your mind, it can be transmuted into a positive or constructive emotion by the simple procedure of changing your thoughts. There is no other road to genius than through voluntary self-effort.

When the emotion of romance is added to those of love and sex, the obstructions between the finite mind and Infinite Intelligence are removed. Then a genius has been born!

SUCCESS REQUIRES NO EXPLANATIONS.

FAILURE PERMITS NO ALIBIS.

THE SUBCONSCIOUS MIND

THE CONNECTING LINK

The Eleventh Step Toward Riches

The subconscious mind consists of a field of consciousness in which every impulse of thought that reaches the conscious mind, through any of the five senses, is classified and recorded. The subconscious receives and files sense impressions or thoughts regardless of their nature.

You can plant in your subconscious mind any plan, thought, or purpose that you desire to translate into its physical or monetary equivalent. Those desires that have been mixed with emotional feeling, and faith in your ability, are the ones that are strongest. Therefore they are the first to which the subconscious responds.

The subconscious mind works day and night, and in some way which is not fully understood, the subconscious seems able to draw upon the forces of Infinite Intelligence for the power to transmute your desires into their physical equivalent. And it does it in the most straightforward and practical way.

$52\overline{)100,000}$

$3 \times 52 = 156$

$160 - 156 = 4$

NOTES & COMMENTS

$100,000 by 12/31/2010

earn average of

$1,923/week

You cannot entirely control your subconscious mind, but you can hand over to it any plan, desire, or purpose that you wish transformed into concrete form. Refer again to the instructions for using the subconscious mind, in chapter 5, Autosuggestion.

COMMENTARY

In the chapter on autosuggestion, the four primary methods for planting and reinforcing suggestions in your subconscious are: (1) by formulation and writing-out of your desire, (2) by repetition of positive affirmations, (3) by creative visualization of your goal, and (4) by acting as though the goal is already yours.

From my research, I have concluded that the subconscious mind is the connecting link between the finite mind of man and Infinite Intelligence. It is the intermediary through which you may draw upon the forces of Infinite Intelligence. Only the subconscious mind contains the process by which mental impulses (thoughts) are modified and changed into their spiritual (energy) equivalent. It alone is the medium through which prayer (desire) may be transmitted to the source capable of answering prayer (Infinite Intelligence).

HOW TO ENERGIZE YOUR SUBCONSCIOUS MIND FOR CREATIVE EFFORT

The possibilities of what you can do when you connect creative effort with the subconscious mind are stupendous. They inspire me with awe.

I never approach the discussion of the subconscious mind without a feeling of littleness and inferiority due to the fact that man's entire stock of knowledge on this subject is so pitifully limited.

First, you must accept as a reality the existence of the subconscious mind and what it can do for you. This will enable you to understand its possibilities as a medium for transmuting your desires into their physical or monetary equivalent, and then you will comprehend the full significance of the instructions given in chapter 3, Desire. You will also understand the importance of making your desires clear and putting them in writing. You will understand, as well, the necessity of persistence in carrying out instructions.

The thirteen principles that are the basis of this book are the stimuli with which you acquire the ability to reach and to influence your subconscious mind. Do not become discouraged if you cannot do this on your first attempt. Remember that the subconscious mind can be directed only through habit. You have not yet had time to master faith. Be patient. Be persistent.

COMMENTARY

There are two aspects to Hill's theory of the subconscious mind. One is the concept of the subconscious as the storehouse of all information and thoughts that you have ever experienced. The second is the concept of the subconscious as the gateway to Infinite Intelligence. In this chapter Hill focuses primarily on the subconscious as a storehouse.

Expanding on the editorial comment about the subconscious mind that appears in the chapter on autosuggestion, proof that the subconscious is a storehouse of information is confirmed in the use of hypnotherapy by psychiatrists. Through hypnosis, psychiatrists are able to help patients open the door to their subconscious so that they can retrieve information about traumatic situations that have been filtered out or repressed by the conscious mind. Further proof is in the use of hypnosis by law enforcement officials to recapture information such as license plate numbers and other details that the conscious mind of a witness has filtered out. Although results vary from person to person, there is no doubt that the subconscious has access to information that the conscious mind does not.

This "storehouse" aspect of the subconscious is what accounts for some ideas that come to us through creative imagination. In some instances, bits of information and ideas that our conscious mind has forgotten will connect with

NOTES & COMMENTS

each other on a subconscious level to create a new idea, and that idea will be received by our creative intelligence, which presents it to us as a flash of inspiration.

You can't completely control this process, but you can condition yourself to come up with more and better ideas. It is a fact that a traumatic experience—the result of which creates a strongly planted idea—can influence the way a person thinks and acts. If that is true, then by intentionally using all of your efforts to powerfully plant an idea in your subconscious, you should be able to create what would amount to a "good" traumatic experience that will influence the way you think and act, in a positive way. This is exactly how you develop what Hill calls a money consciousness.

If you do everything within your power to strongly, firmly, and with complete faith and conviction, plant the idea that you will be successful and achieve your desire, your subconscious will accept and store that idea. If you have planted the idea so strongly that it is the dominant idea in your subconscious, it will influence all of the other ideas and information stored there. When you have given your subconscious this specific direction that it did not have before, it will begin to put together pieces of information, and through your creative intelligence you will find that you are coming up with more and better plans and ideas to accomplish your goal.

But, as Hill says, you can do this only through faith and habit. You must write out the affirmation of your goal, and you must repeat it aloud every day, with absolute faith and conviction that you can achieve it. You must vividly and creatively visualize yourself achieving your goal, and you must do it every day. You must conduct yourself with the attitude that says you can accomplish your goal, and that you deserve the help of those who can help you to accomplish your goal, and you must conduct yourself in that way every day.

If you seriously commit yourself to doing these things, it will change the way you think and act, your subconscious will do everything it can to transmute your desire into reality, and other people will want to do what they can to help you succeed.

Many statements in the chapters on faith and on autosuggestion are repeated here for the benefit of your subconscious mind. Remember, your subconscious mind functions whether you make any effort to influence it or not. This means that thoughts of fear, poverty, and all negative ideas will affect your subconscious mind unless you master these impulses and give it more desirable food on which it may feed.

The subconscious mind will not remain idle. If you don't plant desires in your subconscious mind, it will feed on the thoughts that reach it as the result of your neglect. Both negative and positive thoughts are reaching your subconscious mind continuously. These thoughts come from four sources: (1) consciously from other people, (2) your subconscious, (3) subconsciously from other people, and (4) Infinite Intelligence.

Every day all kinds of thought impulses are reaching your subconscious mind without your knowledge. Some of these impulses are negative, some are positive. Right now you should be specifically trying to shut off the flow of negative impulses, and actively working to influence your subconscious mind through positive impulses of desire.

When you achieve this, you will possess the key that unlocks the door to your subconscious mind. Moreover, you will control that door so completely that no undesirable thought may influence your subconscious mind.

Everything that you create begins in the form of a thought impulse. You can create nothing that you do not first conceive as a thought. Through the aid of the imagination, thoughts may be assembled into plans. The imagination, when under your control, may be used to create plans or purposes that lead to success in your chosen occupation.

All thoughts that you want to turn into success, and have planted in the subconscious mind, must pass through the imagination and be

NOTES & COMMENTS

mixed with faith (your faith in your own abilities). The "mixing" of faith with a plan, or purpose, intended for submission to the subconscious mind can only be done through the imagination.

From these statements, it should be clear that if you want to make use of your subconscious mind, it will call for the coordination and application of all thirteen principles of success that are the basis of this book.

MAKE YOUR POSITIVE EMOTIONS WORK FOR YOU

The subconscious mind is more susceptible to influence by thought mixed with feeling or emotion than it is by thoughts originating solely in the reasoning portion of the mind. In fact, there is much evidence to support the theory that only emotionalized thoughts have any real influence on the subconscious mind. It is a fact that emotions or feelings rule the majority of people. If it is true that the subconscious mind responds better and faster to thoughts that are well mixed with emotion, it is essential to become familiar with the more important of the emotions.

There are seven major positive emotions and seven major negative emotions. The negatives get into your thoughts naturally and go directly to your subconscious without any help from you. The positive emotions must be injected by you, through the principle of auto-suggestion, into the thought impulses that you wish to pass on to your subconscious mind.

These emotions, or feeling impulses, may be likened to yeast in a loaf of bread. They are the action element which transforms thought impulses from the passive to the active state. That is why thought impulses that have been well mixed with emotion are acted upon more readily than thought impulses originating in "cold reason."

COMMENTARY

W. Clement Stone, Napoleon Hill's friend, mentor, and business partner, arranged for the publication of many of Hill's later writings. The following is adapted from material that appears in two of these books, Napoleon Hill's Keys to Success *and* Believe and Achieve.

Enthusiasm is a positive mental attitude—an internal *impelling force of intense emotion, a power compelling creation or expression.*

Being enthusiastic is an impelling external *expression of action. When you act enthusiastically, you accentuate the power of suggestion and autosuggestion.*

The sales manager, public speaker, minister, lawyer, teacher, or executive who acts enthusiastic by speaking in an enthusiastic, sincere manner develops genuine enthusiasm. If you act enthusiastic your emotions will follow.

By filling your conscious mind with enthusiasm, you also impress upon your subconscious mind that your burning obsession and your plan for obtaining it are certain things. Then, if your conscious enthusiasm dims, your subconscious will be there, full of images of your success, to help you stoke your conscious fires of enthusiasm once again.

You are preparing yourself to influence and control the "inner audience" of your subconscious mind in order to hand over to it the desire for money, which you wish transmuted into its physical, monetary equivalent. It is essential, therefore, that you understand the method of approach to this "inner audience." You must speak its language. It understands best the language of emotion or feeling.

Following are the seven major positive emotions and the seven major negative emotions. I am listing them here so that you may draw upon the positives, and avoid the negatives, when giving instructions to your subconscious mind.

The Seven Major Positive Emotions

- The emotion of desire

- The emotion of faith

- The emotion of love

- The emotion of sex

- The emotion of enthusiasm

- The emotion of romance

- The emotion of hope

There are other positive emotions, but these are the seven most powerful and the ones most commonly used in creative effort. Master these seven emotions (they can be mastered only by use) and the other positive emotions will be at your command when you need them. Remember that you are studying a book that is intended to help you develop a "money consciousness" by filling your mind with positive emotions.

The Seven Major Negative Emotions to Be Avoided

- The emotion of fear

- The emotion of jealousy

- The emotion of hatred

- The emotion of revenge

- The emotion of greed

- The emotion of superstition

- The emotion of anger

Positive and negative emotions cannot occupy the mind at the same time. One or the other must dominate. It is your responsibility to make sure that positive emotions constitute the dominating influence of your mind. That is where the law of habit will help you. Form the habit of applying and using the positive emotions. Eventually they will dominate your mind so completely that the negatives cannot enter it.

Only by following these instructions literally, and continuously, can you gain control over your subconscious mind. The presence of a single negative in your conscious mind is sufficient to destroy all chances of constructive aid from your subconscious mind.

COMMENTARY

Napoleon Hill's concern about the susceptibility of the subconscious mind to negative thoughts, emotions, and comments is well known to professionals who work with these techniques. In clinical hypnotherapy there is an axiom referred to as the Law of Reversed Effect, which states that whenever there is a conflict between imagination and willpower, the imagination wins. When you attempt to plant an idea, if the subconscious already harbors a negative, trying to force the new idea has the reverse effect because the subconscious becomes obsessed with defending its established negative idea. And the harder you "try" to do something, the more the subconscious resists and the more difficult it becomes.

Even the use of the word try *is warned against because it gives the suggestion to the subconscious of a preconceived failure. The concept of "trying" implies an ongoing effort. You don't want to try. You want to succeed. If you ask your subconscious to help you "try," it may do just that. It may help you try, but it will prevent you from succeeding—because if you did succeed, then it could no longer help you "try," which is what you asked it to do.*

The cautionary note about using the word try *is just one example of the care that should be taken when formulating affirmations and using autosuggestion. The following are some other rules of thumb that most modern experts agree on.*

NOTES & COMMENTS

1. *Affirmations should always be stated as a positive. Affirm what you do want, not what you don't want.*

2. *Affirmations work best when they are short and very clear about a single desired goal. Take the time to write, rewrite, and polish your affirmation until you can express your desire in a short statement of precise and well-chosen words.*

3. *Affirmations should be specific about the desired goal, but not about how to accomplish it. Your subconscious knows better than you what it can do and how it can do it.*

4. *Do not make unreasonable time demands. Your subconscious can't make anything happen "suddenly" or "now."*

5. *Just saying the words will have little effect. When you affirm your desire you must do it with such faith and conviction that your subconscious becomes convinced of how important it is to you. As you affirm your desire to yourself, visualize it in your mind's eye as big as a billboard. Make it big, powerful, and memorable.*

6. *Repetition of your emotionalized affirmation is crucial. At this time it is your habit to think one way. By repeating your affirmation often every day, your new way of thinking will begin to be your automatic response. Keep reinforcing it until it becomes second nature to you, and your habit will have become to think the new way—the way you want to think.*

We form habits based on the degree of reinforcement we receive. Habits make no moral judgments; they can be either good or bad. Both are formed through repetition. If we try something and like the results, we repeat the action. You can replace negative thoughts with positive ones, you can replace inaction with action, and you can form any habit you choose. Your thoughts are the only thing that you can completely control if you choose to do so. You can control your thoughts to control your habits.

THE SECRET OF EFFECTIVE PRAYER

Most people resort to prayer only after everything else has failed. Or else they pray by a ritual of meaningless words. And because most people who pray do so only after everything else has failed, they go to prayer with their minds filled with fear and doubt. Because fear and doubt are the emotions that are mixed with their prayer, these are the emotions the subconscious mind passes on and these are the emotions that Infinite Intelligence receives and acts upon.

If you pray for a thing, but as you pray you have fear that you may not receive it, or that your prayer will not be acted upon by Infinite Intelligence, your prayer will have been in vain.

Prayer does, sometimes, result in the realization of that for which one prays. If you have ever had the experience of receiving something for which you prayed, go back in your memory and recall your actual state of mind while you were praying, and you will know for sure that the theory here described is more than a theory.

The method by which you may communicate with Infinite Intelligence is very similar to the way the vibration of sound is transmitted by radio waves. Sound cannot be transmitted through the atmosphere until it has been changed into a very high rate of vibration. The radio station takes the sound of the human voice and modifies it by stepping up the vibration millions of times. Only in this way can the energy of sound be sent over distances. After this transformation has taken place, the energy (which originally was in the form of vibrations of sound) is broadcast or transmitted as a radio signal. When a radio set receives the high-speed transmission, it then reconverts that energy back to its original slower rate of vibration, and when it is stepped down to its original rate, it vibrates the diaphragm of the speaker which reproduces the original sound of the voice.

The subconscious mind is the intermediary that translates prayers or desires into terms that Infinite Intelligence can receive. The answer

NOTES & COMMENTS

comes back to you in the form of a definite plan or idea for procuring the object of your prayer. When you understand this principle, you know why mere words read from a prayer book cannot serve as an agency of communication between the mind of man and Infinite Intelligence.

DO NOT EXPECT TROUBLES,

AS THEY HAVE A TENDENCY

NOT TO DISAPPOINT.

THE BRAIN

A BROADCASTING AND RECEIVING STATION
FOR THOUGHT

The Twelfth Step Toward Riches

It was while I was working with the late Dr. Alexander Graham Bell, and Dr. Elmer R. Gates, that I first proposed the idea that every human brain is both a broadcasting and receiving station for the vibration of thought.

In some way similar to the principle behind the operation of a radio receiver, every human brain is capable of picking up vibrations of thought that are being released by other brains *[hunches and flashes of intuition]*.

As was explained in previous chapters, it is your creative imagination that is the "receiving set" of your brain, which receives thoughts from your subconscious and, under certain circumstances, receives thoughts released by the brains of others. Your creative imagination is the interconnection between your conscious or reasoning mind and the four sources from which you receive thought stimuli: (1) consciously from other people, (2) your subconscious, (3) subconsciously from other people, and (4) Infinite Intelligence.

NOTES & COMMENTS

When stimulated, or stepped up to a high rate of vibration, the mind becomes more receptive to thoughts that reach it from outside sources. This stepping-up process takes place through either the positive emotions or the negative emotions. Through the emotions, the vibrations of thought may be increased.

The brain that has been stimulated by emotions functions at a much more rapid rate than it does when that emotion is quieted or absent. The result is the increase of thought to such a pitch that the creative imagination becomes highly receptive to ideas.

On the other hand, when the brain is functioning at a rapid rate it also gives to your own thoughts the emotional feeling that is essential before those thoughts will be picked up and acted upon by your subconscious mind.

The subconscious mind is the "sending station" of the brain, through which vibrations of thought are broadcast. Autosuggestion is the medium by which you may put into operation your "sending station." The creative imagination is the "receiving set" through which the energies of thought are picked up.

COMMENTARY

The following combines the above concept with the related materials from previous chapters to provide a step-by-step recap of Napoleon Hill's view of the process.

1. *The brain is simultaneously both a broadcaster and a receiver.*

2. *Emotion affects both your ability to send and your ability to receive.*

   - *When under the effect of strong emotion, the more powerfully you can send thoughts.*

   - *When under the effect of strong emotion, the more receptive you are to receiving thoughts.*

3. When you "send" thoughts, to where do you send them? You send them to your subconscious by using autosuggestion.

4. When you "receive" thoughts, where do they come from? They come from your subconscious and you receive them through your creative imagination.

5. Your subconscious mind has two aspects:

   - Your subconscious is a storehouse of information (as explained in the previous chapter).

   - Your subconscious is your connection to Infinite Intelligence.

6. Infinite intelligence is the medium through which you receive thoughts from other brains. Infinite intelligence is Hill's term for describing the basic law of physics: Because everything in the universe is either time, space, energy, or matter, and because matter is just energy in a different form, then everything is actually different parts of the same thing. This means that your subconscious mind (energy) has a common base with every other subconscious mind (energy).

7. Thoughts from other brains come to you as follows: When you are under the effect of a strong emotion and your "receiver" is especially receptive, sometimes its "pull" is so strong that it attracts a thought from the subconscious mind of another brain. It is able to do this because Infinite Intelligence interconnects your subconscious with the subconscious of the other brain.

8. These thoughts from other brains are what we refer to as intuition, hunches, déjà vu, and foreknowledge.

Although Hill's explanation depends on the action of an intangible force that cannot be isolated and dissected in a laboratory, neither medical science nor psychology can offer a better explanation for those thoughts that depend on knowledge or information that we do not have.

THE GREATEST FORCES ARE INTANGIBLE

In the past, we have depended too much on our physical senses and have limited our knowledge to physical things that we could see, touch, weigh, and measure.

I believe we have entered the most marvelous of all ages—an age that will teach us more about the intangible forces of the world about us. Perhaps we shall learn that there is an "other self" that is more powerful than the physical self we see when we look in a mirror.

Many people do not take seriously such intangibles—the things that they cannot perceive through any of their five senses. However, to belittle the idea of forces that are intangible or cannot be explained is to ignore the fact that all of us, every day, are controlled by forces that are unseen and intangible.

The whole of mankind has not the power to cope with, nor to control, the intangible force wrapped up in the rolling waves of the oceans. We still do not fully understand the intangible force of gravity, which keeps this little earth suspended in space and keeps us from falling from it, much less have the power to control that force. We are entirely subservient to the intangible force that comes with a thunderstorm, and we are just as helpless in the presence of the intangible force of electricity. We do not understand the intangible force (and intelligence) wrapped up in the soil of the earth—the force that provides us with every morsel of food we eat, every article of clothing we wear, and every dollar we carry in our pockets.

Last, but not least, with all of our culture and education, we still understand little or nothing of the greatest of all the intangibles: thought. However, we have begun to learn a good deal about the intricate workings of the physical brain, and the results are stunning. We know that the central switchboard of the human brain—the number of lines that connect the brain cells to each other—is written as the figure one followed by fifteen million zeros.

Dr. C. Judson Herrick of the University of Chicago says, "The figure is so stupendous that astronomical figures, dealing with hundreds of millions of light years, become insignificant by comparison. . . . It has been determined that there are from 10 billion to 14 billion nerve cells in the human cerebral cortex, and we know that these are arranged in definite patterns. These arrangements are not haphazard. They are orderly."

It is inconceivable to me that such a network of intricate machinery should be in existence for the sole purpose of carrying on the physical functions connected with the growth and maintenance of the physical body. Is it not likely that the same system which gives billions of brain cells the media for communication, one with another, also provides the means of communication with other intangible forces?

COMMENTARY

In the time since Hill wrote the above comments, we have learned a great deal more about the physical brain and how it operates. We understand much about the chemistry of the brain; we can measure the energies it releases; we know which areas control the various functions of the body and which areas affect memory, emotions, reasoning, and many other subtleties related to the thinking process. Through scanning technologies we can even observe the changes that take place in the brain while it is working. Through surgery, medication, and other techniques we know how to prevent the brain from having certain kinds of thoughts, and we know how to encourage the brain to produce certain other kinds of thoughts when we want it to. For instance, a specific area can be stimulated and you will have pleasurable thoughts—but we cannot yet control what those pleasurable thoughts will be, and we have no idea what the bits and pieces of information are that go into your pleasurable thoughts.

With all of our advanced knowledge about the physical brain, we still don't know how to make it have a specific thought or idea. Especially not an original

NOTES & COMMENTS

thought or a creative idea. And medical science offers no better theory than ✱ *Hill's as to how we could have an intuition or hunch made up from information that we don't have and were never exposed to.*

In short, the physical properties of the brain confirm that it is where the thinking process takes place, but it does not offer the answer to the question of how it happens, or how thoughts from one brain might travel to another.

In previous commentaries we pointed to the laws of physics as they relate to Hill's theory about the interconnectedness of all things. And although this is not meant to be a science lesson, it may reassure you to know that the work of renowned scientists lends support to the idea. Quantum theory deals with sub-atomic particles so miniscule that they are almost at the level of the basic "stuff" from which everything is made. Albert Einstein developed what is called the EPR effect (Einstein, Podolski, and Rosen), and Irish physicist John Stewart Bell proposed Bell's Theorem, both of which pertain to the concept that when two linked subatomic particles are separated from each other, when a change is made to particle A, the same change will instantly happen in particle B, even though the two are distant from each other.

Another related concept is called the Holographic Brain or Holographic Universe, and is named after an unusual quality of holograms. It is a fact that if you cut a hologram in half, you don't get two halves of a picture; you get two separate but complete pictures. Cut either one of those in half and you get another two complete pictures. Cut other pieces, and again you get whole images. Every part of a hologram has the whole of the information in the original.

In the 1970s Karl Pribram, a neurophysiologist at Stanford University, announced the results of his studies which suggest that memory is not in a specific part of the brain but is spread throughout the brain like the image on a holographic plate. At almost the same time, renowned physicist David Bohm proposed that the workings of the universe were like a holographic image; that among all things there is total interconnectivity and that all things influence all other things. In effect, every part of the universe contains the whole ✱ *of the universe.*

That is probably more than enough science for most readers. The point is, Hill was not alone in his conclusion that through some intangible force your subconscious shares interconnectivity with everything else in the universe. Previously the example was given of the folds and bumps in a tablecloth all being different but all still tablecloth. Here is another way to envision the intangible interconnection of all things: Suppose you were to drill five holes in a wall and have someone outside the room put their fingers and thumb through the holes and wiggle them. If you then bring into the room someone who only believes in tangible things that he or she can see, that person will see five separate objects that can move independently of each other. You may tell the person that behind the wall the objects are connected and all part of the same hand, but because they cannot see the connection, and disbelieve anything they don't understand, the person will not be convinced.

Neither modern medicine nor psychiatry nor technology can yet, conclusively, show us behind the wall. But the fact remains, we have all had a hunch about somebody and it turns out to be right, a premonition that something will happen and it does, or a feeling that something isn't right with someone who is not there with you and it turns out to be true. How does this information come to us?

As mentioned previously, psychologist Carl Jung called the intangible connection the collective unconscious (also called the universal subconscious). Others call it the Totally Unified Theory, the Great First Cause, the Universal Mind, or Spirit, and some see it as another way of describing God. Napoleon Hill calls it Infinite Intelligence and offers a common-sense explanation that allows you to work with the phenomenon even if it is not completely understood. And that, after all, is what Hill was aiming for: to give you a way to access intangible forces that will help you turn your desire into reality.

After this book had been written, just before the manuscript went to the publisher, the *New York Times* published an editorial showing that at least one great university, and one intelligent investigator in the field of mental phenomena, are carrying on an organized research through which conclusions have been reached that parallel many of those described in this and the following chapter. The editorial briefly analyzed the work carried on by Dr. J. B. Rhine and his associates at Duke University:

WHAT IS 'TELEPATHY'?

A month ago we cited on this page some of the remarkable results achieved by Professor Rhine and his associates in Duke University from more than a hundred thousand tests to determine the existence of "telepathy" and "clairvoyance." These results were summarized in the first two articles in *Harper's Magazine.* In the second, which has now appeared, the author, E. H. Wright, attempts to summarize what has been learned, or what it seems reasonable to infer, regarding the exact nature of these "extra-sensory" modes of perception.

The actual existence of telepathy and clairvoyance now seems to some scientists enormously probable as the result of Rhine's experiments. Various percipients were asked to name as many cards in a special pack as they could without looking at them and without other sensory access to them. About a score of men and women were discovered who could regularly name so many of the cards correctly that "there was not one chance in many a million million of their having done their feats by luck or accident."

But how did they do them? These powers, assuming that they exist, do not seem to be sensory. There is no known organ for them. The experiments worked just as well at distances of several hundred miles as they did in the same room. These facts also dispose, in Mr. Wright's opinion, of the attempt to explain telepathy or clairvoyance through any physical theory of radiation. All known forms of radiant energy decline inversely as the square of the distance traversed. Telepathy and clairvoyance do not. But they do vary through physical cause as our other mental powers do. Contrary to widespread opinion, they do not improve when the percipient is asleep or half-asleep, but, on the contrary, when he is most wide-awake and alert. Rhine discovered that a narcotic will invariably lower a percipient's score, while a stimulant will always send it higher. The most reliable performer apparently cannot make a good score unless he tries to do his best.

One conclusion that Wright draws with some confidence is that telepathy and clairvoyance are really one and the same gift. That is, the faculty that "sees" a card face down on a table seems to be exactly the same one that "reads" a thought residing only in another mind. There are several grounds for believing this. So far, the two gifts have been found in every person who has either of them. If you have the abilities, both seem to be of equal strength. Screens, walls, distances, have no effect at all on either. Wright expresses his "hunch" that other extra-sensory experiences such as prophetic dreams, premonitions of disaster, and the like, may also prove to be part of the same faculty. The reader is not asked to accept any of these conclusions, but the evidence that Rhine has piled up must remain impressive.

COMMENTARY

In 1927 Dr. J. B. Rhine and his wife, Dr. Louisa E. Rhine, joined Professor William McDougall, chairman of the psychology department at Duke University, to create a lab that would apply strict scientific procedures to the study of psychic phenomena. They developed scientific methodologies and procedures to study, identify, and test individuals who demonstrated unusual abilities. It was Dr. Rhine who coined the term extrasensory perception *(ESP), and he adopted the word* parapsychology *to describe their studies. It is fair to say that the research done at the Rhine lab is some of the most advanced work on the entire subject.*

In 1962 they created the Foundation for Research into the Nature of Man, in order to continue their studies independent of the university and to publish related works. In 1995 the name was changed to the Rhine Research Institute.

HOW TO JOIN MINDS IN TEAMWORK

In view of Dr. Rhine's findings about the conditions under which the mind responds to what he terms extrasensory modes of perception, I would like to add my own observations. My associates and I have discovered what we believe to be the ideal conditions under which the mind can be stimulated so that this "sixth sense" can be made to function in a practical way.

To begin with, I should explain that there is a close working alliance between myself and two members of my staff. Through experimentation and practice, we have discovered how to stimulate our minds so that we can, by a process of blending our three minds into one, find the solution to a great variety of problems that are submitted by my clients.

The procedure is very simple. We sit down at a conference table, clearly state the nature of the problem we have under consideration, then begin discussing it. Each contributes whatever thoughts may occur (by applying the principle used in connection with the "invisible counselors" described in the next chapter). The strange thing about this method of mind stimulation is that it places each participant in communication with unknown sources of knowledge definitely outside their own experience.

If you understand the principle described in the chapter on the Master Mind, you of course recognize the roundtable as being a practical application of the Master Mind.

This method of mind stimulation, through the discussion of definite subjects between three people, illustrates the simplest and most practical use of the Master Mind. When you tap into the power of your Master Mind group, you will find that the more you work together, the more each member will learn to anticipate the ideas of others and to connect immediately with their intense enthusiasm and inspiration. You cannot completely control this process, but the more you use it the more it will come into play.

By adopting and following a similar plan, you will be making use of the famous Carnegie formula described in chapter 1. If it means nothing to you at this time, mark this page and read it again after you have finished the last chapter.

GREAT ACHIEVEMENT

IS USUALLY BORN OF GREAT SACRIFICE,

AND IS NEVER THE RESULT

OF SELFISHNESS.

THE SIXTH SENSE

THE DOOR TO THE TEMPLE OF WISDOM

The Thirteenth Step Toward Riches

The thirteenth principle is known as the sixth sense, through which Infinite Intelligence may and will communicate voluntarily without any effort from, or demands by, the individual.

This principle is the apex of the philosophy of success. It can be assimilated, understood, and applied only by first mastering the other twelve principles.

The sixth sense is that portion of the subconscious mind that has been referred to as the creative imagination. It has also been referred to as the "receiving set" through which ideas, plans, and thoughts flash into the mind. The flashes are sometimes called hunches or inspirations.

The sixth sense defies description. It cannot be described to a person who has not mastered the other principles of this philosophy, because such a person has no knowledge and no experience with which the sixth sense may be compared.

After you have mastered the principles in this book, you will be prepared to accept as truth a statement that may otherwise be incredible to you. Through the sixth sense, you will be warned of impending dangers in time to avoid them and notified of opportunities in time to embrace them.

As you develop your sixth sense, it is almost as though a guardian angel comes to you to be of help and assistance; a guardian angel who will open to you at all times the door to the temple of wisdom.

MIRACLES OF THE SIXTH SENSE

I am not a believer in, nor an advocate of, "miracles," for the simple reason that I have enough knowledge of nature to understand that Nature never deviates from her established laws. However, I believe that some of Nature's laws are so incomprehensible that they produce what *appear* to be miracles. The sixth sense comes as near to being a miracle as anything I have ever experienced.

This much I do know—that there is a power, or a First Cause, or an Intelligence, which permeates every atom of matter and embraces every unit of energy perceptible to man. I know that this Infinite Intelligence is the thing that converts acorns into oak trees, causes water to flow downhill in response to the law of gravity, follows night with day, and winter with summer, each maintaining its proper place and relationship to the other. Through the philosophy explained in this book, this Intelligence can help turn your desires into concrete, or material, form. I know this because I have experimented with it—and I have experienced it.

Step by step through the preceding chapters you have been led to this, the last principle. If you have mastered each of the preceding principles, you are now prepared to accept, without being skeptical, the extraordinary claims made here. If you have not mastered the other principles, you must do so before you may determine, definitely, whether or not the claims made in this chapter are fact or fiction.

LET GREAT PEOPLE SHAPE YOUR LIFE

I have never entirely divested myself of the habit of hero worship. While I was passing through the stage of hero worship, I found myself trying to imitate those whom I most admired. My experience has taught me that the next best thing to being truly great is to emulate the great, to try to act like them, be like them, and feel like them as much as I could. I discovered that the faith with which I tried to imitate my idols gave me great capacity to do so quite successfully.

Long before I had ever written a line for publication, or delivered a speech in public, I followed the habit of reshaping my own character by trying to imitate the nine men whose lives and lifeworks had been most impressive to me. These nine men were Emerson, Paine, Edison, Darwin, Lincoln, Burbank, Napoleon, Ford, and Carnegie. Every night, over a long period of years, I held an imaginary council meeting with this group whom I called my "invisible counselors."

This is how I did it. Just before going to sleep at night, I would shut my eyes and see, in my imagination, this group of men seated with me around my council table. Here I had not only an opportunity to sit among those whom I considered to be great, but I actually dominated the group by serving as the chairman.

I had a very definite purpose in using my imagination in this way. My purpose was to rebuild my own character so it would become a composite of the characters of my imaginary counselors. Realizing that I had to overcome the handicap of being born and raised in an environment of ignorance and superstition, I deliberately assigned myself the task of voluntary rebirth through the method I have described above.

NOTES & COMMENTS

_____
_____
_____
_____
_____
_____
_____
_____
_____
_____
_____
_____
_____
_____
_____
_____
_____
_____
_____
_____
_____
_____

Building Character through Autosuggestion

I knew, of course, that we all become what we are because of our dominating thoughts and desires. I knew that every deeply seated desire causes a person to find a way to turn that desire into reality. I knew that self-suggestion is a powerful factor in building character. In fact, it is the sole principle through which character is built.

With this knowledge of how the mind works, I was fairly well armed with the equipment needed to rebuild my character. In these imaginary council meetings I called on my cabinet members for the knowledge I wished each to contribute. I would even speak out loud to each of them, as follows:

Mr. Emerson, I desire to acquire from you the marvelous understanding of nature which distinguished your life. I ask that you impress upon my subconscious mind those qualities you possessed that enabled you to understand and adapt yourself to the laws of nature.

Mr. Burbank, I request that you pass on to me the knowledge that enabled you to so harmonize the laws of nature that you caused the cactus to shed its thorns and become an edible food. Give me access to the knowledge that enabled you to make two blades of grass grow where but one grew before.

Napoleon, I desire to acquire from you the marvelous ability you possessed to inspire men and to arouse them to greater and more determined spirit of action. I desire also to acquire the spirit of enduring faith which enabled you to turn defeat into victory and to surmount staggering obstacles.

Mr. Paine, I desire to acquire from you the freedom of thought and the courage and clarity with which to express convictions, which so distinguished you.

Mr. Darwin, I wish to acquire from you the marvelous patience and ability to study cause and effect, without bias or prejudice, so exemplified by you in the field of natural science.

Mr. Lincoln, I desire to build into my own character the keen sense of justice, the untiring spirit of patience, the sense of humor, the human understanding, and the tolerance that were your distinguishing characteristics.

Mr. Carnegie, I wish to acquire a thorough understanding of the principles of organized effort, which you used so effectively in the building of a great industrial enterprise.

Mr. Ford, I wish to acquire your spirit of persistence, the determination, poise, and self-confidence that have enabled you to master poverty, and to organize, unify, and simplify human effort, so I may help others to follow in your footsteps.

Mr. Edison, I wish to acquire from you the marvelous spirit of faith with which you have uncovered so many of nature's secrets, the spirit of unremitting toil with which you have so often wrested victory from defeat.

The Startling Power of Imagination

My method of addressing the members of my imaginary cabinet would vary, according to the traits of character I was most interested in acquiring. I studied the records of their lives with painstaking care. After some months of this nightly procedure, I was astounded as each time my imaginary counselors started to become more and more real to me.

Each of these nine men developed individual characteristics that surprised me. For example, Lincoln developed the habit of always being late, then walking around in solemn parade. He always wore an expression of seriousness on his face. Rarely did I see him smile.

That was not true of the others. Burbank and Paine often indulged in witty repartee, which seemed at times to shock the other members of the cabinet. On one occasion Burbank was late. When he came, he was excited with enthusiasm, and explained that he had been late because of an experiment he was making, through which he hoped to be able to grow apples on any sort of tree.

Paine chided him by reminding him that it was an apple that started all the trouble between man and woman. Darwin chuckled as he suggested that Paine should watch out for little serpents when he went into the forest to gather apples, as they had the habit of growing into big snakes. Emerson observed, "No serpents, no apples," and Napoleon remarked, "No apples, no state!"

These meetings became so realistic that I became fearful of their consequences, and discontinued them for several months. The experiences were so uncanny, I was afraid that if I continued them I would lose sight of the fact that the meetings were purely experiences of my imagination.

In writing this book, this is the first time that I have had the courage to mention this. I knew, from my own attitude in connection with such matters, that I would be misunderstood if I described my unusual experience.

I now have the courage to put this on the printed page, because I am now less concerned about what "they say" than I was in the years that have passed.

While the members of my cabinet may be purely fictional, and the meetings existed only in my own imagination, they have led me into glorious paths of adventure, rekindled my appreciation of true greatness, encouraged my creativity, and inspired me to be honest and bold in expressing my thoughts.

COMMENTARY

Napoleon Hill's experience with his imaginary counselors is not as uncommon as it may seem on first reading. In fact, it happens to novelists all the time. As an author proceeds with the writing of a book, there will come a point when the characters in the novel become so well-defined in the author's mind that the personalities of the characters themselves begin to suggest plot points and dialogue that the author never planned. Often the thoughts that come to the author when he or she is "in the character" are completely original, and in "real life" would never have occurred to the author.

Psychiatrists, therapists, and motivational experts also use this phenomenon when they work with "role playing." The usual procedure is to ask two people to act out a scenario as if they were in each other's shoes. If this is done in a situation where the participants do not feel embarrassed or self-conscious, and if the people will allow themselves to become submerged and seriously try to become the other person, the results can be stunning. Depending on the faith with which you approach it, you can get not just a general sense of what the other person is going through, but also have flashes of insight, actually "feel" what the other person feels, and gain a real understanding about the reactions or motivations of others.

Why it works is just as much a mystery as why you get hunches. It may be simply that when your imagination creates a character it doesn't give the character inhibitions, so when you think "through" the character your mind is less restricted. Regardless, the fact is that by using your imagination to project yourself into other characters you can open yourself to ideas that you don't normally have access to. And you can use this mental phenomenon as one of the tools that will help you turn your desire into success.

TAPPING THE SOURCE OF INSPIRATION

Somewhere in the cell-structure of the brain is something that receives the vibrations of thought ordinarily called hunches. So far, science has not discovered where this sixth sense is located, but this is not important. The fact remains that human beings do receive accurate knowledge through sources other than the physical senses. Generally, such knowledge is received when the mind is under the influence of extraordinary stimulation. Any emergency that arouses the emotions

NOTES & COMMENTS

and causes the heart to beat more rapidly may bring the sixth sense into action. Anyone who has experienced a near accident while driving knows that the sixth sense often comes to your rescue and, by split seconds, helps to avoid the accident.

I mention this as background to the following statement of fact: On many occasions when I have faced emergencies, some of them so grave that my life was in jeopardy, I have been miraculously guided past these difficulties through the influence of my "invisible counselors."

My original purpose in conducting council meetings with imaginary beings was solely to use autosuggestion to impress upon my subconscious mind certain characteristics that I wanted to acquire. In more recent years, my experimentation has taken on an entirely different trend. I now go to my imaginary counselors with every difficult problem that confronts me and my clients. During my meetings with these "invisible counselors" I find my mind most receptive to ideas, thoughts, and knowledge that reach me through the sixth sense. The results are often astonishing, although I do not depend entirely on this form of counsel.

The sixth sense is not something that one can take off and put on at will. Ability to use this great power comes slowly, through application of the other principles outlined in this book.

No matter who you are, or what may have been your purpose in reading this book, you can profit by it even if you don't fully understand how or why the principle described in this chapter works. This is especially true if your major purpose is that of accumulation of money or other material things.

This chapter on the sixth sense was written because the book is designed to present a complete philosophy by which individuals may unerringly guide themselves in attaining whatever they ask of life. The starting point of all achievement is desire. The finishing point is the kind of knowledge that leads to understanding—understanding of yourself, understanding of others, understanding of the laws of nature, and the recognition and understanding of happiness.

Full understanding of this comes only through familiarity with, and use of, the principle of the sixth sense.

In reading this chapter, you may have found yourself lifted to a high level of mental stimulation. Splendid! Come back to this again a month from now, read it once more, and observe that your mind will soar to a still higher level of stimulation. Repeat this experience from time to time, giving no concern as to how much or how little you learn at the time. Eventually you will find yourself in possession of a power that will enable you to throw off discouragement, master fear, overcome procrastination, and draw freely upon your imagination. Then you will have felt the touch of that unknown "something" that has been the moving spirit of every truly great thinker, leader, artist, musician, writer, or statesman. Then you will be in a position to transmute your desires into their physical or financial counterpart as easily as you may lie down and quit at the first sign of opposition.

NOTES & COMMENTS

THE MAN WHO ACTUALLY KNOWS

JUST WHAT HE WANTS IN LIFE

HAS ALREADY GONE A LONG WAY

TOWARD ATTAINING IT.

16

THE SIX GHOSTS OF FEAR

HOW MANY ARE STANDING IN YOUR WAY?

Before you can put any portion of this philosophy into successful use, your mind must be prepared to receive it. The preparation is not difficult. It begins with study, analysis, and understanding of three enemies that you shall have to clear out—indecision, doubt, and fear.

The sixth sense will never function while these three negatives, or any one of them, remain in your mind. The members of this unholy trio are closely related; where one is found, the other two are close at hand.

Indecision is the seedling of fear. Remember this as you read. Indecision crystallizes into doubt; the two blend and become fear. The "blending" process often is slow. This is one reason why these three enemies are so dangerous. They germinate and grow without their presence being observed.

The remainder of this chapter describes a state of mind that you must attain before the philosophy can be put into practical use. This chapter also analyzes a condition that has reduced huge numbers of

NOTES & COMMENTS

people to poverty, and it states a truth that must be understood by all who accumulate riches, whether measured in terms of money or in terms of a state of mind that may be of far greater value than money.

The purpose of this chapter is to turn the spotlight of attention on the cause and the cure of the six basic fears. Before you can master an enemy, you must know its name, its habits, and where to attack it. As you read, analyze yourself carefully and determine which, if any, of the six common fears have attached themselves to you. And keep in mind that sometimes they are hidden in the subconscious mind, where they are difficult to locate and still more difficult to eliminate.

THE SIX BASIC FEARS

There are six basic fears. At one time or another, every person suffers from some combination of these fears. Most people are fortunate if they do not suffer from the entire six. Named in the order of their most common appearance, they are:

- The fear of poverty

- The fear of criticism

- The fear of ill health

- The fear of loss of love of someone

- The fear of old age

- The fear of death

All other fears are of minor importance, and are in fact just variations on these six.

Fears are nothing more than states of mind. Your state of mind is subject to your control and direction.

You can create nothing that you do not first conceive in the form of an impulse of thought. The following statement is of even greater importance: Thought impulses begin immediately to translate themselves into their physical equivalent, whether those thoughts are voluntary or involuntary. Even thought impulses that are picked up by mere chance (thoughts that have been released by other minds) may determine your financial, business, professional, or social destiny just as surely as the thoughts that you create by intent and design.

This circumstance also explains why some people seem to be lucky, while others of equal or greater ability, training, experience, and brain capacity seem destined to have misfortune. The explanation is that you have the ability to completely control your own mind. With this control, you may open your mind to the thought impulses that are being released by other brains, or you can close the doors tightly and admit only thought impulses of your own choice.

Nature has endowed human beings with absolute control over only one thing, and that one thing is thought. This fact, coupled with the additional fact that everything we create begins in the form of a thought, leads us very near to the principle by which fear may be mastered.

If it is true that all thought has a tendency to clothe itself in its physical equivalent (and this is true, beyond any reasonable room for doubt), it is equally true that thought impulses of fear and poverty cannot be translated into terms of courage and financial gain.

THE FIRST BASIC FEAR: THE FEAR OF POVERTY

There can be no compromise between poverty and riches. The two roads that lead to poverty and riches travel in opposite directions. If you want riches, you must refuse to accept any circumstance that leads toward poverty. (The word *riches* is used in its broadest sense, meaning

NOTES & COMMENTS

financial, spiritual, mental, and material wealth.) The starting point of the path that leads to riches is desire. In chapter 3 you received full instructions for the proper use of desire. In this chapter on fear, you have complete instructions for preparing your mind to make practical use of desire.

Here is the place to give yourself a challenge that will definitely determine how much of this philosophy you have absorbed. Here is the point at which you can tell what the future holds in store for you. If, after reading this chapter, you are willing to accept poverty, you may as well make up your mind to receive poverty. This is one decision you cannot avoid.

But if you demand riches, determine what form and how much will be required to satisfy you. You know the road that leads to riches. You have been given a road map. If you follow it, it will keep you on that road. If you neglect to make the start, or stop before you arrive, no one will be to blame but you. This responsibility is yours. No excuse will save you from accepting the responsibility if you now fail or refuse to demand riches of life. All you need is one thing— incidentally, the only thing you can control—and that is a state of mind. A state of mind is something that is up to you. It cannot be purchased; it must be created.

The Most Destructive Fear

Fear of poverty is a state of mind, nothing else. But it is sufficient to destroy your chances of achievement in any undertaking.

This fear paralyzes your ability to use reason, destroys the imagination, kills off self-reliance, undermines enthusiasm, discourages initiative, leads to uncertainty of purpose, encourages procrastination, wipes out enthusiasm, and makes self-control an impossibility. It takes the charm from your personality, destroys the possibility of accurate thinking, diverts concentration of effort. It defeats persistence, turns willpower into nothingness, destroys ambition, clouds the memory, and invites failure in every conceivable form. It kills love and assassinates the finer emotions of the heart, discourages friendship and invites disaster in a hundred forms, leads to sleeplessness, misery, and unhappiness—and all this despite the obvious truth that you live in a world of overabundance of everything your heart could desire, with nothing standing between you and your desires except lack of a definite purpose.

The fear of poverty is, without doubt, the most destructive of the six basic fears. It has been placed at the head of the list, because it is the most difficult to master. The fear of poverty grew out of our inherited tendency to prey upon our fellow human beings economically. Nearly all animals lower than us are motivated by instinct, but their capacity to "think" is limited and therefore they prey upon one another physically. We, with our superior sense of intuition, with the capacity to think and to reason, do not eat others bodily. Human beings get more satisfaction out of "eating" others financially. Humans are so avaricious that every conceivable law has been passed to safeguard us from one another.

Nothing brings so much suffering and humility as poverty! Only those who have experienced poverty understand the full meaning of this.

It is no wonder that we fear poverty. Through a long line of inherited experiences we have learned, for sure, that some people cannot be trusted where matters of money and earthly possessions are concerned.

So eager are we to possess wealth that we will acquire it in whatever manner we can—through legal methods if possible; through other methods if necessary or expedient.

Self-analysis may disclose weaknesses that you do not like to acknowledge. But this form of examination is essential if you are going to demand of life more than mediocrity and poverty. Remember, as you check yourself point by point, that you are both the court and the jury, the prosecuting attorney and the attorney for the defense, and that you are both the plaintiff and the defendant. You are on trial. Face the facts squarely. Ask yourself definite questions and demand direct replies. When the examination is over, you will know more about yourself. If you do not feel that you can be an impartial judge, call upon someone who knows you well to serve as judge while you cross-examine yourself. You are after the truth. Get it, no matter at what cost, even though it may temporarily embarrass you.

The majority of people, if asked what they fear most, would reply, "I fear nothing." The reply would be inaccurate, because few people realize that they are bound, handicapped, whipped spiritually and physically through some form of fear. So subtle and deeply seated is the emotion of fear that you may go through life and never recognize its presence. Only a courageous analysis will disclose the presence of this universal enemy. When you begin such an analysis, search deeply into your character. The following is a list of the symptoms to look for.

Symptoms of the Fear of Poverty

- *Indifference.* Commonly expressed through lack of ambition, willingness to tolerate poverty, and the acceptance of whatever compensation life may offer, without protest. Also mental and physical laziness, and lack of initiative, imagination, enthusiasm, and self-control.

- *Indecision.* The habit of permitting others to do your thinking. Sitting on the fence.

- *Doubt.* Generally expressed through alibis and excuses designed to cover up, explain away, or apologize for your failures. Sometimes expressed in the form of envy of those who are successful, or by criticizing them.

• *Worry.* Usually expressed by finding fault with others, a tendency to spend beyond your income, neglect of personal appearance, scowling and frowning, nervousness, lack of poise, self-consciousness, and often the use of alcohol or drugs.

• *Overcaution.* The habit of looking for the negative side of every circumstance. Thinking and talking about possible failure instead of concentrating on succeeding. Knowing all the roads to disaster, but never searching for the plans to avoid failure. Waiting for "the right time" to begin, until the waiting becomes a permanent habit. Remembering those who have failed, and forgetting those who have succeeded. Seeing the hole in the doughnut but overlooking the doughnut.

• *Procrastination.* The habit of putting off until tomorrow that which should have been done last year. Spending more time in creating excuses than it would take to do the job. This symptom is closely related to overcaution, doubt, and worry. Refusal to accept responsibility. Willingness to compromise rather than put up a fight. Compromising with difficulties instead of harnessing and using them as steppingstones to advancement. Bargaining with life for a penny instead of demanding prosperity, opulence, riches, contentment, and happiness. Planning what to do if you fail, instead of burning all bridges and making retreat impossible. Weakness of, and often total lack of, self-confidence, definiteness of purpose, self-control, initiative, enthusiasm, ambition, thrift, and sound reasoning ability. Expecting poverty instead of demanding riches. Associating with those who accept poverty instead of seeking the company of those who demand and receive riches.

Money Talks!

Some will ask, "Why did you write a book about money? Why measure riches in dollars alone?" Some will believe, and rightly so, that there are other forms of riches more desirable than money.

Yes, there are riches that cannot be measured in terms of dollars, but there are also millions of people who say, "Give me all the money I need, and I will find everything else I want."

The major reason why I wrote this book on how to get money is that millions of men and women are paralyzed with the fear of poverty. What this sort of fear does to one was well described by Westbrook Pegler:

COMMENTARY

James Westbrook Pegler was a controversial newspaper columnist for the Chicago Daily News *and the* Washington Post. *Although his career lasted into the 1960s, he was most widely read and quoted during the 1930s and 1940s. During that period he went from being a public supporter of Franklin Roosevelt and the New Deal policies, to the opposite end of the political spectrum championing conservative points of view. Pegler was also the author of three books based on his columns, and in 1940 won the Pulitzer Prize for his exposé of union racketeering.*

Money is only clam shells or metal discs or scraps of paper, and there are treasures of the heart and soul which money cannot buy, but most people, being broke, are unable to keep this in mind and sustain their spirits. When a man is down and out and on the street, unable to get any job at all, something happens to his spirit which can be observed in the droop of his shoulders, the set of his hat, his walk and his gaze. He cannot escape a feeling of inferiority among people with regular employment, even though he knows they are definitely not his equals in character, intelligence or ability.

These people—even his friends—feel, on the other hand, a sense of superiority and regard him, perhaps unconsciously, as a casualty. He may borrow for a time, but not enough to carry on in his accustomed way, and he cannot continue to borrow very long. But borrowing in itself, when a man is borrowing merely to live, is a depressing experience, and the money lacks the power of earned money to revive his spirits. Of course, none of this applies to bums or habitual ne'er-do-wells, but only to men of normal ambitions and self-respect.

Women in the same predicament must be different. We somehow do not think of women at all in considering the down-and-outers. They are scarce in the breadlines, they rarely are seen begging on the streets, and they are not recognizable in crowds by the same plain signs which identify busted men. Of course, I do not mean the shuffling hags of the city streets who are the opposite number of the confirmed male bums. I mean reasonably young, decent and intelligent women. There must be many of them, but their despair is not apparent.

When a man is down and out he has time on his hands for brooding. He may travel miles to see a man about a job and discover that the job is filled or that it is one of those jobs with no base pay but only a commission on the sale of some useless knick-knack which nobody would buy, except out of pity. Turning that down, he finds himself back on the street with nowhere to go but just anywhere. So he walks and walks. He gazes into store windows at luxuries which are not for him, and feels inferior and gives way to people who stop to look with an active interest. He wanders into the railroad station or puts himself down in the library to ease his legs and soak up a little heat, but that isn't looking for a job, so he gets going again. He may not know it, but his aimlessness would give him

NOTES & COMMENTS

away even if the very lines of his figure did not. He may be well dressed in the clothes left over from the days when he had a steady job, but the clothes cannot disguise the droop.

He sees thousands of other people, bookkeepers or clerks or chemists or wagon hands, busy at their work and envies them from the bottom of his soul. They have their independence, their self-respect and manhood, and he simply cannot convince himself that he is a good man, too, though he argue it out and arrive at a favorable verdict hour after hour.

It is just money which makes this difference in him. With a little money he would be himself again.

THE SECOND BASIC FEAR: THE FEAR OF CRITICISM

Just how we originally came by this fear no one can say definitely, but one thing is certain—we have it in a highly developed form.

I am inclined to attribute the basic fear of criticism to that part of our inherited nature that prompts us not only to take away other people's goods and wares, but also to justify our actions by criticism of the character of others. It is well known that a thief will criticize the man from whom he steals; that politicians seek office not by displaying their own virtues and qualifications, but by running negative campaigns against their opponents.

Designers and clothing manufacturers have not been slow to take advantage of this basic fear of criticism. Every season styles change. Who establishes the styles? Certainly not the purchaser. It is the designers and manufacturers. Why do they change the styles so often? The answer is obvious. They change the styles so they can sell more clothes.

The fear of criticism robs people of their initiative, destroys their power of imagination, limits their individuality, takes away their self-reliance, and does them damage in a hundred other ways. Parents often do their children irreparable injury by criticizing them. The mother of one of my friends used to punish him with a switch almost daily, always completing the job with the statement, "You'll land in the penitentiary before you are twenty." He was sent to a reformatory at the age of seventeen.

COMMENTARY

Modern psychotherapy is well aware of the circumstance that Hill describes in the preceding paragraph. In the chapters on autosuggestion and hypnosis, reference was made to childhood traumas that result in phobias, compulsive behaviors, fixations, or complexes. However, there are instances in which the implanting of a suggestion is much more subtle. Hypnotherapists have found that common phrases such as "Don't you ever say no to me again," "I'm afraid she'll never get over it," or "You're just like your father" can hamper a person's abilities later in life if such phrases were said often enough, or at a time when a child was particularly vulnerable.

Criticism is the one form of service of which everyone has too much. Everyone has a stock of it, which is handed out gratis whether called for or not. Your nearest relatives are often the worst offenders. It should be recognized as a crime (in reality it is a crime of the worst nature) for any parent to build inferiority complexes in the mind of a child, through unnecessary criticism. Employers who understand human nature get the best there is in people not by criticism but by constructive suggestion. Parents may accomplish the same results with their children. Criticism will plant fear in the human heart, or resentment, but it will not build love or affection.

Symptoms of the Fear of Criticism

This fear is almost as universal as the fear of poverty and its effects are just as fatal to personal achievement, mainly because this fear destroys initiative and discourages the use of imagination. The major symptoms of the fear are:

- *Self-consciousness.* Generally expressed through nervousness, timidity in conversation and in meeting strangers, awkward movements, and shifting of the eyes.

- *Lack of poise.* Expressed through lack of voice control, nervousness in the presence of others, poor posture, poor memory.

- *Personality weaknesses.* Lacking in firmness of decision, personal charm, and ability to express opinions definitely. The habit of sidestepping issues instead of meeting them squarely. Agreeing with others without careful examination of their opinions.

- *Inferiority complex.* The habit of expressing your own self-approval as a means of covering up your feeling of inferiority. Using "big words" to impress others (often without knowing the real meaning of the words). Imitating others in dress, speech, and manners. Boasting of imaginary achievements, and "acting superior" to cover up the fact that you feel inferior.

- *Extravagance.* The habit of trying to "keep up with the Joneses" and spending beyond your income.

- *Lack of initiative.* Failure to embrace opportunities for self-advancement, fear of expressing opinions, lack of confidence in your own ideas, giving evasive answers to questions asked by superiors, hesitancy of manner and speech, deceit in both words and deeds.

- *Lack of ambition.* Mental and physical laziness, lack of self-assertion, slowness in reaching decisions, being too easily influenced, the habit of accepting defeat without protest or quitting an undertaking when opposed by others. Also the habit of criticizing others behind their backs and flattering them to their faces, suspicion of other people without cause, lack of tactfulness of manner and speech, and unwillingness to accept the blame for mistakes.

THE THIRD BASIC FEAR: THE FEAR OF ILL HEALTH

This fear may be traced to both physical and social heredity. It is closely associated with the causes of fear of old age and the fear of death. We fear ill health because of the terrible pictures that have been planted in our minds of what may happen if death should overtake us. We also fear it because of the economic toll that it may claim.

One reputable physician estimated that 75 percent of all people who visit doctors are suffering with hypochondria (imaginary illness). It has been shown that the fear of disease, even where there is not the slightest cause for fear, often produces the physical symptoms of the disease feared. Powerful and mighty is the human mind! It builds or it destroys.

Through a series of experiments my staff proved how susceptible people are to the power of suggestion. We asked three acquaintances to visit separately with the "victim." They were instructed to pose the question, "What ails you? You look terribly ill." The first questioner provoked a grin from him and a nonchalant, "Oh nothing, I'm all right." The second questioner was answered with the statement, "I don't know exactly, but I do feel badly." The third questioner was met with the admission that the victim was actually feeling ill.

COMMENTARY

Hill's experiment is one that you do not want to carry too far. It is not that different from the principle behind certain religious sects whose members take vengeance on their enemies by "hexing" or placing a spell on a victim. The spell only works because the victim believes that spells can be cast and that it is possible he or she could be hexed. When the hex victim is informed that someone has cast a spell on them, they accept that it is possible, and their mind does the rest.

The same theory operated when Hill's associate was told three times that he looked ill. He believed it was possible, being told three times was convincing, and his mind went to work and made it so.

NOTES & COMMENTS

There is overwhelming evidence that disease sometimes begins in the form of negative thought impulse. Such thoughts may be planted in your mind by suggestion, or created by you in your own mind.

Doctors send patients to new climates for their health because a change of "mental attitude" is necessary.

The seed of fear of ill health lives in every human mind. Worry, fear, discouragement, or disappointment can cause this seed to germinate and grow.

Symptoms of the Fear of Ill Health

The symptoms of this almost universal fear are:

- *Autosuggestion.* The habit of negative use of self-suggestion by looking for, and expecting to find, symptoms of all kinds of disease. "Enjoying" your imaginary illness and speaking of it as being real. The habit of trying "fads" and "isms" recommended by others as having therapeutic value. Talking to others of operations, accidents, and other forms of illness. Experimenting with diets, physical exercises, weight-loss systems, without professional guidance. Trying home remedies, patent medicines, and "quack" remedies.

- *Hypochondria* (a medical term for imaginary disease). The habit of excessively talking about illness, and by concentrating the mind on disease you begin to expect it to happen to you. Nothing that comes in bottles can cure this condition. It is brought on by negative thinking, and nothing but positive thought can cure it. Hypochondria is said to do as much damage on occasion as the real disease might do.

- *Exercise.* Fear of ill health often interferes with proper physical exercise, and results in overweight.

NOTES & COMMENTS

- *Susceptibility.* Fear of ill health breaks down your natural resistance, which makes you susceptible to real disease. The fear of ill health is often related to the fear of poverty, especially in the case of the hypochondriac who constantly worries about the possibility of having to pay doctors' bills, hospital bills, etc. This type of person spends much time preparing for sickness, talking about death, saving money for cemetery plots, burial expenses, and such.

- *Self-coddling.* The habit of seeking sympathy. The habit of feigning illness to cover your laziness or to serve as an alibi for lack of ambition. (People often resort to this trick to avoid work.)

- *Intemperance.* The habit of using alcohol or drugs to destroy pain instead of eliminating the cause.

- *The habit of reading about illness* and worrying over the possibility of being stricken by it.

THE FOURTH BASIC FEAR: THE FEAR OF LOSS OF LOVE

Jealousy and other similar forms of neurosis grow out of our fear of the loss of love of someone. This fear is the most painful of all the six basic fears. It probably plays more havoc with the body and mind than any of the other basic fears.

COMMENTARY

By way of introduction to each of the six basic fears, Napoleon Hill usually postulates how the fear originated in humans. In the original edition of this book he suggested that the fear of loss of love may have started with prehistoric man's habit of stealing his neighbor's mate and taking liberties with her whenever he could. Though amusing, this theory does not take into account that women fear the loss of a love just as profoundly as men do. And both men and women fear losing the love of not just their mates but also of family members and others with whom they are close.

How the emotion of love originated may remain a mystery, but there is no mystery about how we feel when we lose it.

Symptoms of the Fear of Loss of Love

The distinguishing symptoms of this fear are:

- *Jealousy.* The habit of being suspicious of friends and loved ones The habit of accusing wife or husband of infidelity without grounds. General suspicion of everyone and absolute faith in no one.

- *Fault-finding.* The habit of finding fault with friends, relatives, business associates, and loved ones upon the slightest provocation, or without any cause whatsoever.

- *Gambling.* The habit of gambling, stealing, cheating, and otherwise taking hazardous chances to provide money for loved ones, in the belief that love can be bought. The habit of spending beyond your means, or incurring debts, to provide gifts for loved ones in order to make a good impression. Also insomnia, nervousness, lack of persistence, weakness of will, lack of self-control, lack of self-reliance, bad temper.

THE FIFTH BASIC FEAR: THE FEAR OF OLD AGE

In the main, this fear grows out of two sources. First, the thought that old age may bring with it poverty. Second, is the concern that many have for what may await them in the world beyond.

The most common cause of fear of old age is associated with the possibility of poverty. "Poorhouse" is not a pretty word. It throws a chill into the mind of every person who faces the possibility of having to spend declining years having to live on some form of charity.

The possibility of ill health, which is more common as people grow older, is also a contributing cause of this common fear of old age, as is concern about diminishing sexuality.

Another contributing cause of the fear of old age is the possibility of loss of freedom and independence, as old age may bring with it the loss of both physical and economic freedom.

Symptoms of the Fear of Old Age

The most common symptoms of this fear are:

- *Lack of Enthusiasm.* The tendency to slow down and develop an inferiority complex, falsely believing you are "slipping" because of age. The habit of killing off initiative, imagination, and self-reliance by falsely believing you are too old to exercise these qualities.

- *Self-consciousness of speech.* The habit of speaking apologetically of yourself as "being old" merely because you have reached the age of forty or fifty, instead of reversing the rule and expressing gratitude for having reached the age of wisdom and understanding.

- *Inappropriate dress and action.* Trying to appear much younger than your age by going overboard in your attempt to keep up with the style and mannerisms of youth.

THE SIXTH BASIC FEAR: THE FEAR OF DEATH

To some this is the cruelest of all the basic fears. The reason is obvious. The terrible pangs of fear associated with the thought of death, in the majority of cases, may be charged to religious fanaticism. So-called "heathens" are less afraid of death than the more "civilized."

For hundreds of millions of years we have been asking the still unanswered questions, Where did I come from? and Where am I going?

During the darker ages of the past, the more cunning and crafty were not slow to offer the answer to these questions, for a price.

"Come into my tent, embrace my faith, accept my dogmas, and I will give you a ticket that will admit you straight into heaven when you die," says the religious leader. "Remain out of my tent," says the same leader, "and the devil will take you and burn you throughout eternity."

The thought of eternal punishment destroys interest in life and makes happiness impossible.

While the religious leader may not actually be able to provide safe conduct into heaven, or send you to hell, the possibility of the latter seems terrible. The very thought of it takes hold of the imagination in such a realistic way that it paralyzes reason and sets up the fear of death.

The fear of death is not as common now as it was during the age when there were no great colleges and universities. People of science have turned the spotlight of truth upon the world, and this truth is rapidly freeing men and women from this terrible fear of death. The young men and women who attend the colleges and universities are not easily impressed by fire and brimstone. Through knowledge, the fears of the dark ages that gripped the mind have been dispelled.

The entire world is made up of only four things: time, space, energy, and matter. In elementary physics we learn that neither matter nor energy (the only two realities known to man) can be created or destroyed. Both matter and energy can be transformed, but neither can be destroyed.

Life is energy, if it is anything. If neither energy nor matter can be destroyed, of course life cannot be destroyed. Life, like other forms of energy, may be passed through various processes of transition, or change, but it cannot be destroyed. Death is mere transition.

And if death is not mere change, or transition, then nothing comes after death except a long, eternal, peaceful sleep, and sleep is nothing to be feared. If you can accept the logic of this, you may forever wipe out your fear of death.

Symptoms of the Fear of Death

The general symptoms of this fear are:

- *The habit of thinking about dying,* instead of making the most of life. This is generally due to lack of purpose, or lack of a suitable occupation. This fear is more prevalent among the aged, but sometimes the more youthful are victims of it. The greatest of all remedies for the fear of death is a burning desire for achievement, backed by useful service to others. A busy person seldom has time to think about dying. A busy person finds life too thrilling to worry about death.

- *Sometimes the fear of death is closely associated with the fear of poverty,* where death would leave loved ones poverty-stricken.

- *In other cases the fear of death is caused by illness,* and the breakdown of physical body resistance.

- *The most common causes of the fear of death* are ill health, poverty, lack of appropriate occupation, disappointment over love, insanity, and religious fanaticism.

THE DISASTER OF WORRY AND DESTRUCTIVE THINKING

Worry is a state of mind based upon fear. It works slowly but persistently. It is insidious and subtle. Step by step it digs itself in until it paralyzes the reasoning faculty and destroys self-confidence and initiative. Worry is a form of sustained fear caused by indecision. Therefore it is a state of mind that can be controlled.

An unsettled mind is helpless. Indecision makes an unsettled mind. Most individuals lack the willpower to reach decisions promptly and to stand by them after they have been made.

We do not worry over conditions once we have reached a decision to follow a definite line of action. I once interviewed a man who was sentenced to be electrocuted two hours later. The condemned man was the calmest of the eight men who were in the death cell with him. His calmness prompted me to ask him how it felt to know that he was going into eternity in a short while. With a smile of confidence on his face, he said, "It feels fine. Just think, brother, my troubles will soon be over. I have had nothing but trouble all my life. It has been a hardship to get food and clothing. Soon I will not need these things. I have felt fine ever since I learned for certain that I must die. I made up my mind then to accept my fate in good spirit."

As he spoke he devoured a dinner sufficient for three men, eating every mouthful of the food brought to him and apparently enjoying it as much as if no disaster awaited him. Decision gave this man resignation to his fate. Decision can also prevent one's acceptance of undesired circumstances.

Through indecision, the six basic fears become translated into a state of worry. Relieve yourself forever of the fear of death, by reaching a decision to accept death as an inescapable event. Eliminate the fear of old age by reaching a decision to accept it not as a handicap but as a great blessing that carries with it wisdom, self-control, and understanding. Master the fear of loss of love by reaching a decision to get along without love, if that is necessary. Defeat the fear of criticism by reaching a decision not to worry about what other people think, do, or say. Overcome the fear of ill health by the decision to forget symptoms. And whip the fear of poverty by reaching a decision to get along with whatever wealth you can accumulate without worry.

Kill the habit of worry, in all its forms, by reaching a general blanket decision that nothing life has to offer is worth the price of worry. With this decision will come poise, peace of mind, and calmness of thought, which will bring happiness.

If your mind is filled with fear you not only destroy your own chances of intelligent action, but you transmit these destructive vibrations to the minds of all who come into contact with you, and you destroy their chances too.

Even a dog or a horse knows when its master lacks courage. It will pick up the vibrations of fear given off by its master, and behave accordingly.

The vibrations of fear pass from one mind to another just as quickly and as surely as the sound of the human voice passes from the broadcasting station to a radio receiver.

The person who constantly speaks of negative or destructive thoughts is practically certain to experience the results of those words in the form of destructive feedback. But even negative thoughts, without words, will come back to you. The release of destructive thought impulses, alone, also produces feedback in more ways than one. First, and perhaps most important to be remembered, the person who releases thoughts of a destructive nature must suffer damage through the breaking-down of creative imagination. Secondly, the presence in the mind of any destructive emotion develops a negative personality, which repels people and often converts them into antagonists. The third source of damage is that negative thoughts not only affect others but they also embed themselves in the subconscious mind of the person releasing them, and there become a part of that person's character.

Your business in life is to achieve success. To be successful you must find peace of mind, acquire the material needs of life, and, above all, attain happiness. All of these indications of success begin in the form of thought impulses.

You control your own mind; you have the power to feed it whatever thought impulses you choose. With this goes the responsibility of using your mind constructively. You are the master of your own earthly destiny just as surely as you have the power to control your own thoughts. You may influence, direct, and eventually control your own environment, making your life what you want it to be. Or you may neglect to make your life what you want, and you will be adrift on the seas of "circumstance" where you will be tossed like a wood-chip on the waves of the ocean.

The Devil's Workshop

In addition to the six basic fears, there is another evil by which people suffer. It constitutes a rich soil in which the seeds of failure grow abundantly. It is so subtle that its presence often is not detected. It is more deeply rooted, and more often fatal, than all of the six fears. For want of a better name, let us call this evil *susceptibility to negative influences.*

Those who accumulate great riches always protect themselves against negative influences. The poverty-stricken never do. Those who succeed in any calling must prepare their minds to resist such influences. If you are reading this book to learn how to grow rich, you should examine yourself very carefully to determine whether you are susceptible to negative influences. If you neglect this self-analysis, you will give up your right to attain the object of your desires.

Make your analysis searching. As you read the following questions, be tough on yourself. Go at the task as carefully as you would if you were searching for any other enemy you knew was waiting to ambush you. You must deal with your own faults as you would with a real and serious enemy.

You can easily protect yourself against real enemies because there are laws, police, and courts to deal with them. But this "seventh basic evil" is more difficult to master because it strikes when you are not aware of its presence, when you are asleep and while you are awake. Moreover, its weapon is intangible because it consists of merely a state of mind. Negative influences are also dangerous because they come in so many different forms. Sometimes they enter the mind through the well-meant words of your friends and relatives. At other times they come from within, through your own mental attitude. Always it is as deadly as poison, even though it may not kill as quickly.

How to Protect Yourself against Negative Influences

To protect yourself against negative influences, whether of your own making or the result of negative people around you, recognize that your willpower is your defense. You must put it into constant use until it builds a wall of immunity against negative influences in your own mind.

Recognize that you and every other human being are, by nature, lazy, indifferent, and susceptible to all suggestions that reinforce your weaknesses.

Recognize that you are, by nature, susceptible to all of the six basic fears, and you must set up habits to counteract all these fears.

Recognize that negative influences often work on you through your subconscious mind and are therefore difficult to detect. Keep your mind closed against all people who depress or discourage you in any way.

Clean out your medicine chest and stop pandering to colds, aches, pains, and imaginary illness.

Deliberately seek the company of people who influence you to think and act for yourself.

Do not expect troubles, as they have a tendency not to disappoint.

Without doubt, the most common weakness of all human beings is the habit of leaving their minds open to the negative influences

NOTES & COMMENTS

of other people. This weakness is all the more damaging because most people do not even know they do it.

The following list of questions is designed to help you see yourself as you really are. You should read through the list now, then set aside a day when you can give adequate time to go through the list again, and thoroughly answer each question. When you do this, I advise that you read the questions and state your answers aloud so you can hear your own voice. This will make it easier for you to be truthful with yourself.

SELF-ANALYSIS QUESTIONS

Do you complain often of "feeling bad," and if so, what is the cause?

Do you find fault with other people at the slightest provocation?

Do you frequently make mistakes in your work, and if so, why?

Are you sarcastic and offensive in your conversation?

Do you deliberately avoid the association of anyone, and if so, why?

Do you suffer frequently with indigestion? If so, what is the cause?

Does life seem futile and the future hopeless to you?

Do you like your occupation? If not, why?

Do you often feel self-pity, and if so, why?

Are you envious of those who excel you?

To which do you devote most time, thinking of success or of failure?

Are you gaining or losing self-confidence as you grow older?

Do you learn something of value from all mistakes?

Are you permitting some relative or acquaintance to worry you? If so, why?

Are you sometimes excited about life, and at other times in the depths of despondency?

Who has the most inspiring influence upon you, and for what reason?

Do you tolerate negative or discouraging influences that you could avoid?

Are you careless of your personal appearance? If so, when and why?

Have you learned how to ignore your troubles by being too busy to be annoyed by them?

Would you call yourself a "spineless weakling" if you permitted others to do your thinking for you?

How many preventable disturbances annoy you, and why do you tolerate them?

Do you resort to alcohol, drugs, cigarettes, or other compulsions to "quiet your nerves"? If so, why do you not try willpower instead?

Does anyone "nag" you, and if so, for what reason?

Do you have a definite major purpose, and if so, what is it and what plan do you have for achieving it?

Do you suffer from any of the six basic fears? If so, which ones?

Have you developed a method to shield yourself against the negative influence of others?

Do you use autosuggestion to make your mind positive?

NOTES & COMMENTS

NOTES & COMMENTS

Which do you value most, your material possessions or your privilege of controlling your own thoughts?

Are you easily influenced by others, against your own judgment?

Has today added anything of value to your stock of knowledge or state of mind?

Do you face squarely the circumstances that make you unhappy, or do you sidestep the responsibility?

Do you analyze all mistakes and failures and try to profit by them, or do you take the attitude that this is not your duty?

Can you name three of your most damaging weaknesses? What are you doing to correct them?

Do you encourage other people to bring their worries to you for sympathy?

Do you choose, from your daily experiences, lessons or influences that aid in your personal advancement?

Does your presence have a negative influence on other people as a rule?

What habits of other people annoy you most?

Do you form your own opinions, or do you permit yourself to be influenced by other people?

Have you learned how to create a mental state of mind with which you can shield yourself against all discouraging influences?

Does your occupation inspire you with faith and hope?

Are you conscious of possessing spiritual forces of sufficient power to enable you to keep your mind free from all forms of fear?

Does your religion help to keep your mind positive?

Do you feel it your duty to share other people's worries? If so, why?

If you believe that "birds of a feather flock together," what have you learned about yourself by studying the friends whom you attract?

What connection, if any, do you see between the people with whom you associate most closely and any unhappiness you may experience?

Could it be possible that some person whom you consider to be a friend is, in reality, your worst enemy because of his or her negative influence on your mind?

By what rules do you judge who is helpful and who is damaging to you?

Are your intimate associates mentally superior or inferior to you?

How much time out of every twenty-four hours do you devote to:

- your occupation
- sleep
- play and relaxation
- acquiring useful knowledge
- plain wasted time

Who among your acquaintances:

- encourages you most
- cautions you most
- discourages you most

What is your greatest worry? Why do you tolerate it?

NOTES & COMMENTS

When others offer you free, unsolicited advice do you accept it without question or do you analyze their motive?

What, above all else, do you most desire? Do you intend to acquire it? Are you willing to subordinate all other desires for this one? How much time daily do you devote to acquiring it?

Do you change your mind often? If so, why?

Do you usually finish everything you begin?

Are you easily impressed by other people's business or professional titles, college degrees, or wealth?

Are you easily influenced by what other people think or say about you?

Do you cater to people because of their social or financial status?

Whom do you believe to be the greatest person living? In what respect is this person superior to yourself?

How much time have you devoted to studying and answering these questions? (At least one day is necessary for the analysis and the answering of the entire list.)

If you have answered all these questions truthfully, you know more about yourself than the majority of people. Study the questions carefully, come back to them once each week for several months, and be astounded at the amount of additional knowledge of great value to yourself you will have gained by the simple method of answering the questions truthfully. If you are not certain about the answers to some of the questions, seek the counsel of those who know you well, especially those who have no motive in flattering you, and see yourself through their eyes. The experience will be astonishing.

THE ONE THING OVER WHICH YOU HAVE ABSOLUTE CONTROL

You have absolute control over only one thing, and that is your thoughts. This is the most significant and inspiring of all facts known to humans. It reflects our divine nature. This ability to control your thoughts is the sole means by which you may control your own destiny. If you fail to control your own mind, you may be sure you will control nothing else. Your mind is your spiritual estate. Protect and use it with the care to which divine royalty is entitled. You were given your willpower for this purpose.

Unfortunately, there is no legal protection against those who, by design or through ignorance, poison the minds of others with negative suggestion.

Those with negative minds tried to convince Thomas A. Edison that he could not build a machine that would record and reproduce the human voice, "because," they said, "no one else had ever produced such a machine." Edison did not believe them. He knew that the mind could produce anything the mind could conceive and believe. That knowledge was the thing that lifted the great Edison above the common herd.

Men with negative minds told F. W. Woolworth he would go broke trying to run a store on five- and ten-cent sales. He did not believe them. He knew that he could do anything, within reason, if he backed his plans with faith. Exercising his right to keep the negative suggestions of others out of his mind, he piled up a fortune of more than a hundred million dollars.

Doubting Thomases scoffed scornfully when Henry Ford tried out his first crudely built automobile on the streets of Detroit. Some said the thing would never become practical. Others said no one would pay money for such a contraption. Ford said, "I'll belt the earth with dependable motor cars," and he did. For the benefit of those seeking vast riches, let it be remembered that practically the sole difference between Henry Ford and a majority of workers is this: Ford had a mind and he controlled it. The others have minds that they do not try to control.

Mind control is the result of self-discipline and habit. You either control your mind or it controls you. There is no halfway compromise. The most practical method for controlling your mind is the habit of keeping it busy with a definite purpose backed by a definite plan. Study the records of those who achieve noteworthy success, and you will see that they have control over their own minds, and that they exercise that control and direct it toward the attainment of definite objectives. Without this control, success is not possible.

FIFTY-FIVE FAMOUS ALIBIS BY OLD MAN "IF"

People who do not succeed have one distinguishing trait in common. They know all the reasons for failure, and have what they believe to be airtight alibis to explain away their own lack of achievement.

Some of these alibis are clever and a few of them are justifiable by the facts. But alibis cannot be used for money. The world wants to know only one thing: Have you achieved success?

A character analyst compiled a list of the most commonly used alibis. As you read the list, examine yourself carefully and determine how many of these alibis you use. Remember, the philosophy presented in this book makes every one of these alibis obsolete.

If I didn't have a wife and family . . .

If I had enough "pull" . . .

If I had money . . .

If I had a good education . . .

If I could get a job . . .

If I had good health . . .

If I only had time . . .

If times were better . . .

If other people understood me . . .

If conditions around me were only different . . .

If I could live my life over again . . .

If I did not fear what "they" would say . . .

If I had been given a chance . . .

If I now had a chance . . .

If other people didn't "have it in for me" . . .

If nothing happens to stop me . . .

If I were only younger . . .

If I could only do what I want . . .

If I had been born rich . . .

If I could meet "the right people" . . .

If I had the talent that some people have . . .

If I dared to assert myself . . .

If only I had embraced past opportunities . . .

If people didn't get on my nerves . . .

If I didn't have to keep house and look after the children . . .

If I could save some money . . .

NOTES & COMMENTS

NOTES & COMMENTS

_____

_____

_____

_____

_____

_____

_____

_____

_____

_____

_____

_____

_____

_____

_____

_____

_____

_____

_____

_____

_____

If the boss only appreciated me . . .

If I only had somebody to help me . . .

If my family understood me . . .

If I lived in a big city . . .

If I could just get started . . .

If I were only free . . .

If I had the personality of some people . . .

If I were not so fat . . .

If my real talents were known . . .

If I could just get a "break" . . .

If I could only get out of debt . . .

If I hadn't failed . . .

If I only knew how . . .

If everybody wasn't against me . . .

If I didn't have so many worries . . .

If I could marry the right person . . .

If people weren't so dumb . . .

If my family were not so extravagant . . .

If I were sure of myself . . .

If luck were not against me . . .

If I had not been born under the wrong star . . .

If it were not true that "what is to be will be" . . .

If I did not have to work so hard . . .

If I hadn't lost my money . . .

If I lived in a different neighborhood . . .

If I didn't have a "past" . . .

If I only had a business of my own . . .

If other people would only listen to me . . .

If—and this is the greatest of them all—I had the courage to see myself as I really am, I would find out what is wrong with me and correct it. And I know that something must be wrong with the way I have done things, or I would already have the success that I desire. I recognize that something must be wrong with me, otherwise I would have spent more time analyzing my weaknesses and less time building alibis to cover them.

Building alibis to explain away failure is a national pastime. The habit is as old as the human race, and is fatal to success. Why do people cling to their pet alibis? The answer is obvious. They defend their alibis because they create them. Your alibi is the child of your own imagination. It is human nature to defend your own brainchild.

Building alibis is a deeply rooted habit. Habits are difficult to break, especially when they provide justification for something we do. Plato had this truth in mind when he said, "The first and best victory is to conquer self. To be conquered by self is, of all things, the most shameful and vile."

Another philosopher had the same thought in mind when he said, "It was a great surprise to me when I discovered that most of the ugliness I saw in others was but a reflection of my own nature."

NOTES & COMMENTS

Elbert Hubbard, philosopher, author, publisher of *The Fra* magazine, and founder of the Roycrofters community of artists, said, "It has always been a mystery to me why people spend so much time deliberately fooling themselves by creating alibis to cover their weaknesses. If used differently, this same time would be sufficient to cure the weakness, then no alibis would be needed."

In parting, I would remind you that "Life is a checkerboard, and the player opposite you is time. If you hesitate before moving, or neglect to move promptly, your men will be wiped off the board by Time. You are playing against a partner who will not tolerate indecision!"

Previously you may have had a logical excuse for not having forced life to come through with whatever you asked. That alibi is now obsolete because you are in possession of the Master Key that unlocks the door to life's riches.

The Master Key is intangible, but it is powerful. It is the privilege of creating, in your own mind, a burning desire for a definite form of riches. There is no penalty for the use of this key, but there is a price you must pay if you do not use it. The price is failure. There is a reward of stupendous proportions if you put the key to use. It is the satisfaction that will come to you when you conquer self and force life to pay whatever is asked.

The reward is worthy of your effort. Will you make the start and be convinced?

"If we are related," said the immortal Emerson, "we shall meet." In closing, may I borrow his thought, and say, "If we are related, we have, through these pages, met."

REMEMBER THAT YOUR REAL WEALTH

CAN BE MEASURED NOT BY WHAT YOU HAVE,

BUT BY WHAT YOU ARE.

Highroads Media, Inc. is the publisher of more books and audiobooks by Napoleon Hill than any other publisher in the world. Other titles available:

NEW BOOKS FROM HIGHROADS MEDIA

Think and Grow Rich: The 21st-Century Edition Workbook (oversized paperback)

The Secret Law of Attraction as explained by Napoleon Hill (hardcover)

Napoleon Hill's First Editions (hardcover)

Selling You! (trade paperback)

REVISED & UPDATED BOOKS

Think and Grow Rich: The 21st-Century Edition (hardcover)

Law of Success: The 21st-Century Edition (trade paperback)

LEATHER-BOUND, GILT-EDGED COLLECTOR'S EDITIONS

Think and Grow Rich (single volume)

Law of Success (available in four volumes)

AUDIOBOOKS AVAILABLE ON CD

The Secret Law of Attraction as explained by Napoleon Hill (unabridged audiobook)

Selling You! (abridged audiobook)

Selling You! (unabridged audiobook)

Think and Grow Rich (unabridged and abridged audiobook editions)

Think and Grow Rich: Instant Motivator (original audiobook)

Law of Success (four-volume unabridged audiobook set)

Your Right to Be Rich (unabridged audiobook)

Napoleon Hill's Keys to Success (unabridged and abridged audiobooks)

Believe and Achieve (abridged audiobook)

The Richest Man in Babylon & The Magic Story (original audiobook)

A Lifetime of Riches: The Biography of Napoleon Hill (abridged audiobook)

For more information about Napoleon Hill books and audiobooks, contact:
Highroads Media, Inc., 6 Commerce Way, Arden, NC 28704
telephone: (323) 822-2676   fax: (323) 822-2686
email: highroadsmedia@sbcglobal.net

visit us at our website: www.highroadsmedia.com

12/9/2010 Bible Reading Wisdom

Gratitudinal Reflections:

waking w/ Friskers
Reading w/ Bella mellow tonight
Pink Christmas Tree
Sunny day
$15 Publix gift card
PPL partners - John Ace & Don Thompson
(Shingle Creek)
Heat Now on!
Food on table & gas in car
Volunteer Moffitt & salting tomorrow
heat hiking boots bought in CT